So You Think You Know George Washington?

STORIES THEY DIDN'T TELL YOU IN SCHOOL !

I0084462

Jack Darrell Crowder

CLEARFIELD

Published for Clearfield Company by
Genealogical Publishing Company
Baltimore, Maryland

ISBN 9780806359656

Cover illustration: George Washington statue by Horatio Greenough in the National Musuem of
American History, Washington, D.C. This work is in the public domain.

Books by Jack Darrell Crowder from Clearfield Company:

Women Patriots in the American Revolution: Stories of Bravery, Daring, and Compassion

The First 24 Hours of the American Revolution: An Hour by Hour Account of the Battles of Lexington, Concord, and the British Retreat on Battle Road

Strange, Amazing, and Funny Events that Happened during the Revolutionary War

The Story of Yorktown: Told by the Men Who Were There

Victory or Death: Military Decisions That Changed the Course of the American Revolution

FOR

MATTHEW DAVID SCOTT

Born ca. 1740-48 in Tyrone County, Ireland and died ca. Jan., 1815 in Montgomery County, Virginia. He joined the 12th Virginia in 1776. In 1777 the 12th was assigned to the 4th Virginia, an element of the main Continental Army. In May of 1779 the 4th Virginia became the 8th Virginia. Sergeant Matthew David Scott served with General Washington during the entire winter at Valley Forge. After his discharge in December 1779, he joined the militia and served until 1783. Matthew is my 4th great grandfather. Below is his discharge found in the National Archives.

Contents

Introduction

"It is not the critic who counts; not the man who points out how the strong man stumbles, or where the doer of deeds could have done them better. The credit belongs to the man who is actually in the arena, whose face is marred by dust and sweat and blood; who strives valiantly; who errs, who comes short again and again, because there is no effort without error and shortcoming; but who does actually strive to do the deeds; who knows great enthusiasms, the great devotions; who spends himself in a worthy cause; who at the best knows in the end the triumph of high achievement, and who at the worst, if he fails, at least fails while daring greatly, so that his place shall never be with those cold and timid souls who neither know victory nor defeat."   ---------Theodore Roosevelt

Most of the drawings and paintings we see of Washington were made years after the Revolution, when he was President. Paintings of Washington continued to be made after his death and well into the 20th century. They usually depicted him looking stiff, stern, and unhappy with his ill-fitting false teeth, and powdered hair. It's hard to imagine Washington any other way. This image of him has become one of a marble character, not of a living person.

George Washington was not on par with a Greek god, or some mythical creature that should be worshipped. He was merely a man who did some great things during much of his life. In the 1700s he physically looked like the classic idea of a hero. He was taller than most men, muscular, and at times graceful. Yet, he was unsure of his abilities, and when he spoke you realized that he was not much of an intellectual. Thomas Jefferson wrote, "His colloquial talents were not above mediocrity, possessing neither copiousness of ideas, nor fluency of words. In public when called on for a sudden opinion, he was unready, short, and embarrassed."[1]

During the years that he was alive, he impressed and inspired others. His life was the history of the early days of this nation. His name was alongside every important event and person during the formation of our country. When times became tough during the Revolution, or when forming a new government and preserving it, people turned to Washington for guidance.

For the first hundred years of our new nation George Washington, like other great men of his day, was a hero that had few faults and defects like the rest of us mere mortals. During those years, Washington became less of a real person. He survived every disease that he contracted, he walked away from every battle unscratched, and even though he had won no battles in his early years, he was made commander of the American Army and was ordered to defeat the greatest nation on earth with few resources. You could say he was like a superhero minus the cape and mask.

Between December 1799 and February 1800, no fewer than 440 eulogies were delivered to an audience that could not get enough of George Washington. As the country moved into the latter part of the 1800s, Washington was still looked upon as a mythical person, but his earlier deeds began to diminish. By the early part of the 1900s, Washington's image began to fade, and it seemed that his most important contribution was being the first president and appearing on the dollar bill.

Washington's image continued to suffer until it has reached the point where today we have a man who once was called first in war, first in peace, and first in the hearts of his countrymen, but has now been reduced to a man who should be forgotten. Some people with narrow vision choose to defame Washington by only focusing on the issues of race, class, and gender. Rather than judge a man by the standards of society he lived under in the 1700s, they choose to judge him by today's standards. They want to dehumanize, not humanize Washington, while trying to convince the rest of us that he and other founders did not get anything right. It is doubtful that the lives of these critics today will be able to stand up to the standards of their critics two hundred years from now.

It is true that Washington and the other great men of his time had some serious flaws in their characters. But, if you look at the entirety of their lives and the contributions they made to their country, the good surely outshines the bad. The critics might believe that Washington and the other founders were great in their day, but today they would be seen as just ordinary men. Even if that is true, their contributions still affect us today.

One uninformed young person said, "George Washington didn't do something big, he was just the first." There lies the greatness of this man, he had no trail to follow so he had to blaze a new trail. How many of us could had done what he did in the early days of the Revolution or during his Presidency?

We don't need more praise of these men like Washington, but rather an understanding of them and their circumstances. So the purpose of this book is to take a closer look at Washington, the man behind the legend, and reveal little known stories that shows us what George Washington was really like. As a god he was a terrible failure, but as a man he had greatness. We will see that he was a man with common frailties that made him human, yet he could inspire those he encountered.

It is important to remove him from the pedestal some have placed him on, peel away the layers of myth, and see him as the man he was in his time or day. Perhaps, if we look at George Washington as more human than he has been portrayed, then we can understand and appreciate the greatness and noble character he possessed and be less critical of his flaws.

Benjamin Franklin summed up Washington's importance to the founding of our country at a dinner with diplomats years after the Revolution. Attending were the French and English Ambassadors along with Benjamin Franklin of the United States.

The English Ambassador rose and gave a toast to his homeland, "To England, the sun whose bright beams enlighten and fructify the remotest corners of the earth." Not to be outdone, the French Ambassador rose and politely said, "To France, the moon whose mild steady, and cheering rays are the delight of all nations, consoling them in darkness and making their dreariness beautiful."

Ben Franklin slowly rose and in a very dignified way he said, "To George Washington, the Joshua who commanded the sun and the moon to stand still, and they obeyed him."[2]

Please note that the spelling and grammar in all quotes and written letters is in the original form and has not been corrected.

1

The Myth of George Washington

"When the legend becomes fact, print the legend" ----from the movie, "The Man Who Shot Liberty Valance"

⸻

Before we can see and understand the real George Washington, we must look at the myth of the man. There are numerous stories that have been told about him over the years that make him appear to be larger than life. Some are based on a small truth, while some are completely fabricated from thin air. Here are a few of the more famous tales spun about George Washington.

Much of Washington's folklore has been fashioned by Parson Weems. Mason Locke Weems was a minister, bookseller, and author who wrote the first biography of George Washington soon after his death. He wrote of the virtues of Washington to provide moral instructions for the youth of the country. To get his message across he exaggerated or invented stories to prove his point.

Pastor Weems, unknown artist, image taken from *Pictorial Field Book of the Revolution, Vol. II by Benson J. Lossing, 1850.*

⸻

The Cherry Tree

These tales were read and told to generations, and for many people they became fact. Historians today look at them as romantic, quaint, and ridiculously false. Probably the most famous of the tales is the story of the cherry tree. According to Weems, the story came from a distant relative who spent much time with the family as a young girl. She chose to remain an anonymous source.

Based on her story, when George was about six he was given a hatchet. Like any six year old he went around chopping everything that he came across, which included a young cherry tree in the family garden. George's father discovered the damaged tree and began to look for the person responsible.

Nobody could provide any information until George appeared with his little hatchet. He was asked by his father if he knew who had chopped the small tree down. According to Pastor Weems, George replied, "I can't tell a lie, Pa, you know I can't tell a lie, I did cut it with my hatchet."

"Run to my arms you dearest boy," cried his father, "run to my arms, glad am I, George, that you ever killed my tree, for you have paid me for it a thousand fold. Such an act of heroism in my son, is more worth than a thousand trees, though blossomed with silver, and their fruits of Arrest gold." [1]

For over two hundred years the story has been repeated to grade school children across the nation. This is a wonderful story about the virtue of honesty, but historians agreed it is false. Today most people believe the story is harmless and contains a good moral lesson.

Riding a Horse to Death

A similar story appeared in the *United States Gazette* on May 13, 1826, as an article written by Washington's step-grandson George Washington Parke Custis. According to the story, young George was determined to ride a wild colt owned by his mother. He managed to capture the horse and put a bit into his mouth and mount the animal.

Once on the wild horse, the animal began leaping to get rid of the rider. The struggle of the horse was so fierce that a blood vessel broke, and the animal fell dead. George's mother called him to breakfast, and knowing that he had been in the field asked about her favorite horse. George told her that the horse was dead, and he told her the story of how he killed the animal. George's mother controlled her anger and said she regretted the loss of her favorite horse, but rejoiced in her son for telling the truth.

Historians have found no evidence that the story is true. Instead, it was just another example to portray George Washington as an honest and truthful person. It became another lovely myth to add to the others about George Washington.

Betsey Ross

Another famous myth we learned in school about George Washington was the Betsy Ross story. In 1870 her grandson, William Canby, told her story for the first time when he delivered a paper about the history of the American flag to the Historical Society of Pennsylvania.

According to his story, Betsy Ross was in her shop one day when several men entered, including General Washington. They said they were from a Committee of Congress instructed to produce a new flag for the country. She agreed to follow the pattern they wanted, and soon the stars and stripes we all know were born.

Historians have debunked this story by pointing out there was never a secret flag committee in Congress, and a Flag Resolution wasn't passed by Congress until a year later in June 1777. In addition, at the time Washington was not a member of Congress as he was busy running the army. Although there is no proof that Betsy ever met Washington, she may have made flags for the Pennsylvania navy. On June 14, 1777, Congress passed the first flag act which stated the flag of the United States should consist of thirteen alternating stripes of red on white with thirteen white stars on a blue field. It did not include anything about the points of the stars or if the stripes were to be vertical or horizontal. It is not known who designed the flag, or why that particular color combination and pattern were chosen.

The first time that the flag was flown was at Fort Stanwix (also called Fort Schuyler) on August 3, 1777. When Massachusetts reinforcements arrived at the fort, they brought the news of the flag's adoption. The soldiers cut up their shirts to make the white stripes, and the red stripes were made from the red flannel petticoats of the officers' wives. The blue area was made from Captain Swartwout's blue cloth coat. Three days later on October 6 the flag was flown under fire for the first time at the Battle of Oriskany.[2]

Praying

Another popular story about Washington was him praying at Valley Forge. According to the story, Isaac Potts, a local farmer, stumbled upon Washington kneeling in the snow and heard him praying to God for his army's deliverance. He observed this until Washington finished praying, and then Potts rushed home to tell his wife what he heard and observed which later caused Potts, a Quaker, to convert to the Revolutionary cause.

The Prayer at Valley Forge, from Library of Congress. The famous painting by John C. McRae shows Potts hiding behind a tree and listening.

The first version of this story came from Mason Locke Weems who wrote about it in 1804. Another version appeared after Potts allegedly revealed his experience to his pastor, Reverend Nathaniel Snowden, who then copied it down in his journal.

Later, a number of artists painted Washington kneeling in prayer, some in the snow, and some in the grass in the woods. There was even a guide in the 1920s and 1930s who would give tours and show the "exact spot upon which the General kneeled in prayer."

There is no evidence any of this took place. In 1918, the Valley Forge Park Commission refused to allow a patriotic group to place a marker on the spot where it was claimed Washington knelt in prayer. The Commission's report reviewed thousands of pages of correspondence and diaries of the Commander-in-Chief and his staff; which included generals of divisions and brigades, officers and privates of regiments, the Congressional Committee who were at the camp, manuscripts in the Library of Congress, and other institutions where Revolutionary matter is preserved. It concluded that none of these contained a single paragraph that would substantiate the tradition of the Prayer at Valley Forge.

Isaac Potts, 26 years old, was a real person and a Quaker who opposed war. He, however never had a change of heart about the war. In addition, family history records have proven that the Potts' family did not move to the Valley Forge area until 1800. During the time the Americans were at Valley Forge, Potts was living in Pottsgrove, Pennsylvania. Also, it is highly unlikely that Reverend Snowden ever knew or associated with Isaac Potts. Several critics of Snowden claimed the Reverend recanted his story when presented with the evidence.

In addition, there is the simple fact that George Washington refused to pray on his knees. Historians and biographers of Washington have pointed out that Washington chose standing instead of kneeling when praying. Also, Washington made it clear to his military advisers that he detested anything that brought a man to his knees. Since Washington was very concerned about keeping a neat appearance, especially while in uniform, it would be unlikely for him to kneel and soil his pants in wet snow.

Was Washington Baptized?

Another religious story about Washington, which occurred at Valley Forge, was that Washington came to Pastor John Gano and asked to be baptized. The pastor served as chaplain of the 19th Continental Infantry commanded by Charles Webb and later the 5th Regiment commanded by Colonel Louis Dubois. John Gano's grandchildren signed affidavits in the 1870s and 1880s attesting to the baptism. They said that Gano's older daughter told them that it actually happened. In 1932 *Time* magazine published an article about the event and stated that 42 people witnessed it. There is even a famous painting hanging in the Gano Chapel at William Jewell College depicting the baptism. It is a lovely story and a beautiful painting, but it probably never happened.[4]

When the army spent the winter at Valley Forge, Gano had returned home. He did not join the army in winter quarters, because he believed that the men were not properly clothed to stand out in the harsh cold weather to hear him preach.

Also, had this Baptism taken place, Gano surely would have written about it in his memoirs, which he did not do. Washington's church believed in infant Baptism, and Washington's christening was recorded as having taken place on April 3, 1732, when he was six weeks old. In addition, there is no written account by the 42 onlookers. The legend is popular, because it is used to prove that Washington's religion was open and active.

Nude Washington?

The myth of Washington was so great at times, that if you even mention George Washington in a play it could draw the wrath of critics. For example, William Thackeray used Washington as a character in his novel *The Virginians, A Tale of the Last Century* (1858).[5] Some of the critics of the day were outraged he did this.

One critic felt that it was only permissible for Washington to make a very brief appearance and then not be mentioned again. Another critic was annoyed that Washington appeared in the story just like any other common man. He felt that Washington was not like any other man, and that he should not be brought down to the level of ordinary men.[6]

In 1832, Congress commissioned a marble statue of Washington that was completed in 1840. It had Washington sitting in a chair, stripped to the waist, and wearing a toga. Critics were not very pleased having Washington looking like he was about to bathe. Some said that he looked like an early Roman in a toga.

Nathaniel Hawthorne wrote, perhaps half-kidding, "Did anybody ever see Washington nude? It is inconceivable. He had no nakedness, but I imagine he was born with his clothes on and with his hair powdered."[7]

George Washington statue by Horatio Greenough in the National Museum of American History. Public domain

2

Young George Washington

"The good thing about being young is that you are not experienced enough to know you cannot possibly do the things you are doing."......Anonymous

❧❀❧

Background

Inside George Washington mother wrote inside the family Bible, "George Washington, son to Augustine Washington, and Mary, his wife, was born ye 11th day of February, 1731-2, about ten in the morning, and was baptized ye 3d of April following. Mr. Beverly Whiting and Captain Christopher Brooke, godfathers, and Mrs. Mildred Gregory, godmother."[1] This was before the adoption of the Gregorian calendar, which made February 22 his birthday.

Even without the entry in the family bible, it would have been certain that young George was baptized. His family was very religious, but even if they weren't they would have followed the law. According to a law passed in Virginia in 1661, parents of every free child had to report the birth to a minister within twenty days. Following this, the child would be required to be baptized.

The future president was born in Virginia on February 11, 1732, and had no middle name. His grandfather (John) was an Englishman, who came over and settled in Virginia in 1657. George's father, Augustine, married his second wife, Mary Ball, and George was the first of six children born to the couple. He also had three half-brothers and one half-sister from his father's first marriage to Jane Butler who died in 1728.

Education:

George Washington grew up in a wealthy family. His father, a land speculator, was frequently absent leaving George and his older brothers on their own. The first school that young George was sent to was a "field school". It was run by one of his father's tenants, named Hobby, who was an honest and poor old man.

[Note: a field school was set up by parents or teachers, and individuals funded the school and selected the teachers. They were built on old worn-out farm fields and the school term was about three months in the winter.]

George Washington's father, Augustine, sent his eldest son, Lawrence, to England for his education. In 1737, Augustine came home from England bringing a shipload of convicts to use as labor, which included a teacher for five-year-old George. The Reverend Jonathan Boucher, an English clergyman who later tutored Jack Custis, Martha and George's son, wrote, "George, like most people thereabouts at that time, had no other education than reading, writing and accounts, which he was taught by a convict servant whom his father bought for a schoolmaster." [2]

Although George did not have the formal education his older brothers had, he later received a surveyor's license from the College of William & Mary in 1749. Washington's formal education ended when he was around eleven after his father died. Because of his death, George was not able to be educated in England like his half-brothers. As a result, all through his life he felt embarrassed and inferior by his lack of schooling. Most of his later learning would be self-attained.

There were some early historians that claimed that Washington was a Latin scholar, however, he never learned a word of Latin. Even with limited education, his spelling improved over time and he developed a large, handsome, and impressive handwriting. Later in life he rarely ever discussed his education. He might not have written about his childhood because he was ashamed of his lack of education.

It is true that compared to the common people of his day, he was well-educated, for, as a rule, they could hardly read and write. However, he was not educated up to the average level of people of his own aristocratic class. Literary and classical allusions seldom appear in his writings, although it was the custom of his time to sprinkle the written word liberally with the words of Greece and Rome. He knew no French, and years later he would have a great deal to do with the French, as enemies and as friends. He seemed to have had no curiosity whatever about their language. Now and then, on rare occasions, he used a French word or phrase in his writings, which were almost always spelled wrong.

He did not destroy his childhood school work and kept it in three notebooks. Much of what he read, studied and copied to learn were manners and customs which can be found in these books. Below are some samples from Washington's favorite book, *Rules of Civility and Decent Behavior*, which he studied and followed during his life. He would later insist that others also follow these guidelines as well. There were 110 rules in all and Washington followed them closer than any religion. Below are some examples,

Rule 4: In the present of others, sing not to yourself with a humming noise nor drum with your fingers,

Rule 11: Shift not yourself in the sight of others nor gnaw your nails.

Rule 49: Use no reproachful language against anyone; neither curse nor revile.

Rule 110: Labor to keep alive in your breast that little spark of Celestial fire called conscience.[3]

However, George's lack of a formal education did not hamper him being elected in 1788 as Chancellor of William and Mary College. The honor came to him as a sudden surprise and it was of great concern,

Not knowing particularly what duties, or whether any active services are immediately expected from the person holding the office of chancellor, I have been greatly embarrassed in deciding upon the public answer proper to be given. My difficulties are briefly these. On the one hand, nothing in this world could be farther from my heart, than . . . a refusal of the appointment provided its duties are not incompatible with the mode of life to which I have entirely addicted myself; and, on the other hand, I would not for any consideration disappoint the just expectations of the convocation by accepting an office.[4]

George thought it over and wrote back a week later to accept the post, which he held until his death until 1799. He had been asked to serve because the president of the college felt that the position needed a national figure to occupy it.

Mary Ball Washington

Washington's mother:

George's mother, Mary Ball was Augustine's second wife. Mary's mother was illiterate, and had received no education worth mentioning. According to many accounts, Mary was a strict mother. Once her husband died, she had George and the other children help her run the farm. Raising five children by herself, she emphasized obedience in all her children, and although strict, she was in her own way a loving mother. Mary was an imposing woman, large, and vigorous, with an explosive temper, which she passed down to George.

One of George's young friends said that George was very afraid of her, and the same boy said that he himself was ten times more afraid of her than his own parents. Washington and his mother were not particularly affectionate toward each other. In letters he sent his mother throughout his early years, George often addressed her as "Honored Madam." Some might claim that this showed a lack of affection, but more likely it was showing respect and courtesy that she expected from her children.

George was a dutiful rather than an adoring son of a woman who had a reared a brood of children, and who believe that her exertions were not fully appreciated. Mary was extremely protective of her family but seldom exhibited pride in achievements of any of her children, including George.

The portrait on the left is Mary Ball Washington as a young woman. It is from the book *George Washington the Human Being & the Hero* by Rupert Hughes, 1926, page 15. On the right is a 1916 portrait of her around 80 years old from the Library of Congress.

An example of her lack of pride would be how she reacted when she learned that George had become president of the United States. "I am not surprised at what George has done, for he was always a good boy," is the remark that General Washington's mother made. At the time he was the greatest man in America.[5]

Mary Washington hated to display any of her emotions. George Kiger, a letter carrier, told how he galloped a long way to bear a letter from Washington to his mother, during the latter part of the revolution. He found her in her garden in her usual short yellow gown, occupied with her vegetables. Kiger gave her the letter and waited, but the old lady went on with her work, without opening the letter. At length the youth said, "Madam, this whole community is interested in that letter." Thereupon she opened the dispatch, which announced a victory; but all the news she shared with the messenger was the smiling remark, "George generally carries through anything he undertakes."[6]

As Mary became older, she depended on George to help her with her domestic needs. On June 7, 1755, she wrote to him while he was serving in the British army on the Virginia frontier. George replied back to her letter,

> "I was favored with your letter, by Mr. Dick, and am sorry it is not in my power to provide you with a Dutch servant, or the butter, agreeably to your desire. We are quite out of the part of the country where either is to be had, there being few or no inhabitants where we now lie encamped, and butter cannot be had here to supply the wants of the army." "I hope," he also says, "you will spend the chief part of your time at Mount Vernon, as you have proposed to do, where I am certain ever thing will be ordered as much to your satisfaction as possible."[7]

There is no record of what was in Mary's letter other than she wanted some butter and a servant. At the time George wrote this letter he was with the British army and soon would be engaged in a battle with French troops and their Indian allies. Five weeks later the British were defeated by the enemy and nearly 1,000 men had been killed or wounded. Washington was very lucky to escape with his life since officers were targeted in the fight. Mary must have known that her son was in a dangerous position, yet her concern was about butter and a servant.

―――――⁂―――――

Washington Visits his Mother after Yorktown:

After the defeat of Cornwallis in 1781, Washington's son Jacky, who was with him at Yorktown, took sick and died the first of November. Now, both of George's step-children were dead. On his way back to Mount Vernon, Washington stopped at Fredericksburg to visit his mother. The town turned out to cheer their hero, all except his mother. She had left town, so he left her a little money and rode off for home. Days later she wrote him a thank you, but in her note she made no mention of the death of Jacky or Patsy. She also failed to extend any sympathy to Martha or Eleanor despite being aware of the death of the two children.[8]

―――――⁂―――――

Mary hints about living with George and Martha:

Mary never visited George and Martha at Mount Vernon, which was probably fine with George. When Mary was eighty years old, she was living alone in Fredericksburg, Virginia. She decided that due to her advanced age she should go live her son John. Before the move took place, John died and she hinted that she might come to live with George and Martha.

George became fearful she would, so he wrote the following letter to her in hopes of convincing her to stay away. Like a lawyer, George made a strong case as to why she would not be happy at Mount Vernon [the original spelling and grammar have not been changed],

> My House is at your service, & would press you most sincerely & most devoutly to accept it, but I am sure and candor requires me to say it will never answer your purposes, in any shape whatsoever—for in truth it may be compared to a well resorted tavern, as scarcely any strangers who are going from north to south, or from south to north do not spend a day or two at it—This would, were you to be an inhabitant of it, oblige you to do one of 3 things, 1st to be always dressing to appear in company, 2d to come into in a dishabille or 3d to be as it were a prisoner in your own chamber The first you would not like, indeed for a person at your time of life it would be too fatiguing. The 2d I should not like because those who resort here are as I observed before strangers and people of the first distinction. and the 3d, more than probably, would not be pleasing to either of us—nor indeed could you be retired in any room in my house; for what with the sitting up of Company; the noise and bustle of servants—and many other things you would not be able to enjoy that calmness and serenity of mind, which in my opinion you ought now to prefer to every other consideration in life. If you incline to follow this advice the House and lots on which you now live you may rent, and enjoy the benefit of the money arising there from as long as you live—this with the rent of the land at the little falls & the hire of your Negros would bring you in an income which would be much more than sufficient to answer all your wants and make ample amends to the child you live with; for myself I should desire nothing, if it did not, I would, most cheerfully contribute more. A man, a maid.
>
> There are such powerful reasons in my mind for giving this advice, that I cannot help urging it with a degree of earnestness which is uncommon for me to do. It is I am convinced, the only means by which you can be happy.
>
> Mrs. Washington, George & Fanny Join me in every good wish for you and I am honored Madam, Yr. most dutiful & affe. Son.[9]

Mary took George's advice and stayed where she was. He visited her in the spring of 1789 one last time, and she died from breast cancer six months later. He was President when she died, and he did not learn of her death until a week after she passed. Because of this, he was unable to attend the funeral. In her will she left George her entire estate which included her prized bedroom furniture.

During the Revolution Mary Washington had been suspected of "Toryism" because she hated war and declared, "This fighting and killing" a bad business, and wished that "George would come home and attend to his plantation."[10] This rumor of her allegiance began because some of the French troops stationed in Virginia claimed they heard her criticize some of Washington's policies during the war. This could have resulted in her being run out of town except she was General Washington's mother.

There is no proof that Mary was a Tory sympathizer, in fact her other three sons served in the Virginia militia. Also, her son-in-law, Fielding Lewis, was in charge of a gunnery works that made muskets for use by the American troops.

Lawrence Washington

George lived with his half-brother Lawrence after the death of their father:

George's father, Augustine Washington died in 1743 when George was eleven. He inherited the farm acquired by his father in 1738. The farm was later named the Ferry Farm after the near-by ferry that crossed the Rappahannock River in Virginia. In addition to the farm, George became an eleven year old that now owned ten slaves. Since his father died before the age of fifty, and his grandfather died at thirty-seven, George had a lasting impression that the Washington men were not long lived.

George went to live with his brother Lawrence in 1746. It is not known exactly why he left his mother's home. Perhaps Mary found it difficult to provide for all her children. Perhaps he wanted to get away from the woman he feared, or it may have been that George needed an elder brother's guidance. His school-days were over and he did not appear to have advanced in school beyond the elementary grades.

Now that young George was no longer under the watchful and often disapproving eye of his mother, the young lad began to bloom. He met the upper fringes of the colony, the Lees, the Masons', the Fauntleroy's, and the Fairfax's. He assisted his brother around the plantation, developed his talent at surveying, discovered his love of fox hunting, and flirted with the girls of high society.

Lawrence Washington around 30 years old, public domain.

George wants to join the Royal Navy:

When George was about fourteen he decided he might join the Royal Navy. In the early 1740s, Lawrence had spent time aboard the flagship of British Admiral Edward Vernon during the War of Jenkins' Ear. When he returned to Virginia, he told George exciting stories of his naval adventures which spiked the impressionable young man's interest of life at sea.

In the fall of 1746, Lawrence sent two letters, one to George and one to his mother Mary that some historians believe suggested that George join the navy. George was to give Mary's letter to her and keep secret the letter given to him. The two letters are lost to history, but William Fairfax, a family friend wrote to Lawrence on September 9, 1746,

> George has been with us, and says He will be steady and thankfully follow your Advice as his best Friend. I gave him his Mother's letter to deliver with Caution not to shew his. I have spoken to Dr. Spencer who I find is often at the Widow's and has some influence, to persuade her to think better of your advice in putting Him to Sea with good Recommendation.[11]

It sounded as if Lawrence and William Fairfax were suggesting that George join the navy and they were quietly working behind Mary's back to make this happen. Mary's half-brother,

Joseph Ball, advised her that she should not let George join the merchant service or the Royal Navy, because he considered the ships to be nothing more than floating prisons. In this letter to her he made a very compelling argument against the idea of going to sea,

> I understand that you are advised and have some thoughts of putting your son George to sea. I think he had better be put apprentice to a tinker, for a common sailor before the mast has by no means the common liberty of the subject; for they will press him from ship to ship, where he has fifty shillings a month, and make him take twenty-three, and cut and slash and use him like a negro, or rather like a dog. And as to any considerable preferment in the navy, it is not to be expected, as there are so many gaping for it here who have interest, and he has none. And if he should get to be master of a Virginia ship (which is very difficult to do), a planter who has three or four hundred acres of land, and three or four slaves, if he be industrious, may live more comfortably, and have his family in better bread than such a master of a ship can.[12]

It appeared that Robert Jackson, a good friend of the Washington family, also became involved in the naval plot from a letter he wrote to Lawrence September 18, 1846,

> I am afraid Mrs. Washington will not keep up to her first resolution. She seems to intimate a dislike to George's going to sea and says several persons have told her it's a very bad scheme. She offers several trifling objections such as fond and unthinking mothers naturally suggest, and I find that one word against his going had more weight than ten for it.[13]

Robert admitted that Mary's word on the matter carried more weight than the others combined. He was correct, because Mary appeared to be the only person objecting against George going to sea and she told her son no. George, knowing all too well his mother's temper, obeyed her, and his dream of life on the ocean, evaporated. One can only speculate what would have happen with the American Revolution if Mary had agreed to let her son join the British navy.

Washington's First Job

George Washington the surveyor:

At the age of 16, Washington joined a surveying party sent to the Shenandoah Valley by Lord Fairfax, a land baron and family friend. George went on to perfect his skills and used some of the income from various surveying jobs to obtain a surveyor's license in the summer of 1749. Two days after becoming licensed, and largely through the influence of William Fairfax, Washington secured an appointment as county surveyor for the newly created frontier county of Culpeper, where he served until November 1750. Before he was eighteen, he was earning 125 pounds a year from surveying, which was more cash than most Virginian planters saw in a year and as much as any skilled artisan in Williamsburg.

He continued to work in the area from July 1749 to November 1752. During these three years on the frontier Washington established a reputation for fairness, honesty, and dependability. Records showed that he had 199 professional surveys in Culpeper, Frederick, and Hampshire counties. His close relationship with the Fairfax family gave him an advantage over other local surveyors. Some of these surveys were for the purpose of buying new land for himself, defending his own boundaries, or dividing his property into profitable farms.

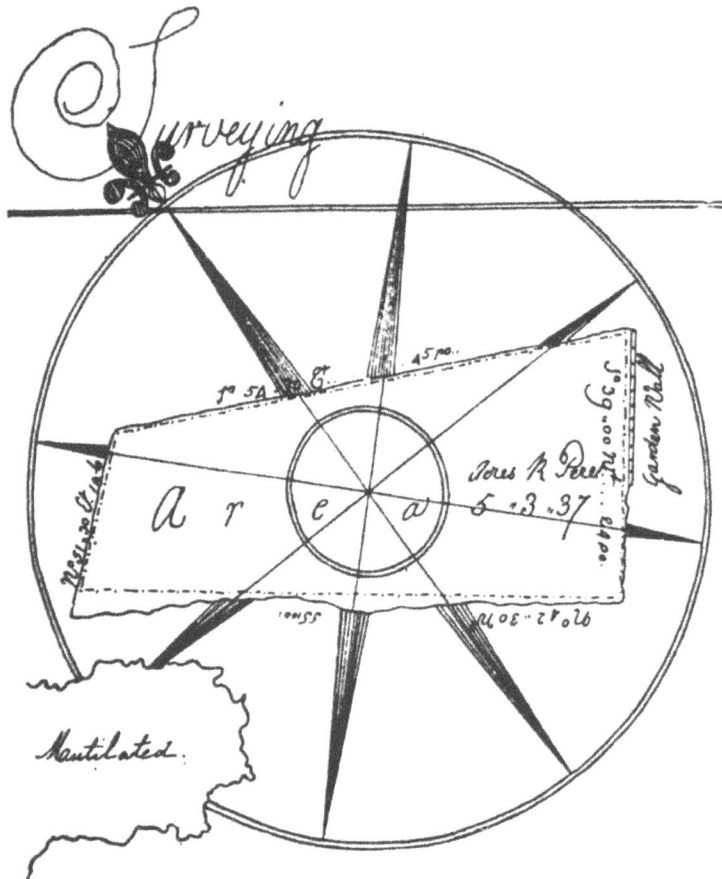

A survey of a turnip patch belonging to Lawrence Washington, from George Washington's school copy book, volume 2, 1745. Library of Congress.

Barbados

The only time Washington left the United States:

In 1751, Lawrence Washington developed tuberculosis and his doctors recommended a change of climate. Lawrence's cough had grown more persistent and he knew that another cold Virginia winter could kill him, so he decided to move to Barbados in the West Indies. There was a long standing medical tradition of treatment of lung disease on the island. Since Lawrence's wife could not make the trip due to a difficult pregnancy, George traveled with Lawrence and they arrived on the island in November 1751. They hoped to stay at the resident of Gedney Clarke's home, who was Lawrence's wife's uncle.

Once they arrived, they had to rent a house due to the Clarke household having smallpox. Even so, the two boys were invited to the Clarke home to visit which proved to be a mistake. Soon, George became ill with smallpox and was confined to bed for three weeks. In addition to the smallpox, he also developed malaria.

Having smallpox later prove to be a blessing. When George took command of the army, smallpox existed among his men, but he was immune to it. Unfortunately, his treatment for smallpox likely resulted in making him sterile and would later cause tooth loss. Additionally, for the rest of his life his face was disfigured by pockmarks.

Lawrence did not get any better, so he moved to Bermuda, where his condition worsened. Meanwhile George returned home in December 1751. The voyage back was difficult and stormy causing George to suffer from seasickness. For the rest of his life he refused to take another ocean crossing.

The Plantation

George inherits Mount Vernon:

Lawrence later returned home from Barbados and died at Mount Vernon in July 1752. Lawrence's will stipulated that his widow, Anne, should own a life estate, meaning she would own it until she died, and the remaining interest would go to George.

Anne remarried five months after the death of Lawrence into the Lee family and moved out of Mount Vernon. When her daughter by Lawrence died in 1754, Washington leased the plantation from Anne. In 1761, Anne died and now George was the sole owner of Mount Vernon. It was estimated that he now owned about 5,000 acres of land cleared and not cleared, and forty-nine slaves. Much of the time he had little cash, as it was all in land, equipment, and slaves. He once wrote, "To keep myself out of debt; I have found it expedient now and then to sell Lands, or something else to effect this purpose."[14]

The Gambler

George plays the lottery:

One way he tried to raise money was to purchase chances in lotteries and raffles, which at the time were not merely respectable, but even fashionable. In 1760, five pounds and ten shillings were invested in one lottery. Five pounds purchased five tickets in Strother's lottery in 1763. Three years later six pounds were risked in the York lottery and produced prizes to the extent of sixteen pounds. Fifty pounds were put into Colonel Byrd's lottery in 1769. Washington even sponsored a lotter in 1769 to build a road across the Blue Ridge Mountains. Unfortunately it was not successful.

Love for his plantation:

In the early 1750s, George spent much time in the army and was away from Mount Vernon. The property became run down during his absence, so upon his return he immediately went to work to restore the plantation. George made renovations to the house in 1758 and continued doing so for the next twenty years. All the work was done by slaves and artisans. He also purchased more land in the surrounding area until the 1780s. He had done so many improvements to the home over the years that one visitor once said, "It's a pity he did not build a new one at once, for it has cost him nearly as much to repair his old one."[15]

He kept the original name of the plantation, Mount Vernon, which was named for Admiral Edward Vernon, of the British Navy. He developed a strong affection for Mount Vernon and during his later years of service would return to it whenever he could. In writing to an English correspondent, he showed his feeling for the place by saying, "No estate in United America, is more pleasantly situated than this. It lies in a high, dry and healthy country, three hundred miles by water from the sea, and, as you will see by the plan, on one of the finest rivers in the world."[16]

George Washington Body and Soul

"It was impossible to mistake for a moment his majestic figure and deportment; nor was he less distinguished by the noble affability of his manner."-----Marquis De Lafayette

∼≪◈◉◈≫∼

Physical Appearance of Washington

The earliest known description of Washington was written in 1760 by his companion-in-arms and friend George Mercer,

> He may be described as being as straight as an Indian, measuring six feet two inches in his stockings, and weighing 175 pounds when he took his seat in the House of Burgesses in 1759. His frame is padded with well-developed muscles, indicating great strength. His bones and joints are large, as are his feet and hands. He is wide shouldered, but has not a deep or round chest.

> He is neat waisted, but is broad across the hips, and has rather long legs and arms. His head is well shaped though not large, but is gracefully poised on a superb neck. A large and straight rather than prominent nose, blue -gray penetrating eyes, which are widely separated and overhung by a heavy brow. His face is long rather than broad, with high round cheek bones, and terminates in a good firm chin. He has a clear though rather a colorless pale skin, which burns with the sun. A pleasing, benevolent, though a commanding countenance, dark brown hair, which he wears in a cue. His mouth is large and generally firmly closed, but which from time to time discloses some defective teeth. His features are regular and placid, with all the muscles of his face under perfect control, though flexible and expressive of deep feeling when moved by emotion. In conversation he looks you full in the face, is deliberate, deferential and engaging. His voice is agreeable rather than strong. His demeanor at all times composed and dignified. His movements and gestures are graceful, his walk majestic, and he is a splendid horseman.[1]

He had light blue eyes and reddish brown hair, and he powdered it white. Unlike many men of the time, he never wore a wig. A British officer who met Washington some years later reported that he had a dark complexion and a foreign look, which probably meant that Washington was tanned at the time. Washington was only sixteen, but he looked much older. He had large hands and feet, and he wore a size thirteen shoe. His head appeared small for such a large body, and when Washington ordered a hat, he asked for one for a large head.

Washington enjoyed wearing fine clothes and looking the part of a gentleman. In 1763 he wrote to his London tailors to, "take measure of a gentleman who wares well-made cloths of the following size: to wit, 6 feet high and proportionally made, if anything rather slender than thick, for a person of that height, with pretty long arms and thighs. You will take care to make the breeches longer than those you sent me last, and I would have you keep the measure of the cloths you now make, by you, and if any alteration is required in my next it shall be pointed out." At the same time of this order, he ordered 6 pairs of men's riding gloves larger than the middle size and several dozen pairs of stockings, "to be long, and tolerably large."[2]

One time in 1773, the British governor of New York, William Tyron, was having dinner with several colonials. The governor bragged that a British regiment that had just landed contained some officers that were the most handsome that could be found in the colonies. Mrs. Morris, an

American lady replied, "I wager you a pair of gloves, that I will show you a finer man in the procession tomorrow, than your Excellency can select." "Done, madam!" replied the governor.

The next day, June 4th, there was a procession in honor of the birthday of the King. There were a number of British soldiers marching down Broadway to the military music. The governor pointed out several troops by name, and remarked how handsome they looked in their uniforms. Following in the rear was a band of colonial officers, and the attention of the governor was drawn to one tall looking warrior. Mrs. Morris remarked, "I perceive that your Excellency's eyes are turned to the right object; what say you to your wager now, sir?" "Lost madam. When I laid my wager, I was not aware that Colonel Washington was in New York."[3]

A giant of a man:

George Washington at six foot two was a towering figure in most crowds, because the average height of a male American during the Revolution was five feet eight inches. This was nearly two inches taller than the average British soldier. Young Washington weighed around 175 pounds and was a strong and powerful man, as demonstrated in a story told by the artist Charles W. Peale, a friend of Washington,

> One afternoon several young gentlemen, visitors at Mount Vernon, and myself were engaged in pitching the bar, one of the athletic sports common in those days. [Pitching the bar was a game of strength, a log-throwing, or pole-throwing, competition similar to the tossing game played by Highland Scots.]
>
> Suddenly Colonel Washington appeared among us. He requested to be shown the pegs that marked the bounds of our efforts; then, smiling, and without putting off his coat, held out his hand for the missile. No sooner did the heavy iron bar feel the grasp of his mighty hand that it lost the power of gravitation, and whizzed through the air, striking the ground far, very far, beyond our outmost limits. We were indeed amazed, as we stood around, all stripped to the buff, with shirt sleeves rolled up, and having thought ourselves very clever fellows, while the Colonel, on retiring, pleasantly observed, 'When you beat my pitch, young gentlemen, I'll try again.[4]

Abigail Adams described George Washington on July 16, 1775,

> I was struck with General Washington. You had prepared me to entertain a favorable opinion of him, but I thought the one half was not told me. Dignity with ease, and complacency, the Gentleman and Soldier look agreeably blended in him. Modesty marks every line and feature of his face.[5]

During Lafayette's visit to Mount Vernon in 1825, he said to a writer, "I never saw so large a hand on any human being, as the generals. It was in this portico, in 1784, that you were introduced to me by the general. You were a very little gentleman, with a feather in your hat, and holding fast to one finger of the good general's remarkable hand, which was all you could do, my dear sir, at that time."[6]

In 1797 one man wrote of sixty-five year old George Washington, "His chest is full; and his limbs, though rather slender, well-shaped and muscular. His head is small, in which respect he resembles the make of a great number of his countrymen. His eyes are of a light grey color; and in proportion to the length of his face, his nose is long. Mr. Stewart, the eminent portrait painter, told me, that there were features in his face totally different from what he ever observed in that of any other human being; the sockets for the eyes, for instance, are larger than what he ever met with before, and the upper part of the nose broader."[7]

An officer of the Life-Guard had been often heard to observe, that the Commander-in-Chief was thought to be the strongest man in the army. In 1781 a company of riflemen from the county of Augusta in Virginia reinforced the troops of Lafayette. As the stalwart band of mountaineers, marched before the general, the astonished and admiring Frenchman exclaimed, "Mon Dieu! What a people are these Americans; they have reinforced me with a band of giants!"[8]

Stories of his strength:

One story that made the rounds in Virginia may or may not be true. At one time there were many athletes engaged in a number of games in Virginia. Washington chose not to take part, but rather he sat under a shade tree to read a book. The champion of the games got into the ring calling for someone to challenge him in wrestling. Washington closed his book, walked over, and got into the ring with the man. Washington soon had the man in his grasp rendering him helpless. In a quick motion he hurled the man to the ground. While the people shouted of Washington's victory, he simply returned to the shade tree and resumed his reading.[9]

As a teenage boy in the 1740s, Washington was a head taller than most boys his age. In addition to being a good wrestler and rail-splitter, he was especially proud of his throwing arm. He believed that he could throw a stone farther than anyone he knew.

The power of Washington's arm was displayed in several memorable instances: in his throwing a stone from the bed of the stream to the top of the Natural Bridge, another over the Palisades into the Hudson, and yet another time across the Rappahannock at Fredericksburg. In the article where he spanned the stream, there were various accounts. He probably threw a piece of slate, fashioned to about the size and shape of a silver dollar, and it not only spanned the river but struck the ground at least thirty yards on the other side.[10]

Washington's Likes and Dislikes

Washington's grandson said that he could not endure smoke from tobacco. Even when it was necessary in meeting with Indians to take a puff of the peace pipe, he made a foul face and took in as little smoke as possible. Liquor, on the other hand, was a different story. He manufactured and imported it, gave it away to friends, and consumed it in vast quantities. Washington enjoyed drinking but was never drunk.

Washington enjoyed being outdoors and taking part in fox hunting, fishing, and picnics. Sometimes he would spend the day riding over his vast property and interacting with the people. When he had the time, he liked to take part in an afternoon tea.

If there was anything that Washington detested, it was tardiness. Once he went to Philadelphia to visit artist Charles Wilson Peale, who had painted his portrait at Mount Vernon before the war. This led to the two men developing a long friendship. Washington arrived five minutes early according to his pocket watch, and so he paced around outside until the exact moment of his appointment.

Washington was particularly fond of clothes, which was the sign of a true aristocrat. Early in life he was a bit of a dandy, and the fondness for fine clothes never left him. In the 1750s he wrote to his London agent, "Whatever goods you may send me. Let them be fashionable, neat and good of there several kinds."[11]

Part of keeping a gentlemanly appearance was the proper maintaining of the hair. Washington's ledgers shown constant expenditures to the barber. This involved more than just cutting hair. It included the proper care of perfume, powder, pomatum (ointment that was scented to give hair a shiny appearance and to hold it in place), powder bags, and puffs. The barber did not shave George, because this was probably done by a valet or even himself. The paintings of Washington always show his natural hair, never a wig.

Washington the dancer:

Washington loved to dance and he once compared dancing to war and the "gentler conflict."[12] Unfortunately, Martha did not enjoy dancing as much as her husband. Philip Fithian, known for his journals and letters in 1773-1774, wrote about Virginians and dancing, "Blow high, Blow Low, the Virginians are genuine blood they will Dance or die."[13] Washington welcomed dancing teachers to Mount Vernon, and he encouraged his step-children to take part in the lessons. At times, the dancing teacher who gave the lessons found it necessary to tap a boy on the shoulders and warn the lad that he was "insolent and wanton."

Since Washington was so graceful on a horse, dancing probably came easy to him. French officers during the Revolution attested to his great ability in the minuet, marveled that any American could learn its graceful intricacies so well. The officers would also comment that they had never seen anyone at Versailles who danced better than George Washington.

During the Revolution, when he was about fifty years of age, Washington danced once with Catherine Greene, the wife of General Greene, for three hours without stopping. As the other dancers paused and looked on, it seemed to them to have been a kind of endurance contest between Washington and Mrs. Greene. The Virginia balls were stately parties that were enjoyed by the upper class. There were quadrilles and minuets and men and women bowing and curtseying to the music of violins and tambours. The dances had such interesting names such as High Betty Martin and Leather-the-Strap. Like intricate figures, the dancers would weave in and out, and barely touched finger tips in passing. On any given evening you could see perfumed and powdered hair, silks and laces, glancing eyes, words with subtle meanings, and constant flirting between the sexes, while all under the soft yellow light of candles.

George Washington dancing in celebration of the victory at Yorktown, 1781. He is depicted dancing the minuet with Mrs. Henry Willis of Fredericksburg, while his mother, seated on the left, looks on. His mother really was not there.

Washington the gambler:

While at home Washington enjoyed card playing almost daily, especially if the weather was bad. Card games at Mount Vernon were usually played for small sums. Washington kept note of his winnings and losses in a ledger book. They were so evenly balanced that his total losses, after deducting the sums won, were only £6.3s.3d. in four years. Also noted in the ledger were many purchases of one dozen packs of playing cards.

In 1748, when he was sixteen years old, he won two shillings and three pence from his sister-in-law at the card game Whist (a forerunner of Bridge), and five shillings at "Loo" from his brother in another card game. It appeared that he usually played for small stakes, but sometimes it lead to fairly sizable sums. The largest gain found in his records, was three pounds, and the largest loss was nine pounds fourteen shillings and nine pence. He seemed to have lost more often than he won.

Purchases in his ledgers also mentioned his fondness for honey, and sugar candy was mentioned several times. The candy may have been shared with some children. There were also multiple purchases for all kinds of fruits, melons, and nuts.

27

Entertainment he likes:

On fox hunting days, which were frequent, Washington would occasionally hunt all day and then joined with others for a snack at a neighbor's house. Sometimes slaves followed the hunt on jogging mules with picnic baskets crammed full of food and bottles of wine. Outside of fox-hunting, he appeared to have loved the theatre more than any other form of amusement. He went to every play, good or bad, that was produced within his area. Some of the theatres of the day were rough, barnlike affairs, and there were not many of them. However, the acting was good most of the time, because the actors, were usually well trained, from England.

One English theatre group, Lewis Hallam's Company, went to Williamsburg, Virginia in 1752. It remained there for eleven months and played to profitable houses. This was quite unusual because Williamsburg had less than a thousand residents. Washington attended the theater in Williamsburg several evenings a week, when he was visiting there as a member of the House of Burgess.

He took fencing lessons in Fredericksburg, which was over forty miles away, but it had the closest dedicated instructor. He was the Dutch mercenary and translator, Jacob Van Braam, who entered the British naval service and served as a lieutenant with Lawrence Washington. Jacob and George Washington later fought together in 1754. Washington Irving, in his book on George Washington, wrote the following,

> Another of Lawrence [Washington]'s campaigning comrades was Jacob Van Braam, a Dutchman by birth, who had been in the British Army, but was now out of service, and, professing to be a complete master of fence, recruited his slender purse in this time of military excitement, by giving the Virginian youth lessons in the sword exercise.[14]

Washington carried his sword into battle, since it was considered a part of his attire. Gentlemen did not often unsheathe their swords over a small dispute but rather kept them on hand as showpieces, or for ready use in case of a great insult to their honor. George was not known to engage in a sword duel despite numerous slights and insults from gentlemen of his own class. He was courageous in battle but did not seek to settle disputes with a gun or sword. During the Revolution he worked to discourage dueling. If he had not done this, dueling would have cost the American army the lives of many fine officers, since there were constant squabbles and disagreements among them.

Washington also enjoyed letter writing, and he usually devoted much of Sunday to writing to his friends. Many times he would write a rough draft of the letter, then copy it neatly, making changes as he went along. Sunday was also a day of worship, and George attended church on the average of about one Sunday in four. He always enjoyed receiving visitors on Sunday. Most every weekend you would find guests at Mount Vernon, who sometimes staying for several days if they had traveled a long distance.

Washington's Character

Washington's greatness:

He was not a man of first rate ability, but he was a very great man. The greatness of Washington lay in his character. Thomas Jefferson wrote, "I think I knew General Washington intimately and thoroughly; and were I called on to delineate his character it should be in terms like these,"

> His mind was great and powerful, without being of the very first order; no judgment was ever sounder. It was slow in operation, being little aided by invention or imagination.

> He was incapable of fear, meeting personal dangers with the calmest unconcern. Perhaps the strongest feature in his character was prudence, never acting until every circumstance, every consideration was maturely weighed.

> His integrity was most pure, his justice the most inflexible I have ever known, no motives of interest or consanguinity, of friendship or hatred, being able to bias his decision. He was indeed, in every sense of the words, a wise, a good, & a great man.[15]

Washington's greatness was recognized by some as early as 1774 when on the floor of Congress it was stated, "…if you speak of solid information and sound judgment Colonel Washington is unquestionably the greatest man on the floor." [16]

There were several stories that exemplified Washington's character. One was a story that *Harper's Monthly* magazine published in December of 1864, and it was re-published several times after that. Some historians have serious doubts if the story is true. If it is not true, then it should be.

> When Colonel Seth Warner died just after the revolution, his farm was heavily mortgaged. Seth had spent all his energies supporting the Revolution, and the family finances had suffered. Seth's untimely death left his family facing a certain loss of their farm. George Washington, who held Seth Warner in high regard as a Patriot, personally rode to the Warner farm in 1789 and counted out the silver coins to the exact sum required to retire the mortgage and save the farm. Washington wanted this act of Generosity kept a secret.[17]

During the first year of his command he devoted his waking time in organizing the new army, trying to get more recruits, and supplying the demanding needs of thousands of troops. Yet, even though this momentous task was time consuming, he still had time to worry about the less fortunate back home. On November 26, 1775, he wrote to Lund Washington, the distant cousin he appointed to care for Mount Vernon while he was commanding the army,

> Let the hospitality with respect to the poor be kept up. Let no one go hungry away. If any of this kind of people should be in want of corn, supply their necessities, provided it does not encourage them in idleness ; and I have no objection to your giving my money in charity to the amount of forty or fifty pounds a year, when you think it well bestowed.[18]

George Washington was noted as a modest man. He was having dinner on October 22, 1776, with sixty-one year old Captain Roger Lyon and his wife Mary. The Captain, who was blind, handed a drinking cup to Washington and remarked, "General, the ladies say that you are a handsome man, but I cannot see." Washington took the cup and replied, "Tell the ladies I am afraid they are as blind as yourself."[19]

In 1754, when Washington was twenty-two, there was an election that summer. George Fairfax, Washington's good friend, and William Payne had opposing views in the election and began to quarrel. Payne had several of his friends with him at the time. Washington, there with some of his militiamen, became angry and said something that offended Payne, who was much smaller than Washington. Payne struck Washington and surprisingly knocked him down.

To make it worse, some men in Washington's regiment came to his aid ready to get revenge on whoever knocked their beloved leader down. Several officers in Washington's militia pulled out their pistols to defend their commander.

Luckily for Mr. Payne and his friends, Washington stopped his soldiers from engaging in a fight. He thanked them for coming to his aid, but assured them it was not necessary. All the parties involved then moved on. Washington later, after some reflection on the matter, felt that he was the aggressor in the incident and wanted to ask Mr. Payne for his pardon.

The next day Washington went to a tavern and sent a note to Payne to meet him there. Payne soon arrived thinking that he was going to see some dueling pistols to settled what had occurred the previous day. He was much surprised when Washington offered his hand and said, "Mr. Payne, to err is nature; to rectify is glory. I find that I was wrong yesterday; but I was right today. You have had some satisfaction; and if you think that sufficient, here's my hand; let us be friends."

Payne was extremely impressed with Washington's noble jester, and at that moment became an admirer and friend of Washington. Years afterwards, George introduced Payne to his wife as "the little man…who had the resolution, to knock me down, big as I am."[20]

In 1769, Colonel Washington wrote to his distant relative and friend William Ramsay, a merchant at Alexandria, Virginia, "Having been informed of the studious habits of your son William, I will allow him twenty-five pounds annually to assist him in his education at Princeton College. No other return is expected or wished for this offer, than that you will accept it with the same freedom and good will with which it is made, and that you may not even consider it in the light of an obligation on, or mention it as such, for be assured that from me it will never be known."[21]

Respected by his troops:

General Washington had the love, respect, and support of his men. They were willing to stay with him and fight, even when they received no pay for months. In 1776, after losing several battles, his army in full retreat and the enlistment of many of his men up in a few weeks, Washington did the impossible. He rallied his troops to win victories at Trenton and Princeton and was able to keep his small army together. Most historians believe that these victories saved the Revolution.

A large part of Washington's strength of character was that he displayed good judgement concerning the talents of the men around him. By making Marquis de Lafayette a general, he trusted the twenty year old young man from France to lead men into battle. In 1780 Washington appointed Nathanael Greene as Southern Commander of the Continental Army. This move helped to turn the tide of the war in the south in favor of the Americans. His appointment of Baron Von

Steuben at Valley Forge, to train the American troops in the basics of military drills, tactics, and discipline, enabled the Americans to later face the British troops in battle as equals. The Baron also established standards of sanitations and camp layouts that made the army healthier.

Washington certainly was not perfect, for at times he could be vain, overly fond of adulation and power, and greatly disturbed by criticism. Yet, he appeared to be ashamed of his vanity and concealed it under an appearance of great modesty.

Washington was a man that did not seek personal glory. In victory he gave credit to his men and officers and was not threatened by taking the advice of others. Also, he was not afraid to make tough and dangerous decisions. One of his best decisions was to inoculate his troops for smallpox while encamped at Valley Forge. This probably saved his army and the Revolution.

The greatness of his character allowed him to share his power with others and pass on the credit to them. Washington, without doubt, took great satisfaction when the British surrendered at Yorktown and on his terms. Yet, though he was pleased, he made no demonstration of it, no prideful letter came from his pen, or any sentiments ever left his lips. He sent glowing reports of the conduct of his men to Congress, but never once took personal credit for any victory.

At Yorktown in 1781, Washington ceded the intellectual leadership of the siege to General Rochambeau. The French knew much more about how to conduct one than he did. Rochambeau had led, or at least participated in, fourteen sieges in Europe. Washington's pride was not involved, and he did not have to be persuaded to yield to the French suggestions on how to go about squeezing Cornwallis into surrendering. Most of the French troops had a high regard for Washington. Going into battle with him was, for many of the French troops an honor, and not just as opportunity to inflict revenge on an old enemy.

He certainly was not a great general, but, the army stayed together by the force of his great character. He showed flexibility in the means to hold his men. He agreed to temporary furloughs to enable soldiers to go home for short periods of time in order to find winter clothing for themselves, offered a month's pay for those in desperate need, and advised men who were paid to spend it on shirts, stockings, shoes, and leather breeches. He also constantly appealed to Congress for more money in which to pay his troops.

The men loved him and stayed with him throughout hard times, battle losses, and lack of pay. Washington led from the front, and the men knew that he looked out for their welfare and he suffered as they suffered.

Washington as a friend:

At Yorktown during one of Washington's visits to the main battery, a soldier of Colonel Lamb's artillery had his leg shattered by the explosion of a shell. As they were taking him to the rear for treatment, the wounded man recognized Washington and he cried out, "God bless your Excellency, save me if you can, for I have been a good soldier, and served under you during the whole war." Washington immediately ordered the wounded man taken to Doctor Craik (Washington's personal physician). However, it was too late and after an amputation was done, the man died.[22]

After the Battle of Germantown on October 4, 1777, a stray dog was found by some American troops. The dog was wearing an inscription on its collar indicating that he was the property of British General Howe, who was the man that had just defeated them. General Washington had the dog returned to Howe with a polite note. This was an indication of how respectable gentlemen, even in war, were supposed to act.

After the surrender of British General Cornwallis at Yorktown, Baron Von Steuben left for Philadelphia around the first of November. During the war he received very little pay for his services, so the only money he had for the 300 mile journey was one gold coin. George Washington insisted that the Baron take twenty guineas as a loan, and he knew that it was a small amount to give compared to the contribution von Steuben had made to the cause of liberty. Congress later gave the Baron a pension and some land for all he had done.

The true measure of Washington's character occurred when the peace treaty was finally signed and it officially ended the war. Washington always claimed that he sought no power or wealth during the Revolution. When it finally ended he was the most popular person in the United States. Any amount of power or wealth was his for the asking.

At the time it was widely believed that if he had asked, he could have become king or a dictator of the country. Yet, when it was all over, Washington surrendered his sword to Congress on December 23, 1783, and left for his home in Virginia. In his farewell address to Congress he said,

> The great events on which my resignation depended having at length taken place; I have now the honor of offering my sincere Congratulations to Congress and of presenting myself before them to surrender into their hands the trust committed to me, and to claim the indulgence of retiring from the Service of my Country.
>
> Having now finished the work assigned me, I retire from the great theatre of Action; and bidding an Affectionate farewell to this August body under whose orders I have so long acted, I here offer my Commission, and take my leave of all the employments of public life.[23]

When King George asked what Washington was going to do after the war, he was told that the General was going back to his farm. The King replied that if he did that, "he would be the greatest man in the world."[24]

Washington's Reputation

Washington orders the death of an innocent man:

Washington was always aware of his reputation and showed concern for it, by sometimes making a decision based on how it would impact it. This occurred when he was accused of cruelty in the Charles Asgill case in 1782.

In 1782 a Loyalist group executed Continental Army Captain Jack Huddy, in retaliation for the death of a Loyalist soldier, Philip White, on March 30, 1782. Huddy had been turned over to the Loyalists from the British under the false notion that he was going to be used in a prisoner exchange.

In retaliation for the death of Captain Huddy, patriot citizens pressured Washington to act, or they would take action. Washington responded by ordering that a British prisoner be selected to hang in retribution. Twelve British prisoners were chosen and lots drawn. British Captain Charles Asgill, age nineteen, was selected to be hung in retribution for the death of Huddy. In Britain, Asgill's mother, began an intense letter writing campaign on behalf of her son.

Washington began to have second thoughts about the matter, and he wrote to Elias Dayton, June 4, 1782,

> I am just informed by the Sectry at War that Capt. Asgill of the British Guards, the unfortunate Officer who is destined to be the unhappy Victim to atone for the Death of Capt. Huddy, was arrived in Philadelphia, & would set off very soon for the Jersey Line, the place assigned for his Execution. I most devoutly Wish his Life maybe saved—this happy Event may be attained. In the Mean Time while this is doing, I must beg, that you will be pleased to treat Capt. Asgill with every tender Attention & politeness (consistent with his present Situation) which his Rank, Fortune & Connections, together with his Unfortunate State, demand.[25]

Washington did not want to make the decision alone, so wrote to Congress about the dilemma on August 19, 1782, "It is a great national concern, upon which an individual ought not to decide. I shall be glad to be favored with the determination of Congress as early as possible, as I shall suspend giving any answer to Sir Guy Carleton, until I am informed how far they are satisfied with his conduct hitherto."[26]

Asgill wrote to Washington on October 18, 1787, and in the letter gave no indication of horrible treatment by his captors,

> I have been honored with your Excellys Letter & am exceedingly obliged by the attention which mine received. I will not intrude on your time by repetitions of my Distress, which has lately been increased by accounts that my Father is on his Death Bed. I have only to entreat as it may be a long while ere Congress finally determine, that your Excellency will be pleased to allow me to go to New York on Parole & to return in case my reappearance should hereafter be deemed necessary—if this request cannot be granted I hope your Excellency will give orders that my Parole may be withdrawn, as that Indulgence without a prospect of further Enlargement affords me not the least satisfaction, I had rather endure the most severe confinement, than suffer my Friends to remain as at present deceived, fancying ever since my first admission on Parole, that I was entirely liberated & no longer the Object of retaliation-- if your Excelly could form an Idea of my sufferings I am convinced the trouble I give would be excused.[27]

After deliberation, Congress and Washington decided to release the British officer. Washington notified the young man by letter on November 13, 1782,

> It affords me singular pleasure to have it in my power to transmit you the enclosed Copy of an Act of Congress of the 7th instant, by which you are released from the disagreeable circumstances in which you have so long been—supposing you would wish to go into New York as soon as possible, I also in close a passport for that purpose.
>   Your letter of the 18th of October came regularly to my hands—I beg you to believe, that my not answering it sooner, did not proceed from inattention to you, or a want of feeling for your situation—I daily expected a determination of your case, & I thought it better to await that, than to feed you with hopes that might in the end prove fruitless.[28]

Captain Asgill received the letter and returned to England. Later, Asgill began spreading rumors that while a prisoner he was treated with cruelty. This would be a blight on the impeccable reputation Washington had during the war. A letter from James Tilghman was sent to George Washington on May 26, 1786, containing the complaint made against him. It said that Asgill alleged,

> ....that a Gibbet was erected before his prison Window and often pointed in an insulting manner as good, and proper for him to atone for Huddy's death And many other insults all of which he believes were countenanced

by General Washington who was well inclined to execute the Sentence on him but was restrained by the French General Rochambeau.[29]

Washington replied to the letter on June 5, 1786, and denied that he had done anything wrong in the treatment of the British officer,

> I felt for him on many accounts, & not the least, when viewing him as a man of humor & sentiment how unfortunate it was for him that a wretch who possesses neither, should be the means of causing in him a single pang, or a disagreeable sensation._ My favorable opinion of him, however, is forfeited if, being acquainted with these reports, he did not immediately contradict them.
>
> That I could not have given countenance to the insults which *he says* were offered to his person, especially the *groveling* one of creating a gibbet before his prison window, will, I expect, readily be believed when I explicitly declare that I never heard of a single attempt to offer an insult, & that I had every reason to be convinced that he was treated by the officers around him with all the tenderness & every civility in their power.[30]

The problem with a gift:

One difficult test of Washington's reputation occurred in 1785 before he became president. As early as 1772, Washington felt the Potomac and James Rivers were promising locations for canals to be built that would join with the western rivers. The project to accomplish this began in 1785, with the formation of the James River and Potomac Canal Companies.

The state of Virginia decided to show Washington their gratitude for his war service by giving him 150 shares in the company. The act they passed read, "Be it enacted by the Genl. Assembly that the Treasr. be directed in addition to the subscriptions he is already authorised to make to the respective undertakings for Opening the Navigation of Potowmac & James Rivers, to subscribe to the amt. of 50 shares to the former and 100 Shares to the latter, to be paid in like manner with the subscriptions above mentioned: and that the shares so subscribed be & the same & are hereby vested in George Washington."[31]

Washington was afraid that this action might tarnish his reputation. In a letter to Benjamin Harrison, he thought if he "accepted the gift it might be viewed by the public as a pension given to him. On the other hand his reputation might be harmed by refusing the honor. Some might consider this act as being disrespectful to the generous intent of the people."[32]

Washington wanted the project to be successful, but he feared being misunderstood even though he was a private citizen. Besides writing to Benjamin Harrison, he also wrote to other important men for guidance. He explained to Patrick Henry that he would accept the honor but have the funds be for public use, "But if it should please the General Assembly to permit me to turn the destination of the fund vested in me from my private emoluments, to objects of a public nature."[33]

The stock given to Washington amounted to a hefty $20,000 which would be over $600,000 in today's money. It was given as an endowment to Liberty Hall Academy. This university, in Lexington, Virginia was renamed Washington College and was later changed to Washington and Lee University. This proved to be a wonderful compromise for all parties concerned.

Just a Common Man:

Just before Washington was elected president, Elkanah Watson paid him a visit at Mount Vernon in 1785. Watson wrote, "I was extremely oppressed with a severe cold and excessive coughing, contracted from the exposure of a harsh winter journey. He pressed me to use some remedies, but I declined doing so. As usual after retiring, my coughing increased. When some time had elapsed, the door of my room was gently opened and, on drawing my bed-curtains, to my utter astonishment, I beheld Washington himself, standing at my bedside, with a bowl of hot tea in his hand. I was mortified and distressed beyond expression."[34]

During Washington's first term as president, he was down with a fever, when the wife of his vice-president, Abigail Adams, visited Martha Washington. The next day Washington was still ill, but he felt compelled to accompany his wife to return the visit to Abigail.

The Washingtons took a large carriage drawn by six horses to the Adam's residence. The president had ordered the carriage outfitted to accommodate his illness by placing a bed in back. As they drove through the crowded streets with Washington in the bed, he was coughing and blowing his nose. It was important to him that he go with Martha to return Abigail's visit.

Abigail was so impressed that she wrote to her friend Mary Smith Cranch about it on July 12, 1789, "The President has a Bed put into his Carriage and rides out in that way, always with six Horses in his Carriage & four attendants, Mrs. Washington accompanies him."[35]

In 1796, Boston merchant Thomas H. Perkins visited Washington at Mount Vernon, and they sat outside at the back of the house overlooking the river. Rather than talking about the Revolution, his Presidency, or current affairs, Washington chose to talk about nature.

The former president asked Perkins if he had ever observed a toad swallowing a fire-fly. Perkins assured him that he never had. Washington was delighted to tell him that due to the thinness of the toad's skin, he had once seen the light of the fire-fly after it had been swallowed. Perkins later wrote, "I need not remark how deeply I was interested in every word which fell from the lips of this great man."[36]

In June during the early part of the war, a stranger rode into a small village. He stopped at a farmhouse and told the farmer that he was lost and was looking for shelter due to the approaching darkness. The farmer invited the traveler inside and introduced him to his wife. The man's wife was concerned that the stranger might be there to rob them, but after talking with the visitor she believed him to be a good man and was no longer worried. She mentioned that their son Peter was in the Continental Army.

The next morning when the stranger arose, he declined the family's invitation to have breakfast with them and offered them money for allowing him to spend the night. The couple refused any money for their hospitality. The stranger then told them, "I was out yesterday trying to obtain some information on our enemy. I was alone and I ventured too far from the camp. On my return I was surprised by an enemy foraging party, and managed to escape due to my knowledge of the woods and my fast horse. My name is George Washington."[37]

Chasing Fire Wagons:

A few months before his death, George Washington was riding down King Street in Alexandria, Virginia, when a fire bell rang out. Not many of the locals answered the call, but Washington on his horse shouted out, "It is your duty to lead in such matters. Come!" Washington was one of the first to the fire.

He then jumped from his horse and helped man the pumps. Cheering citizens ran to help him, and in a few minutes the fire was under control. Washington had been running to fires since he was a boy, and he continued during his old age.[38]

George Washington as a volunteer fireman in colonial America. Wood engraving, American, 19th century.

4

The Emotions of George Washington

"Yes, sir, he swore on that day, till the leaves shook on the trees, charming, delightful. Never have I enjoyed such swearing before or since. Sir, on that ever-memorable day, he swore like an angel from heaven."----General Charles Scott about Washington at the Battle of Monmouth.

❧

The George Washington most of us grew up with was portrayed as stoic, never smiling, and without a hint of humor. He was a man that was always in complete control of his emotions, and certainly would never had shed a tear in front of others. Most of his portraits showed a man with a grim look on his face, much like the vice-principal we feared at school. All business, no nonsense, a man that looked like he never had any fun, this was the Washington we learned about in school.

Washington the Actor:

In the winter of 1782-83 the United States was still negotiating a peace treaty with England. British troops remained on American soil and Washington's biggest problem was holding his army together to face any threats. American officers were unhappy with Congress because they still had not raised money to pay their salaries, and there was talk that the promise of pensions after the war would be broken. If the officers were to revolt, the army would likely disband and the Revolution would be in danger of failing.

At Washington's headquarters in Newburgh, New York, word got out that there would be a grievance meeting among the officers and they would take strong action. The officers met on March 15, 1783, and as the meeting opened, Washington made a surprise appearance, and faced the group of angry and brooding men. These were officers who he had fought alongside of for years, and now they were the enemy. He urged the men to be patience, explaining that Congress moved slowly.

Washington realized that the men were in no mood to listen to excuses and they were not willing to show him the respect that they had showed in the past. He pulled from his coat pocket a letter from a member of Congress to read to the officers. He fumbled with the letter as if he had trouble reading it, he then pulled out a pair of reading glasses, which only a few of the men had ever seen him wear on occasion.

Washington slowly put the glasses on and said, "Gentlemen, you will permit me to put on my spectacles, for I have not only grown gray but almost blind in the service of my country." This simple sentence caused the officers to recall that their leader had sacrificed much during the Revolution, just as they had. They remembered that he had stood with them during hardship and dangerous times. Many of the men were moved to tears as he struggled to read the letter.

After Washington read the letter he left the room. At that moment the rebellion collapsed and the men were willing to try and work the problems out with Congress. General Knox and other officers offered resolutions of their loyalty to the country, and a committee was formed to write a solution to the problem to present to Congress. The officers' rebellion had been dissolved and the Union was saved.

General Philip Schuyler wrote, "Never through all the war did his Excellency achieve a greater victory than on this occasion, a victory over jealousy, just discontent, and great opportunities. The whole Assembly was in tears at the conclusion of his address."[1]

The Stiffness of Washington:

During the Constitutional Convention, Alexander Hamilton remarked to Governor Morris that George Washington was reserved even to his intimate friends. Morris replied that he could be as familiar with Washington as with any other friend. Hamilton bet Morris a wine supper for himself and a dozen friends if Morris, at the next reception, would gently slap Washington on the back and say, "My dear General, how happy I am to see you, you look so well."

Morris accepted the bet, and at the next reception he made the required remark to Washington and placed his hand on the General's shoulder. Washington withdrew Morris's hand with an angry glance. Washington stared at Morris for a minute or so until Morris retreated and sought refuge in the crowd which was watching in silence.[2] At the supper, which was provided by Hamilton, Morris said, "I have won the bet, but paid dearly for it. Nothing could induce me to repeat it."[3]

Surprisingly, when you read Washington's personal diaries, private letters, and the numerous first hand stories of the man, you learn that he was quite different than the way we imagine him. For the majority of the time, Washington contained and controlled his emotions. In doing so, he could use them at opportune times to induce fear, compassion, understanding, courage, or direction for the people around him.

His early years at Mount Vernon may have provided the atmosphere that helped the young Washington to learn control as a man. Managing a large plantation helped him to develop patience, moderation, and how to effectively deal with subordinates. Being part of the aristocratic class help to train him in the use of persuasion and diplomacy to gain his goals.

Washington's Temper

There is no doubt that George Washington displayed a hot temper, which he inherited from his mother, Mary Ball Washington. The woman was easily displeased, exacting, and was noted for her fiery temper.

Thomas Jefferson wrote of George Washington's temper, "His temper was naturally irritable and high toned; but reflection & resolution had obtained a firm and habitual ascendancy over it. If ever however it broke its bonds he was most tremendous in his wrath."[4]

Gilbert Stuart painted several portraits of Washington over the years. The most famous one was the unfinished portrait that later was portrayed on the one dollar bill. Gilbert's daughter Jane, told a story about Washington's temper, "While talking one day with General Lee, my father happened to remark that Washington had a tremendous temper, but held it under wonderful control. General Lee breakfasted with the President and Mrs. Washington a few days afterward."

"I saw your portrait the other day," said the General, "but Stuart says you have a tremendous temper."

"Upon my word," said Mrs. Washington, "Mr. Stuart takes a great deal upon himself, to make such a remark."

"But stay, my dear lady," said General Lee. He added that the President "had it under wonderful control."

With something like a smile, General Washington remarked, "He is right."[5]

Gilbert Stuart's unfinished 1796 painting of George Washington is also known as the *Athenaeum Portrait*, his most celebrated and famous work. He left it unfinished so that he could refer to it when producing future paintings. Public domain.

Battle of Long Island:

In battle Washington was usually in control of his emotions in order to lessen the effects on the actions of his men. However, there were several occasions in which his temper emerged for all to see, and in those cases, it proved to be just what his men needed at the time. When an officer told World War II General George Patton, who was known to have a temper, that sometimes the men couldn't tell when he was acting and when he was not. He supposedly replied that it was not important for them to know, only important for him to know. It is possible that Washington, too, may have done a little acting when exhibiting his temper.

There were several times during the Battle of Long Island in 1776, that Washington lost his temper. On August 22, when the British were landing their troops on Long Island, Washington became outraged at what he saw. The British had been landing troops and preparing for battle in a precise and orderly manner. The American troops facing them were scattered, walking around as if they were on a Sunday stroll, and discharging their weapons as if celebrating. Washington later wrote a letter to General Israel Putnam and lectured him the way he might talk to a raw officer,

It was with no small degree of concern I surprise yesterday a scattering, unmeaning & wasteful fire, from our people at the enemy, a kind of fire that tended to disgrace our own men as soldiers, and to render our defense contemptible in the eyes of the enemy; no one good consequence can attend such irregularities, but several bad ones will inevitably follow on it.

I must therefore Sir, in earnest terms, desire you to call the Colonels & commanding officers of corps, (without loss of time) before you; and let them afterwards do the same by their respective officers, and charge them, in express & positive terms, to stop these irregularities, as they value the good of the service, their own honor, and the safety of the army.

The distinction between a well-regulated army, & a mob, is the good order & discipline of the first, & the licentious & disorderly surprise of the latter.[6]

The secret retreat:

On August 19, 1776, Washington's army was trapped by the British in Brooklyn Heights and their only hope was to retreat, in secret, across the East River to Manhattan. That evening Washington ordered his 9,000 men to quickly board boats and retreat across the river. For the retreat to be successful, if would need to be accomplished with order and in silence.

Washington noticed that the troops on the beach were no longer following orders. The beach had become clogged with men and disorder prevailed. The men were in a panic and some were trying to board boats and leave out of turn. Washington saw what was happening and raced to the edge of the water where the boats were, and in apparent anger, bent down and picked up a large rock, held it over his head and shouted to the men trying to get in one of the boats, "Damn you!" The stunned men stopped and looked and their general.

"Leave this boat immediately or I will sink it to hell."[7] The men, never seeing their general angry, left the boat, lined up and began following the orders of their officers. By morning all 9,000 men had been transported safely across the river, and the army was saved.

Later that same evening Washington again became angry, this time with an officer, General Thomas Mifflin. As the Americans retreated toward the East River, General Mifflin was ordered to establish a rear guard in the American camp to keep the camp fires burning, so that the British would think that Americans were still in camp and not retreating. At about four in the morning, on August 30, Mifflin was informed by Major Alexander Scammell that it was his unit's turn to evacuate. Mifflin told Scammell that he must be mistaken, but Scammell insisted that he was not, so Mifflin ordered his troops to move out. When Mifflin's troops were within a half mile of the ferry landing, Washington rode up and demanded to know why they were not at their defenses.

Edward Hand, who was leading the troops, tried to explain what had happened, just as Mifflin rode up. Washington exclaimed "Good God, General Mifflin, I am afraid you have ruined us." Mifflin explained that he had been told that it was his turn to evacuate by Scammell. Washington told him it had been a dreadful mistake, and told Mifflin to take his troops back to the outer defenses. Luckily, the British were not aware of what had transpired and the American retreat proved successful.[8]

Anger at Kip's Bay:

The next month on September 15, 1776, Washington once again lost his temper when the British landed their troops on the East River shore of Manhattan at Kip's Bay. Washington was four miles to the north of the landing and upon hearing cannon fire he decided to ride toward the sounds. He wrote to John Hancock the next day telling what he encountered,

As soon as I heard the Firing, I road with all possible dispatch towards the place of landing when to my great 41surprise and Mortification I found the Troops that had been posted in the Lines retreating with the utmost precipitation and those ordered to support them, parson's & Fellows's Brigades, flying in every direction and in the greatest confusion, notwithstanding the exertions of their Generals to form them. I used every means in my power to rally and get them into some order but my attempts were fruitless and ineffectual, and on the appearance of a small party of the Enemy, not more than Sixty or Seventy, their disorder increased and they ran away in the greatest confusion without firing a Single Shot.[9]

Washington could not stop the men from running from the battle. There were some reports that he lost control of himself, ran his horse into their midst, and even threated them with his pistol and sword. Finally, in anger he threw his hat on the ground and yelled, "Are these the men with which I am to defend America? "[10]

Near the spot where the Public Library now stands, at the corner of Fifth Avenue and Forty-Second Street, he met a stream of wild-eyed, breathless soldiers in flight, some of whom had thrown away their weapons. It was reported that an officer came panting along in white-faced terror and recognized Washington. "Save yourself, General," the officer called out, "the redcoats are coming!"[11]

The sight of this officer in flight so enraged Washington that he swung his pistol at him, and tried to run over him with his horse. The terrified officer hurried away more frightened than ever. The British advanced within a hundred yards of capturing Washington, forcing his aids to grab the bridle of his horse and making him flee the field. Had they not, Washington, who was angry and trying in vain to rally his men, would have likely been captured or shot.

Washington's anger at Kip's Bay, from the book *Graham's American Monthly Magazine of Literature & Art, Vol. XLV.* 1854, page 14.

The general's anger did not go away, five days later he issued this order of the day, "Any soldier or officer who upon the approach or attack of the enemy's forces by land or water, shall presume to turn his back and flee, shall be instantly shot down, and all good officers are hereby authorized and required to see this done, that the brave and gallant part of the army may not fall a sacrifice to the base and cowardly part, nor share their disgrace in a cowardly and unmanly retreat."[12]

These outburst of anger in such a short period of time would not occur again during the war. At New York, Washington may have been angry at himself, because the landing was a tactical surprise that caught him off guard. In addition, this was the first time his men had been tested in battle and their discipline was severely lacking. Washington continued to make several mistakes during this encounter and British General Howe had made him look foolish. Fortunately, one of the great things about Washington was that he quickly learned from his mistakes. In the future he would make less blunders and losing his temper would become a rarity.

Salty Language

Cursing at the Battle of Monmouth:

Washington's next big outburst was directed towards one man's lack of courage rather than the lack of support from Congress or the men under his command. It occurred in June of 1778, after the bleak winter at Valley Forge. His new army had undergone new training under the leadership of the Prussian taskmaster, Baron Von Steuben. On June 28, 1778, Washington and his army approached the British army under the command of General Henry Clinton at Monmouth Courthouse, New Jersey. It was one of the hottest days of the year and the heat would almost claim as many victims as bullets. The Americans were outnumbered, but, with the exception of perhaps one soldier, they were anxious to engage the British, to prove that all of their training would pay off.

General Charles Lee, who was never a supporter of General Washington, was offered command of the attacking vanguard. Lee turned it down because he did not like Washington's battle plan and thought the force would be too small, so Washington turned over the command to 20 year old General Lafayette, the wonder boy from France. Lee then decided that perhaps the force was large enough, and decided that he wanted the command back. Since Lee was a senior officer to Lafayette, the request was granted.

When the fighting began, Lee misjudged the size of the British force he had encountered. After a few shots, Lee ordered a retreat, without any apparent cause. He was unaware that most of the British soldiers were over three miles away and posed no immediate threat to him. He was unable to control his men and the retreat became a disorganized flight.

Washington saw the retreat and rode into it. When he encountered Lee, he shouted in fierce tones, "What is the meaning of all this, Sir?" Lee hesitated for a moment, and Washington again demanded, "I desire to know the meaning of this disorder and confusion!" The fiery Lee, stung by Washington's manner, made an angry reply, and the chief, unable to control himself, called Lee "a damned poltroon" [a spiritless coward]. "This," said Lafayette, when relating this story to Governor Tompkins, in 1824, while on his visit to this country, "was the only time I ever heard General Washington swear."[13]

Lee attempted a hurried explanation, and after a few more angry words between the two men, with most of the talking being done by Washington, the angry general departed to form his line and began to rally the men to attack. Then, riding back to Lee in a calmer mind, he offered Lee the choice to fall back or remain and organize the rear guard. Lee chose to remain, however after the battle he said that what he did earlier was right and that Washington was guilty of an act of a cruel injustice toward him. He continued to protest, which later resulting in his being brought up on charges for ordering a retreat and being disrespectful to the Commander-in-Chief. He was found guilty of all charges and was removed from the army for a year.

Painting titled *Washington Rallying the Troops at Monmouth*; depicts George Washington at the 1778 Battle of Monmouth. In 1857, Leutze painted a copy one-third of this size for the Monmouth County Historical Association. Public domain.

Lee could not let the matter rest, and for years he continued to make verbal attacks on Washington. Washington's friend, Colonel John Laurens, could no longer take the attacks on his commander and challenged Lee to a duel. Lee was wounded in the duel, and in 1780, Lee was permanently removed from the army.

Another account of what took place between Lee and Washington, claimed that Washington's language "shook the leaves off the trees."[14] There were other soldiers present at the occurrence and it was the first time that anyone could recall Washington cursing since the retreat at Manhattan.

Cursing once again:

Henry Cabot Lodge received a letter from the sculptor William Story on March 15, 1877, and it contained a story his father, Joseph, told him about George Washington. The story illustrates Washington's violent temper and sometimes salty language,

> It was at one of the most anxious periods of the War and if my memory serves me right immediately after the Battle of the Brandy Wine when there was great doubt as to the exact position and movement of the British. Washington called a meeting of all the officers to discuss the situation and determine the best course to pursue. The consultation took place in Washington's tent. The night was very stormy and wild. Different views were taken by the officers and it became exceedingly important to know the exact position of the British across the river. Washington accordingly sent for an officer and directed him at once to cross the river and endeavor to discover where the British forces were and whether they were in movement and in what direction. The officer received his orders and departed and Washington and his officers remained together in the tent awaiting his report.

Hours passed by of impatience and anxiety. At last he returned. Washington was sitting at a little table on which were writing materials and a large heavy leaden inkstand. "Well," he said, as the officer returned, "What is your report?" The officer in answer and with some hesitation replied that he regretted to say that he had found it impossible to cross the river on account of the severe storm, the violence of the wind and rain, and the swollen condition of the river; that he had done his best but had found it impossible. Washington at this report glared at him an instant and then seizing the great leaden inkstand launched it at his head exclaiming "God damn your soul to Hell, be off with you and send me a man." The officer vanished. He had had enough. In an hour or two he returned and gave his report. Washington had made it possible for him to cross the river and he was able to state the position of the enemy. Those, I think, were the exact words Washington used. They remain fixed and clear in my memory. They made Washington to me a more real and distinct person, and accounted for his personal power and absoluteness of character more than all the dignified narratives of the buckram historians.[15]

Even though General George Patton believed that you can't run an army without profanity, Washington was not the type of man to make it a habit of using bad language. In fact, he really despised himself or anyone else using it. On August 3, 1776, while in New York he issued the General Orders for the day by stating,

The General is sorry to be informed that the foolish, and wicked practice, of profane cursing and swearing [a Vice heretofore little known in an American Army] is growing into fashion; he hopes the officers will, by example, as well as influence, endeavor to check it, and that both they, and the men will reflect, that we can have little hopes of the blessing of Heaven on our Arms, if we insult it by our impiety, and folly; added to this, it is a vice so mean and low, without any temptation, that every man of sense, and character, detests and despises it.[16]

A Friend Turns Traitor

Benedict Arnold had conspired with Major John Andre to turn traitor for money and a commission in the British Army. After the capture of British spy Major John Andre, the major was taken to Colonel John Jameson and he soon convinced the colonel to send him to Arnold at West Point. Colonel Jameson, at this time, was unaware that Arnold was a traitor. Andre was sent to Arnold, but luckily for the Americans he was intercepted and brought back. Meanwhile, Colonel Jameson had sent the incriminating papers that Andre carried to General Washington. Then Jameson sent a note to Arnold telling him of Andre's arrest. This alerted Arnold that the plot had been uncovered and gave him the chance to avoid capture.

When Washington learned that Benedict Arnold had turned traitor he showed mixed emotions. This author believes that most of his emotion about the event was really more of disappointment, than anger. Arnold had been popular with Washington, despite the fact that Arnold could act like a diva at times and was sometimes be a thorn under Washington's saddle.

Washington's real anger showed when he learned that Arnold had escaped capture. After going to Arnold's home and learning of his escape, Washington ordered Alexander Hamilton and James McHenry to go after him. Soon after, Lafayette came into the room and saw Washington sitting with his head down, hand trembling holding the captured treasonous papers, and murmuring to Henry Knox, "Arnold has betrayed me, who can I trust now?"[17]

When Washington learned that Arnold escaped, he exploded with anger at Colonel Jameson for his "egregious folly." He also stated, "Had it not been for Jameson's bewildered conception of his duty to tell Arnold that he had capture Andre, I should as certainly have got Arnold."[18]

On September 27, 1780 Colonel Jameson wrote to his apology to Washington for losing Arnold,

I am very sorry that I wrote to G———Arnold I did not think of a British Ship being up the River and expected that if he was the Man he has since turned out to be, that he wou'd come ⟨down⟩ to the Troops in this Quarter in which case I sho⟨u'd⟩ have secured him (I mentioned my intention to Major Tallmage and some others of the Field Officers all of who(m) were clearly of Opinion that it wou'd be right) until I could hear from your Excellency.[19]

—·····─

The President's Temper

As Washington grew older, the outburst of temper lessen. Washington was later selected to be the first president of the United States by a unanimous vote. He was by far the most loved and popular person in the country. You might think that this would be a period of calm for Washington and the temper he inherited from his mother would not be seen. Unfortunately, Washington was loved by all until he became president.

His first term was a much enjoyed honeymoon period, most things that Washington did started a precedent. In addition, he was still idolized by the masses as the savior of the country. During the years after the Revolution, more newspapers began to spring up and soon they started printing opinions and critical comments that they were not free to do under the previous British rule. By the end of Washington's first term, printed stories were appearing attacking his domestic and foreign policy. Washington had always been sensitive to criticism and these attacks troubled him. It became especially hard when some of the attacks questioned his reputation.

Washington managed to keep control of his temper in the public eye, however behind closed doors it was another matter. It was reported that at one cabinet meeting the President's temper got the best of him that he ripped off his hat, threw it on the ground, and stomped on it. The public never really knew that President Washington ever lost his temper. John Adams explained why in a letter written to Benjamin Rush in 1897, "Whenever he lost his temper as he did Sometimes, either love or fear in those about him induced them to conceal his weakness from the world."[20] This was the same John Adams who had a terrible temper of his own, and once in a fit of rage called Washington a muttonhead.

In Washington's second term as President, he was criticized by friend and foe alike for his neutral stand towards France when the British went to war against them after the French revolution. In 1796, at the end of Washington's second term as president, Thomas Paine attacked him in a series of letters sent to the president, such as the one written on July 30, 1796,

Being now once more abroad in the world I began to find that I was not the only one who had conceived an unfavourable opinion of Mr. Washington. It was evident that his character was on the decline as well among Americans as among foreigners of different nations. From being the chief of a government, he had made himself the chief of a party; and his integrity was questioned, for his politics had a doubtful appearance.[21]

Thomas Jefferson and the Democrat-Republicans were happy about the downfall of the French monarchy and the establishment of a republic. Washington, with his aristocratic beliefs, did not agree with the views of Jefferson toward France, but he said little about it. His wife Martha was not so quiet, she called Jefferson's followers "filthy Democrats."

After a particularly harsh attack in a newspaper by Benjamin Franklin's pro-French grandson, Washington flew into a rage. He pounded his desk and shouted that he was tired of being treated like a "common pickpocket." He swore that he would rather be in the grave than put up with another day of this thankless job.[22] It took a full half hour for him to regain his composure. The general public never saw or heard this outburst by Washington.

Washington's frustrations were understandable. After all, he wanted to live out his life at Mount Vernon after serving his country. Yet, every time a national problem came up it was Washington who was called upon for guidance. When the Constitutional Convention was formed, the delegates said Washington was needed to lead it. When a president was needed, he was talked into the job. After his first term, he wanted to go back home, but it was insisted that he serve again. Washington never sought these jobs after the war, he simply wanted to go back to his farm and live out his days there. And now the same people who earlier praised him and begged him to lead the country were now attacking him, his policies, and his character.

—☙❧—

Controlling His Temper

A good example of Washington controlling his emotions occurred in October 1777. Washington had just begun sitting for his portrait when war dispatches were brought to him. He glanced at them, and continued the sitting without remark. The dispatches announced the capture of Burgoyne at Saratoga.[23]

This was the first great victory against the British and it proved to be the turning point of the American Revolution, yet Washington received it as if he had been notified that a small skirmish had occurred. The commanding general, Gates, had notified Congress first of the victory instead of following the chain of command and notifying Washington. Perhaps Washington was angry about that, regardless he still showed no emotions.

After learning of the victory second hand, Washington had the chance to admonish Gates for not following the chain of command and notifying him first. Washington knew this was not only proper military protocol, but should have done out of respect for your commanding officer. Washington wrote to General Gates on October 30, 1777, to congratulate him on the victory and to call his attention to the fact that he should have notified Washington first. Once again Washington held his temper in check and politely wrote,

> Event that does the highest honor to the American Arms, and which, I hope will be attended with the most extensive and happy consequences. At the same time, I cannot but regret, that a matter of such magnitude and so interesting to our General Operations, should have reached me by report only, or through the channel of Letters not bearing that authenticity, which the importance of it required, and which it would have received by a line under your signature, stating the simple fact.[24]

—☙❧—

Receiving a disturbing letter:

In November of 1791, Washington was entertaining guests at a dinner when he received a distressing letter. He left the dinner table to read the letter in private, which informed Washington that the army under General Arthur St. Clair, who had been operating in the west, was ambushed and cut to pieces.

His aide, Tobias Lear was alone in the room with Washington when he read the letter and the aid later said, "The chief paced the room in hurried strides. In his agony, he struck his clenched hands with fearful force against his forehead. Washington then exclaimed, 'That brave army so officered, Butler, Ferguson, Kirkwood, such officers are not to be replaced within a day.'"[25] Washington then told Lear that in this very room he had told St. Clair to not trust the Indians and to be careful of a surprise.

Once Washington gained control of his composure he told Lear that this news must not go beyond this room. He then sat down for a few moments and later returned to the dinner party showing no change in his manner.

The great snowball fight:

There were times that controlling his temper in front of his men made a bigger impression than losing it. One such time happen on a snowy day in December of 1775. General George Washington had the task of molding men from different regions into a single American Army. American troops fortifying Cambridge during the Siege of Boston needed places to stay, so the president of Harvard, Samuel Langdon, offered his campus to Washington's troops. The five Harvard buildings were used to house 1,600 troops during the winter months, and the Harvard students moved their studies to Concord. Tents and barracks were assembled in Harvard Yard for the troops.

The first troops to move in were from New England such as the 27th Continental Regiment. One day in December a rifle corps from Virginia came into the American camp. The Virginia boys were mainly backwoods and mountain boys, and this was their first time to venture out of their communities. They acted differently and dressed differently from that of the regiments from New England.

The Virginia troops excited the curiosity of the troops from New England, particularly the Marblehead Regiment from Massachusetts. This regiment was composed of seafaring men who were always full of fun and mischief. The Marblehead boys wore heavy round jackets and loose fisherman trousers compared to the buckskins and white linen frocks with ruffles and fringe that the boys from Virginia wore. To make matters worse the Massachusetts troops had some black troops with them. The Virginia troops saw the black soldiers as slaves rather than equals, which caused even more tension.

The two groups began making remarks about how silly the other group dressed. Soon the men began to get serious with each other, and since there was snow on the ground they began throwing snowballs. In no time the playing developed into a heated battle with snowballs flying everywhere. In a matter of minutes the battle escalated with biting, hitting, and gouging. The yard quickly filled with hundreds of combatants engaged in hand-to-hand combat.

A ten year old boy, Israel Trask, was a witness to the event and wrote about what happened next,

> At this juncture General Washington made his appearance, whether accident of design I never knew. I only saw him and his colored servant, both mounted. With the spring of a deer he leaped from his saddle, threw the reins of his bridle into the hands of his servant and rushed into the thickest of the melee with an iron grip seized two, brawny, athletic, savage looking riflemen by the throat keeping them at arm's length alternately shaking and talking to them. In the position the eye of the belligerents caught sight of the General. Its effect on them was instantaneous flight at the top of their speed in all directions from the scene of conflict. Less than fifteen minutes time had lapsed from the commencement of the row before the general and his two criminals were the only occupants of the field of action.[26]

Most people thought that the General would have taken the two men and imprisoned them, court martialed them, and perhaps given them the lash. Instead, Washington released the men and left. The hostile feeling between the two groups ceased due to the mere presence of the physical and mental strength displayed by Washington. The fact that Washington grabbed two fellow Virginians showed the men that he would not be influenced by regional loyalties.

In 1778, there was another snowball fight, this time between Virginia and Pennsylvania troops. General Washington quickly issued a General Order forbidding, on pain of severe punishment, any person belonging to the army throwing snowballs at each other.[27]

Feelings of Despair and Discouragement

Many times, especially during the first few years of the war, Washington felt discouraged and bitter about the course the war was taking. He was in command of a large group of rabble that had surrounded the British in Boston after the Battles of Lexington and Concord in April 1775. The militia he commanded was not a trained army, and the officers were not, in most cases, trained to lead men in battle. To make matters even worse, he had almost no supplies, including powder. Washington now realized that he has been given an almost impossible task. Yet, he always tried to keep his glum feelings from the common soldier under his command.

In his frustration he would express his feelings of despair to others in private letters. One such letter was written to Lieutenant Joseph Reed, one of his trusted aids. At the end of the letter he appeared to have regretted taking command of the army.

> I am perswaded, endulge as many more—The Connecticut Troops will not be prevail'd upon to stay longer than their term (saving those who have enlisted for the next Campaign, & mostly on Furlough) and such a dirty, mercenary Spirit pervades the whole, that I should not be at all surprizd at any disaster that may happen—In short, after the last of this Month, our lines will be so weakend that the Minute Men and Militia must be call'd in for their defence—these being under no kind of Government themselves, will destroy the little subordination I have been labouring to establish, and run me into one evil, whilst I am endeavouring to avoid another; but the lesser must be chosen. could I have foreseen what I have, & am like to experience, no consideration upon Earth should have induced me to accept this Command.[28]

On January 14, 1776 Washington again wrote an extremely despairing letter to Reed. For the past nine months the American army had surrounded the British in Boston, the men were sick, short of supplies and were starting to leave to go home. Washington had requested help from

Congress and the state governments, a message which had fallen on deaf ears. Washington was downcast and feeling sorry for himself when he wrote to Reed,

> We are now without any Money in our treasury—Powder in our Magazines—Arms in Our Stores—We are without a Brigadier (the want of which has been twenty times urged)—Engineers—Expresses (though a Committee has been appointed these two Months to establish them)—and by & by, when we shall be called upon to take the Field, shall not have a Tent to lay in—a propos, what is doing with mine?
>
> These are Evils, but small in comparison of those, which disturb my present repose. Our Inlistments are at a stand—the fears I ever entertaind are realiz'd—that is, the discontented Officers (for I do not know how else to acct for it) have thrown such difficulties, or Stumbling blocks in the way of Recruiting that I no longer entertain a hope of compleating the Army by Voluntary Inlistments, & I see no move, or likelihood of one, to do it by other mean's.
>
> In consequence of the Assurances given, & my expectation of having at least Men enough Inlisted to defend our lines, to which may be added my unwillingness of burthening the caus(e) with unnecessary expence, no relief of Militia has been order'd.
>
> I Issued an Order directing three judicious Men of each Brigade to attend—review—and appraise the good Arms of every Regiment—& finding a very great unwillingness in the Men to part with their Arms, at the same time, not having it in my power to pay them for the Months of Novr & Decr I threatned, severely, that every Soldier who carried away his Firelock, without leave, should never receive pay for those Months; yet, so many have been carried of, partly by stealth, but cheefly as condemn'd, that we have not, at this time 100 Guns in the Stores of all that have been taken in the Prize Ship, and from the Soldiery notwithstanding our Regiments are not half compleat.
>
> Few People know the Predicament we are In, on a thousand Accts—fewer still will beleive, if any disaster happens to these Lines, from what causes it flows—I have often thought, how much happier I should have been, if, instead of accepting of a command under such Circumstances I had taken my Musket upon my Shoulder & enterd the Ranks, or, if I could have justified the Measure to Posterity, & my own Conscience, had retir'd to the back Country, & livd in a Wig-wam..
>
> Could I have foreseen the difficulties which have come upon us—could I have known that such a backwardness would have been discoverd in the old Soldiers to the Service, all the Generals upon Earth should not have convinced me of the propriety of delaying an Attack upon Boston till this time.[29]

This certainly does not sound like the confident, take charge leader we learned about in school. This was the side of Washington that the early biographers of the general would either downplay or overlook completely.

Misery at Valley Forge:

In 1777 at Valley Forge, Washington once again felt that he was not up to the challenge of leading the army. He had just lost two battles and was losing troops to desertion and disease. Recruitment was down and it appeared that by the spring of 1778, he would no longer have an army. The men around him were not aware that their general felt like giving up. He was thinking that all may be lost. His anger broke through his usual restraint, prompting him to expose much of what he thought of the war and the soldiers who were fighting it. He wrote a series of letters from Valley Forge to Henry Laurens, president of the Continental Congress

In a letter written on December 22, 1777 he said,

> It is with infinite pain & concern, that I transmit Congress the enclosed Copies of Sundry Letters respecting the state of the Commissary's Department. In these matters are not exaggerated. I do not know from what cause this alarming deficiency, or rather total failure of Supplies arises: But unless more vigorous exertions and better regulations take place in that line and immediately, This Army must dissolve. I have done all in my power, by remonstrating—by writing to—by ordering the Commissaries on this Head from time to time,

but without any good effect, or obtaining more than a present scanty relief. Owing to this, the march of the Army has been delayed upon more.[30]

After thinking of what he wrote the day before, Washington wrote to Laurens again the next day. This letter expressed even less hope,

> Full as I was in my representation of matters in the Commissary's department yesterday, fresh and more powerful reasons oblige me to add, that I am now convinced beyond a doubt that unless some great and capital change suddenly takes place in that line this Army must inevitably be reduced to one or other of these three things. Starve—dissolve—or disperse, in order to obtain subsistence in the best manner they can. Rest assured, Sir, this is not an exaggerated picture, and that I have abundant reason to support what I say.[31]

Washington realized that he was running out of time, because in a few months the British, camped just eighteen miles away, would begin the spring campaign against him. His letter to Laurens on January 1,

> You must be fully sensible that very little time is left between this and the opening of the next Campaign for the provision of Field Equipage, Carriages, Horses and many other articles essentially necessary, towards which I cannot find that any Steps have yet been taken.[32]

This may well have been the very lowest point in Washington's military career. The fortunes of war, however, change rapidly in the course of a war. By spring his army would be stronger and better trained than ever, thanks to a Prussian officer, Baron Von Steuben. The Baron volunteered, without pay, to train the American army and turn them into a fighting machine. He also passed regulations that improved the sanitation problems the army faced, resulting in a much healthier army. In addition, Washington received the much awaited news that France would enter the war on the side of the Americans. This would mean more supplies and French troops sent to combat the British.

Losing hope again:

For the next few years conditions did improve for the American army, however as late as 1781, the war was still in the balance. General George Washington warned anyone that would listen that his army was tired and the supporters of the war had grown discontent. The support of France was in jeopardy and some Americans were calling for a negotiated end to the fighting. In a letter to John Laurens dated January 15, 1781, Washington wrote, "The people are discontented, but it is with the feeble and oppressive mode of conducting the war, not with the war itself."[33]

John Adams feared that France, faced with growing debts and the lack of progress in the war, might stop her support within the year. It appeared that if there was not a major American victory in 1781, the fate of the country would be decided at a conference table consisting of the great European powers.

The fighting had put the American government deeply in debt, and because most of the soldiers had not been paid, there were desertions and occasionally mutinies. In 1781, pay for the soldiers of the Continental Army was suspended. It was decided that the army would be paid in debt certificates or land grants until the peace treaty was signed. This did not sit well with the soldiers, for they had bills back home to pay.

On April 9, 1781, George Washington wrote a letter to John Laurens, who was in France assisting with the work of Benjamin Franklin. The letter paints a bleak picture for the hope of independence,

> As an honest & candid man—as a man whose all depends on the final and happy termination of the present contest, I assert this—While I give it decisively as my opinion, that without a foreign loan our present force (which is but the remnant of an Army) cannot be kept together this Campaign; much less will it be increased, & in readiness for another. And, if France delays a timely, & powerful aid in this critical posture of our affairs it will avail us nothing should she attempt it hereafter; for we are at this hour, suspended in the Balle—not from choice, but from hard and absolute necessity—for you may rely on it as a fact, that we cannot transport the provisions from the States in which they are assessed to the Army, because we cannot pay the Teamsters—Who will no longer work for Certificates—It is equally certain that our Troops are approaching fast to nakedness & that we have nothing to clothe them with—That our Hospitals are without Medicines, & our Sick without Nutriment except such as well men eat—That all our public works are at a stand, & the Artificers disbanding. but why need I run into the detail, when it may be declared in a word, that we are at the end of our tether, & that now or never deliverance must come.[34]

Tears From The General

In the 1700s most boys were discouraged to cry in public. They believed crying over disappointments or the death of a loved one should be done in private. George Washington had two step-children that died young and caused him much grief. Jack died at the age of 27 shortly after the British surrendered at Yorktown. Patsy died at the age of 17 after suffering from seizures throughout much of her life. He loved the two children as if they were his very own, and no doubt he shed tears at the time of their death. According to various sources, at the death of Patsy, "He knelt at her dying bed and with a passionate burst of tears…"[35]

Crying in private is one thing, but would the father of our country, the stern looking George Washington shed a tear in public? Would a man so concerned about his reputation risk being thought of as weak? Even Washington would sometimes get emotional and allow his guard to drop.

Washington gathered his officers together on December 4, 1783, in the long room of Fraunces Tavern in lower Manhattan. The sad purpose was to say farewell to the men who had been so close to him for the past eight years. Washington entered the room and a toast was drunk.

Washington's farewell to his men. National archives.

Washington then asked for each officer to come to him and shake his hand. As General Knox took his commander's hand, he saw tears running down the cheeks of Washington. Others also reported Washington weeping at the final good-by. In the eight years that many had served him, this was the first time they had seen Washington shed tears.

On December 23, 1783, George Washington stood before Congress to give his brief, and emotional speech announcing his retirement as Commander-in-Chief. The ceremony that took place before the Continental Congress revealed Washington's capacity for deep emotion.

Washington came into the chambers of Congress, and sat down facing the speaker's platform. The President of Congress nodded and the doors at the back of the chamber swung open and a large group of women spectators led by Martha Washington entered. The women were escorted upstairs to the visitor's gallery.

The nod was given for Washington to speak. He then stood up facing the delegates and withdrew, with trembling hands, a paper from his coat pocket. The entire speech lasted a little over three minutes. While reading the speech with a voice that hesitated at times, and as some of the members of Congress shed tears, he resigned his commission from the army. Some claimed that Washington, himself had tears as he neared the end of his speech.

At the back of the chamber, Molly Ridout was present for the event and wrote to her mother, "many tears were shed." Some accounts reported that tears were seen running down Washington's face.

After he finished his speech, Washington bowed and engaged in several formal goodbyes. He quickly left in order to make in back to Mount Vernon in time to spend Christmas with his family.

General George Washington Resigning His Commission. Washington stands with two aides-de-camp addressing the president of the Congress, Thomas Mifflin. Mrs. Washington and her three grandchildren are shown watching from the gallery, although the grandchildren were not in fact present at the event. Public domain.

Tears in battle:

It was reported that Washington shed tears on August 27, 1776 in New York. During the Battle of Long Island, the outnumbered American army began to retreat to Manhattan. Washington had members of the 1st Maryland Regiment cover the retreat of his troops. Called the "Maryland 400," they held the British off until the American army was safely across the river in Manhattan. Of the 400 Maryland troops, only a few dozen survived to rejoin the army.

Washington observed the sacrifice of the 1st Maryland and said, "Good God! What brave fellows I must lose this day!" It was reported that the general was overwhelmed with grief and despair, and his manly features were bathed in tears.[36]

Did Washington weep when he learned of the surrender of Fort Washington near the north end of Manhattan Island on November 16, 1776? The Americans lost over 3,000 troops and it was one of the worst defeats they suffered during the war. Some historians claim that after the surrender Washington turned away and began to weep as a child. Other historians claimed that he wept within his soul. It is very likely that Washington did indeed weep at what he saw. He watched the battle through a telescope and was able to see up close individual men being killed by musket shots and bayonets.

Washington was already in a depressed mood about his army. A few weeks earlier he had witnessed the lack luster performance and retreat of the Americans at Kip's Bay. He wrote to his cousin, Lund Washington on September 30, 1776, "In confidence I tell you that I was never in such an unhappy, divided state since I was born."[37] This combined with the devastating surrender of Fort Washington could very well have brought tears to even the strongest man.

5

The Humor of George Washington

"A sense of humor is part of the art of leadership, of getting along with people, of getting things done."

----Dwight D. Eisenhower

~∞◎◉◎∞~

Sense of Humor

An entire chapter has been devoted to show that Washington had a sense of humor because it seems almost a sacrilege to think of George Washington as laughing and displaying a sense of humor. His paintings cast him as humorless and stone-faced. Gods were supposed to rule with anger and sternness. Yet, sometimes Washington did step out of character and showed a sense of humor. He found humor useful in wartime to relieve the daily stress of anxiety and danger. He used humor to put himself and others around him at ease. His humor can be found in his letters, and from personal accounts of people he encountered during this time.

He certainly was not a comedian nor did he engage in slap-stick humor. For most of us, his displays of humor would not be very funny by today's standards. But in the 1700s, and coming from a man who was typically serious, these examples would indeed fall into the category of mild humor. Washington was a believer in laughing as he noted in his letter to Theodorick Bland on August 15, 1786, "I commend you, however, for passing the time in as merry a manner as you possibly could; it is assuredly better to go laughing than crying thro' the rough journey of life."[1]

Humor was especially useful in time of war. George Washington took command of the Continental Army in June of 1775, and spent the next seven and a half years living with the anxiety and physical dangers of war. The war years were naturally not times of gaiety and laughter, yet he used humor to put himself and others at ease. Washington's use of humor helped to convey an air of confidence and optimism, thus helping the American cause. His jesting is documented in some of his wartime letters, and further attested by personal accounts from many people who spent time with him during the Revolution.

~⟶⋯⟨⟩⋯⟵~

Playful with the ladies:

An example of Washington being playful occurred in the winter camp at Morristown in 1779. Martha was there and she was joined by Kitty, the wife of General Nathanael Greene. One evening several of Washington's staff and their wives gathered for an evening of companionship. As the evening progressed the women retired to one room to talk and perhaps to sew, and the men to another room to drink and talk.

One of the men was not a drinker so he joined the ladies. The other men thought it would be funny to try to capture the non-drinker and take him away from the ladies. The men tried to convince the man to join them, and his while wife held on to his arm. Washington, being playful, grabbed her wrist, causing the woman to scream, "Let go of my hand or I'll pull every hair out of you head! Even if you are a general you are still just a man!"[2] Washington, realizing the woman did not see the humor in what he was doing, let her hand go.

"The story so often repeated of his never laughing," James Madison said, was "wholly untrue, no man seemed more to enjoy gay conversation, though he took little part in it himself. He was particularly pleased with the jokes, good humor, and hilarity of his companions."[3]

When Washington entered Boston after the British evacuated in March 1776, he took resident at an inn on King Street. He noticed a little girl playing out front and he asked her, "You have seen soldiers on both side, which do you like best?" The girl said in all frankness that she like the redcoats best. Washington laughed and replied back, "Yes, my dear, the redcoats do look the best, but it takes the ragged boys to do the fighting."[4]

⁓

Fun with horses:

John Bernard, an English comedian and writer, spent many years in colonial American and became friends with Washington. In his book he noted that he had heard of but one jest by Washington, which was related by his friend Colonel Humphreys. Humphreys, an aide to the general told him that Washington prided himself on his riding ability.

One day the two were out riding and Humphreys bet Washington that he would not follow him over one particular high hedge. Washington enjoyed gambling and accepted his challenge. Humphreys led the way and boldly took the leap over the hedge. He quickly discovered that he mistook the spot and rider and horse ended up in a quagmire.

Washington either knew the ground better, or suspected something was not right because, at an easy pace, he rode up to the hedge and looked over at his engulfed aide and said, "No, no, colonel, you are too deep for me!"[5]

When the Democrats charged the Federalists with stealing from the treasury, Washington wrote to a Cabinet official, "and pray, my good sir, what part of the $800.000 have come to your share? As you are high in Office, I hope you did not disgrace yourself in the acceptance of a paltry bribe—a $100.000 perhaps."[6]

During winter camp at Morristown, Washington had been given a young, bucking horse. One of the soldiers, who was very cocky in his manner, asked if he could break the animal for the general. Washington, an excellent horseman, agreed to allow the young braggart to ride the horse. The general, with some of his officers, watched as the young man made a great show of his preparations to ride the horse.

The young man mounted the horse and within seconds the animal planted his forefeet, threw his back legs up in the air, and sent the young rider flying. Washington, it was said, was so convulsed with laughter, that tears ran down his cheeks.[7]

One afternoon Chief Justice John Marshall and the nephew of George Washington, Associate Justice Bushrod, were traveling to Mount Vernon. Traveling with them was a servant with a trunk of clothing. The group stopped to dig a ditch for bathroom purposes and the men became very dirty in the process. Marshall and Bushrod removed their clothing so they could change into fresh garb.

The servant open the truck to get fresh clothes and discovered that it contain cakes of various types of soap and a large assortment of fancy articles. The servant had mistakenly picked up a trunk that resembled theirs, except this one belonged to a traveling peddler. The servant became extremely upset at the problem, however the two men broke out in loud burst of laughter.

Washington happen to be near the area and heard the commotion and went to investigate. When he saw his two friends standing there naked and dirty, it was said that Washington actually rolled on the grass laughing.[8]

In Washington Irving's book about Washington, he wrote of a time when the president mentioned to Henry Lee that he wanted a pair of horses for his carriage. Lee told him he had a pair but Washington could not get them. When he asked why Lee said, "Because you will never pay more than half price for anything, and I must have full price."

Mrs. Washington started laughing at Lee's reply, and a parrot perched near her joined in the laughing. Washington looked at the bird and then at Lee and said, "Ah Lee, you are a funny fellow, see, that bird is laughing at you."[9]

Laugh at simple things:

In a postscript to a letter written to Joseph Reed on November 8, 1775, Washington amusingly wrote, "A blundering Lieutenant of the blundering Captain Colt, who had blundered upon two vessels from Nova Scotia, just came in with the account of it, and before I could rescue my letter without knowing what he did, picked up a candle and sprinkled it with grease."[10]

Today, these examples would certainly not deliver belly laughs to a reader. They contain a little dry humor that Washington displayed at times. But, these examples and others show that George Washington was capable of expressing a little humor and enjoyed a light moment with others.

"Washington certainly did enjoy a joke." Nelly Custis, his step-granddaughter, said, "I have sometimes made him laugh most heartily from sympathy with my joyous and extravagant spirits. There are many other instances of his laughing recorded."[11]

A dirty look:

Shortly after George Washington was named Commander of the Continental Army, an anonymous printmaker produced an engraving of Washington displaying an intense scowl on the battlefield. The work attempted to capture Washington's ferocity on the battlefield. The engraver, who was possibly cashing in on the popularity of General Washington as a subject, had never seen Washington. So to protect his identity, the artist claimed that the image was drawn from life by Alexander Campbell, a resident of Williamsburg, Virginia.

Colonel Joseph Reed sent Martha Washington a copy of one of these prints which was inscribed: "Done from an original Drawn from the Life by Alex Campbell of Williamsburg in Virginia." No painter of that name had been identified. When Washington saw the image he wrote to Lieutenant Colonel Reed on January 31, 1776, "Mrs. Washington desires I will thank you for the Picture sent her. Mr. Campbell whom I never saw (to my knowledge) has made a very formidable figure of the Commander in Chief giving him a sufficient portion of Terror in his Countenance."[12]

"Alexander Campbell," painting of George Washington, Esqr. General and Commander in Chief of the Continental Army in America, mezzotint and line engraving, 1775. Photo: New York Public Library. Public domain

The joke is on death:

Once Washington joked about his own death. "As I have heard," he said after Braddock's defeat in which he was one of the few officers that escaped injury, "since my arrival at this place, a circumstantial account of my death and dying speech, I take this early opportunity of contradicting the first, and of assuring you, that I have not as yet composed the latter."[13]

An evening with humor:

One time during his presidency some theater goers receive a very unexpected and rare treat. Washington was attending a play in Dunlap's Theater, called *Poor Soldier* in which he, as a Continental, was described in good-humored comic verse. Everybody looked at his box, and hundreds of people were witness to his laughter. The next day it was big news in the newspapers that Washington indeed had laughed.

When having dinner, Washington preferred to have a neat but plain style meal. In 1783, he attended a military banquet and one of the men present, Mr. Peters from Pennsylvania, said that the rather gaudy silver cups on the table were made by a man who had recently become a Quaker preacher. Washington knew Quakers were noted for preferring things that were plain and simple, so he said, "I wished the man had been a Quaker preacher before he made the cups."[14]

French humor:

A French writer who had been a farmer in America, J. Hector St. John de Crèvecoeur, crossed British-American lines to enter into British controlled New York. He was arrested as a spy for the Americans and spent three months in jail. He later wrote of Washington that he was not known for laughing during the Revolutionary War, and rarely smiled among friends. This contributed to the myth many had of Washington as stoic and without humor, however the French officers and officials who actually spent extended time with Washington during the war attested otherwise. Francois Marbois secretary of the French legation and of the Chevalier de la Luzerne, noted that Washington "is serious in business," but that "outside of that, he permits himself a restricted gaiety."

A letter written by Peter Stephen Du Ponceau, the secretary for Baron von Steuben, contained an anecdote about Washington. Du Ponceau remembered from Valley Forge in the winter of 1777-1778,

> I must relate an anecdote which happened to Captain Benjamin Walker while he was in the family of General Washington, and which is strongly descriptive of his honest heart. He had long been engaged to a Quaker young lady who resided in the state of New York and whom he afterwards married. He once asked the General to give him leave of absence for a few days to go and see her. The General told him that he could not at that time dispense with his services. Walker insisted, begged, entreated; but all in vain. "If I don't go," said he, "she will die." "Oh! no," said Washington, "women do not die for such trifles." "But General, what shall I do? What would you do?" "Why, write to her to add another leaf to the book of sufferings." This was related to me by Walker himself. General Washington had a great deal of that dry humor which he knew how to make use of on proper occasions.[15]

The Comte de Ségur stated that Washington "is affable and converses with his officers familiarly and gaily, and that "the expressions on his face was pleasant and kind; his smile was gentle.[16] One Frenchman said that Washington relaxed his expression after a couple glasses of wine.

At times Washington managed to make light of war and the stress he encountered from leadership. Frenchman Mathieu Dumas wrote of a difficult crossing of the Hudson River in September 1779. "We coasted the rocks which lined the right bank of the Hudson, between West Point and New Windsor, at the foot of which it is impossible to land. General Washington perceiving that the master of the boat was very much alarmed, took the helm, saying, 'Courage, my friends, I am going to conduct you, since it is my duty to hold the helm.' After having with much difficulty made our way against the stream and the ice, we landed, and had to walk a league before we reached the headquarters."[17]

This incident was corroborated by Francois Marbois, secretary of the French legation, writing of the river crossing near West Point: "The general held the tiller, and during a little squall which required skill and practice, proved to us that this work was no less known to him than are other bits of useful knowledge."[18]

By this jest recorded by Dumas, Washington meant not that it was literally his duty to hold the helm, but that he was at the helm of the whole American cause, and his taking on the helm of the boat was to be understood as a little symbol.

During the war Washington's humor also appeared in private moments as recounted by Marquis de Chastellux, a major general in the French forces. At a meeting in 1782, the Frenchman was experiencing a fever accompanied by chills. "The General observing it, told me he was sure I had not met with a good glass of wine for some time, an article then very rare, but that my disorder must be frightened away; he made me drink three or four of his silver camp cups of excellent madeira at noon, and recommended to me to take a generous glass of claret after dinner, a prescription by no means repugnant to my feelings, and which I most religiously followed." The marquis recognized the kidding nature of Washington's "medical" prescription and echoed it with mock reverence in his account through his claim to follow Washington's advice "religiously."[19]

Wartime humor:

Washington was at West Point on August 16, 1779, and had asked two ladies to dine with him the next day. One was Mrs. Livingston and the other woman was the wife of John Cochran, Gertrude, the sister of General Schuyler. Even though the war was not going well at the time, he wrote a letter to John Cochran in a light vein,

> I have asked Mrs Cockran & Mrs Livingston to dine with me tomorrow; but ought I not to apprize them of their fare? As I hate deception, even where the imagination only is concerned—I will.
>
> It is needless to premise that my table is large enough to hold the ladies—of this they had occular proof yesterday—To say how it is usually covered is rather more essential, & this, shall be the purport of my Letter.
>
> Since our arrival at this happy spot, we have had a Ham (sometimes a shoulder) of Bacon, to grace the head of the table—a piece of roast Beef adorns the foot—and, a small dish of Greens or Beans (almost imperceptable) decorates the center. When the Cook has a mind to cut a figure (and this I presume he will attempt to do to morrow) we have two Beef-stake Pyes, or dishes of Crabs in addition, one on each side the center dish, dividing the space, & reducing the distance between dish & dish to about Six feet, which without them, would be near twelve a part—Of late, he has had the surprizing luck to discover, that apples will make pyes; and its a question if, amidst the violence of his efforts, we do not get one of apples instead of having both of Beef.
>
> If the ladies can put up with such entertainment, and will submit to partake of it on plates—once tin but now Iron—(not become so by the labor of scowering) I shall be happy to see them.[20]

A great problem facing the army during the war involved funding for arms and provisions, a difficulty exacerbated by the reluctance of the Continental Congress to provide the needed support. The money often had to come from loans, and in that regard financier Robert Morris was instrumental in helping to arrange loans for the struggling Congress to support the armed forces. Continental Congress representative David Howell of Rhode Island recorded a witty remark by Washington. When the President of the Congress said he believed that, "*Mr. Morris had his HANDS full,*" the General replied at the same moment, "*He wished he had his POCKETS full, too.*"[21]

British General Charles Cornwallis, after his surrender to Washington, dined with the American victor. This anecdote appeared in a British magazine in 1782. French General Rochambeau asked for a toast and gave, "The United States." Next, Washington gave, "The King of France." It was now the turn of Cornwallis who raised his glass and gave, "The King." Washington quickly added to the toast, "of England, and confine him there, and I'll drink him a full bumper!"[22] [Bumper means a glass full or overflowing.] There was no record of a response by Cornwallis.

During the Convention of 1787, Elbridge Gerry proposed an amendment to place a constitutional limit on the size of the American standing army at 5,000 troops. George Washington, who was the chairperson of the convention and therefore could not make a motion, whispered to a delegate near him. He suggested to the man that he should move to amend the motion so as to provide that "no foreign enemy should invade the United States at any time, with more than three thousand troops." Gerry's motion was unanimously rejected.[23]

⚔

Humor in art:

During his life, Washington had to sit for many portraits, which must have at times driven him almost mad. He dislike sitting still for long periods of time, especially when it was a busy day. He expressed his feeling regarding this in a letter to Francis Hopkinson on May 16, 1785,

> In for a penny, in for a pound, is an old adage. I am so hackneyed to the touches of the Painters pencil, that I am *now* altogether at their beck, and sit like patience on a Monument whilst they are delineating the lines of my face.
>
> It is a proof among many others, of what habit & custom can effect. At first I was as impatient at the request, and as restive under the operation, as a Colt is of the Saddle—The next time, I submitted very reluctantly, but with less flouncing. Now, no dray moves more readily to the Thill, than I do to the Painters Chair. It may easily be conceived therefore that I yielded a ready obedience to your request, and to the views of Mr Pine.[24]

[Robert Pine was one of the first artists to paint history paintings of the events of the American Revolution.]

In January, 1785, artist Joseph Wright came to Mount Vernon to make a plaster of Paris model of Washington's face. Wright oiled Washington's features over, placing him flat upon his back upon a cot, and proceeded to daub his face with the plaster. When Martha entered the room and saw what was happening she let out a cry. Washington thought it was funny and gave a small smile. As a result his plaster image shows a slight twist, or compressions of his lips in the final image of the bust.[25]

Upon Thomas Jefferson's return from France, he asked Washington why the Constitutional Convention had established two house in the legislature. The question was raised at the breakfast table and Washington asked, "Why did you pour that coffee into your saucer?" "Too cool it," replied Jefferson. Washington answered back, "Even so, we pour legislation into the senatorial saucer to cool it."[26]

Henry Cabot Lodge received a letter from the sculptor William Story on March 15, 1877, and it contained a story his father, Joseph, told him about George Washington,

> Washington and Marshall had gone down into the country to visit a family of friends. They were alone and on horseback. The ride was a long one and night had come on. As they were approaching the house, Marshall by a sudden movement on his horse, perhaps to avoid a tree or other obstacle, split his breeches. What was to be done? It was too late and the distance was too long for him to return and he was in an unpresentable condition. How to make his appearance before the ladies of the family was a question. Washington insisted on his going on, insisted so strongly that he was forced to comply and on they went. The only device to conceal his disastrous condition that occurred to Marshall was to open his handkerchief and hold it by the two ends before him like an apron and this he did. On entering the room Washington turned and looked at him and then suddenly broke into an uncontrollable fit of laughter which was so violent and exhausting that it was said he actually rolled on the floor and could not for a time recover himself."[27]

61

A warning with humor:

Writer John Watson wrote in 1853, "Washington was extremely punctual. His cabinet councils were appointed to meet him precisely at eleven o'clock on set days. On such occasions Alexander Hamilton was usually late and after the appointed time, he would bustle in, draw out his watch, and exclaim it had deceived him. This occurred a number of times, when the General successfully prevented it by rising and looking firmly at Mr. Hamilton. He said in stern voice, 'Sir, you must provide yourself a new watch, or I a new secretary.'"[28]

In 1794, while Washington was president, his step-granddaughter, Nelly Custis kept a green parrot as a pet. She wrote to a friend that she was trying to teach the bird to sing, which apparently was disturbing Washington. When he was packing for the family's return to Mount Vernon, Washington complained to Tobias Lear in a letter on March 9, 1797, "On one side I am called upon to remember the Parrot, on the other to remember the dog. For my own part I should not pine much if both were forgot."[29]

This is probably the same dog he wrote about to William Stoy, on October 14, 1797,

> On monday last, the bearer was Bit by a Small Dog belonging to a Lady in my house, then as was supposed a little diseased—And Yesternight died (I do think) in a State of Madness1—As soon as the Boy (Christopher) was Bit application was made to a medical Gentleman in Alexandria who has cut out so far as He could, the place Bit—applyed Ointment to keep it open, And put the Boy under a Course of mercury.[30]

The boy was a young slave, Christopher, who survived the illness, and was present when Washington died in 1799.

Odd humor:

Architect William Thornton wrote in a letter in 1797, "As Washington sat at table after dinner, the fire behind him was too large and hot. He complained and said he must remove. A gentleman observed it behoove the General to stand fire. Yes, said Washington, but it does not look well for a General to receive the fire behind."[31]

Polish Count Julian Niemeewicz visited Mount Vernon in 1797 as a guest of George Washington. He recorded in his diary this story of a conversation Washington had about a recent duel, "Did you know Mr. Jones, who was recently killed in a duel by Mr. Livingston," asked Mr. Law.

"I believe I have seen him, but I was never on intimate terms with him," replied Washington.

"They say the shot he fired at his opponent had grazed his nose."

Washington answered back, "How could he miss it, you know Livingston's nose; what a target."[32]

On November 13, 1798, Washington gave an amusing account of a call at his lodgings in Philadelphia. "I was informed that Dr. Blackwell, and Dr. Logan were in the parlor and desired to see me. Dr. Logan supported the French revolution, which Washington did not support. He thought the revolution was anarchy that might spread to the United States."

"After a few minutes I went down, and I advanced towards, and gave my hand to the Dr. Blackwell. Dr. Logan came toward me and offered his hand. In a very cool manner and with an air of indifference, I gave him my hand, and asked Dr. Blackwell to be seated. Dr. Logan took a seat without being invited to sit. I addressed all my conservation to Dr. Blackwell, and gave negative or affirmative answers, as few words as I could, except to ask how Mrs. Logan was doing."[33]

Humor in writing:

During the siege of Boston, Washington took time to joke with his brother-in-law Burwell Bassett in a letter dated February 28, 1775, "Mrs. Washington says that she has wrote all the news she could get (and ladies you know are never at a loss) to Mrs. Bassett."[34]

On rare occasions Washington used a little romantic humor in his letters. Washington wrote to the Marquis de Lafayette in September, 1779 about the young officer's separation from his wife, and he wrote the line that "no distance can keep anxious lovers long asunder."[35]

In the same letter he wrote with humor to reassure Lafayette that his young wife would not fall for Washington, because "amidst all the wonders recorded in holy writ no instance can be produced where a young Woman from *real inclination* has preferred an old man,"[36]

Annis Boudinot Stockton, the American poet, sent poems and letters to George Washington. On September 2, 1783, he wrote back using a comparison from the Bible, "Once woman has tempted us and we have tasted the forbidden fruit, there is no such thing as checking our appetites, whatever the consequences may be."[37]

6

George Washington the Ladies Man

"A youth with his first cigar makes himself sick; a youth with his first girl makes everybody sick."----Mary Little

~∞◎◎∞~

Was Martha His first Love?

Washington and romance:

Martha was not the first, second, or third love of George, and perhaps she was never his real love. Washington had a soft heart for pretty women, especially if they had wealth. There were several women that Washington, or as some called him "the stallion of the Potomac," took a liking too. He was never obsessed by the women he romanced and did not have an overwhelming love affair with any of them.

It is very difficult to visualize George Washington as a lover. Early in life he was awkward with love and was not at ease around women. Sometimes in their presence he could suddenly either become pompous or turn spell-bound and silent. Because he was so shy, he found it much easier to put his thoughts and sentiments on paper. Later in life when the passions of youth were under control he wrote,

> Love is said to be an involuntary passion, and it is, therefore, contended that it cannot be resisted. This is true in part only, for like all things else, when nourished and supplied plentifully with aliment, it is rapid in its progress; but let these be withdrawn and it may be stifled in its birth or much stinted in its growth. For example, a woman (the same may be said of the other sex) all beautiful and accomplished will, while her hand and heart are undisposed of, turn the heads and set the circle in which she moves on fire. Let her marry, and what is the consequence? The madness ceases and all is quiet again. Why? Not because there is any diminution in the charms of the lady, but because there is an end of hope. Hence it follows, that love may and therefore ought to be under the guidance of reason for although we cannot avoid first impressions, we may assuredly place them under guard.[1]

~∞◎◎∞~

George the Poet:

While still a school-boy, Washington was caught one day "romping with one of the largest girls," and very quickly more serious flirtations followed.[2] He was in love with one girl after another in his youth. Unfortunately for him, he was not considered a good catch. George, with little education, may have tried to use poetry to woo the young ladies he met. Here is an early sample of his prose:

> "Oh, Ye Gods why should my Poor resistless Heart
> Stand to oppose they might and Power
> At last surrender to Cupid's feather'd Dart
> And now lays bleeding every Hour
> For her that's Pityless of my grief and Woes,
> And will not me pity take.

I'll sleep among my most inveterate Foes
And with gladness never to wish to wake,
In deluding sleepings let my eyelids close
That in an entraptured dream I may
In a rapt fulling sleep and gentle repose
Possess those joys denied by Day."[3]

The swimming incident:

An interesting encounter occurred between George and two young ladies in the summer of 1750. He was robbed while swimming or bathing in the Rappahannock River. Two girls decided to take the clothes of eighteen year old George while he was in the water. The case came to court in December 1751. Transcript of the case is as follows,

3 Dec. 1751. "Ann Carrol and Mary McDaniel Servts of Fredericksburgh, being Committed to the Goal of this County by William Hunter Gent., on Suspicion of Felony, & Charged with robing the Cloaths of Mr George Washington when he was washing in the River some time last Summer, the Court having heard Severall Evidences Are of Oppinion that the said Ann Carroll be discharged, & Admitted an Evidence for our Lord the King Against the said Mary McDaniel.

And Upon Considering the whole in Evidence, & the prisoners defense, the Court are of Oppinion that the said Mary McDaniel is Guilty of petty Larceny, whereupon the said Mary desired Immediate punishment for the said Crime & relied on the Mercy of the Court, therefore it is ordered that the Sheriff carry her to the Whipping post & Inflict fifteen lashes on her bare back, And then she be discharged &."[4]

Washington was out of the country when the case came to court. In September of 1751, he and his brother Lawrence had sailed to Barbados, and did not return until January. This author wonders what George thought about giving a female fifteen lashes. Also, did this start out as a prank that went too far? If his clothes were taken, how did the modest Washington make it home unnoticed?

The mysterious "Low Land Beauty":

As early as 1749, when George was seventeen years of age, he showed his feelings to his youthful correspondent "Dear Robin" (who may have been his cousin Robert Washington). A young lady is mentioned in the letter as staying at Lord Fairfax's house. A draft of the letter was in the note book which he used to record his survey of the Fairfax estate. This is part of the letter,

> My place of Residence is at present at His Lordships where I might was my heart disengag'd pass my time very pleasantly as theres a very agreeable Young Lady Lives in the same house (Colo George Fairfax's Wife's Sister) [His wife was Sarah and she had three sisters. George is probably referring to Mary Cary who was sixteen at the time] this is probably but as thats only adding Fuel to fire it makes me the more uneasy for by often and unavoidably being in Company with her revives my former Passion for your **Low Land Beauty** whereas was I to live more retired from young Women I might in some measure eliviate my sorrows by burying that chast and trouble.[5]

The mysterious "Low Land Beauty" had been identified with half a dozen young women of Westmoreland, among them were Mary Bland, Lucy Grymes, Ann Eilbeck, and Betsy

Fauntleroy. The most convincing possibility is that the Lowland beauty was Miss Lucy Grymes, who afterwards married Henry Lee, and became the grandmother of Gen. Robert E. Lee. She was also the third cousin of George Washington. Whoever she may have been, it is evident that she had left our hero in a state of despair. Getting nowhere with her, Washington was through with women at seventeen, at least for awhile. "Whereas was I to live more retired from young Women I might in some measure eliviate my sorrows by burying that chast and troublesome Passion in the grave of oblivion or etarnall forgetfulness."[6]

In the same notebook that records his thoughts to Dear Robin, we find a few pages further on this cryptic entry: "Twas Perfect Love before But Now I do adores, Young M. A. his Wife." It would appear from this sentimental note that he was adoring somebody's wife. [7]

The Many Loves of George Washington

Lucy Grymes:

Lucy Grymes, one of the possible "lowland beauty" candidates was a beauty; described as fair, blue eyes, and soft blond hair. Her son was Henry Lee III, known in revolutionary history as "Light Horse Harry", who was always a favorite of Washington, probably due to the recollections of his early tender feelings for the boy's mother. In 1906 there was a one act comedy, *Washington's First Defeat,* about the romance between Washington and Lucy.[8]

Frances Alexander:

Around the age of sixteen, George fell in love with Frances Alexander. History only knows her name and nothing about who her family was or where they lived. The young lady and the first two lines of a poem were first mentioned in the book, *Colonial Virginia*, by Mary Newton Custons.[9] The poem below was attributed to Washington, although there is no proof he wrote it. Note that it is an acrostic poem, and the first letter of each line spells out most of the young girl's name. If Washington did write this, for some reason he did not complete her name.

> From your bright sparkling Eyes, I was undone;
> Rays, you have, more transparent than the sun,
> Amidst its glory in the rising Day,
> None can you equal in your bright arrays;
> Constant in your calm and unspotted Mind;
> Equal to all, but will to none Prove kind,
> So knowing, seldom one so Young, you'l Find.
> Ah! woe's me, that I should Love and conceal,
> Long have I wish'd, but never dare reveal,
> Even though severely Loves Pains I feel;
> Xerxes that great, wasn't free from Cupids Dart,
> And all the greatest Heroes, felt the smart.[10]

Betsy Fauntleroy:

When Washington went to Barbados with his brother Lawrence in 1751, he noted in his journal a meeting with a Miss Roberts, "an agreeable young lady."[11] The couple later went to see some fireworks on Guy Fawkes Day. Nothing more was written of her. After his return to Virginia, he began to show an interest in Betsy Fauntleroy.

Betsy Fauntleroy an early love interest of George Washington. Painting, 18th century.

In 1752, at the age of twenty, Washington asked sixteen year old Betsy Fauntleroy to marry him. George had an early relationship with the Fauntleroy family. The family owned land not far from Washington's birthplace and down the river from his childhood home near Fredericksburg. Washington sent a letter to her father, William, with his proposal to court Betsy. The letter was dated May 20, 1752,

I should have been down long before this, but my business in Frederick detained me somewhat longer than I expected, and immediately upon my return from thence I was taken with a violent pleurise which has reduced me very low; but purpose as soon as I recover my strength, to wait on Miss Betsy, in hopes of a revocation of the former cruel sentence, and see if I cannot obtain an alteration in my favor. I have enclosed a letter to her, which should be much obliged to you for the delivery of it. I have nothing to add but my best respects to your good lady and family.[12]

Betsy reply to George's proposal of marriage was no. Several months later Washington asked her again and received the same reply. Betsy was pretty and charming and had numerous suitors. She later married Bowler Cocke and after his death she married Thomas Adams. Washington, rebuked once again, remained single for the next six years.

—·····——

Mary Cary:

After the episode with "the Lowland Beauty," people in the area declared that around 1752, young Washington was in love with fourteen year old Mary Cary. Her elder sister, Sally, had married George Fairfax who was a good friend of Washington. Young Washington would later fall in love with Sally. Some historians believe that Washington's involvement with Mary is confused with his attraction with her older sister, who will be discussed later.

The ever-shy Washington, visited Mr. Cary and asked him to talk to his daughter Mary before he talked to her about romance. The old man told Washington, "If that is your business here, sir, I wish you to leave the house, for my daughter has been accustomed to ride in her own coach."[13] Mary rejected Washington's advances and later married Edward Ambler.

Mary Philipse:

In 1756, the next romance for twenty four year old George Washington was Mary Philipse. Mary, usually called Polly, was a beautiful girl of twenty-six, two years older than Washington. She also had over 51,000 acres coming to her in inheritance. In those days a woman lost her legal rights to land upon marriage, this meant that the land would go to her husband. So Mary was not only pretty, but stood to inherit a large amount of land.

Mary Philipse from the book, *George Washington*, published in 1896, page 90.

Washington knew Joseph Chew who lived in New London, Connecticut, through Chew's brother Colby, who served with Washington in his Virginia Regiment. Chew was a friend of the Robinson and Philipse families. Washington was friends with Captain Beverley Robinson and his wife Susanna, Mary's older sister.

The beauty and possible wealth of Mary had caught Washington's eye when he stayed with the Robinson family in New York. In early 1756, George stayed with the family on his way to Boston to see William Shirley. Washington quickly fell for Mary's charms and remained as a guest, and during the stay he made reference in his diary to spending money on the ladies. He also mentioned having to pay a rather large tailor's bill. You certainly can't court a beauty without the proper clothes and George did try to look his very best.

The next year while Washington was in Philadelphia, Joseph Chew wrote two letters to George trying to encourage him to court Mary before she commits to the British officer, Roger Morris. The first letter was dated March 14, 1757, "I am now at Mr. Robinson's, he, Mrs. Robinson, and his Dear Little Family are all well they desire their Compliments to you. Pretty Miss Polly is here."[14]

MARY PHILIPSE

The second letter was sent on July 13, 1757. Chew was trying to get Washington to leave Philadelphia and return to New York to see Mary,

> I often had the Pleasure of Breakfasting with the Charming Polly, Roger Morris was there (dont be startled) but not always, you know him he is a Ladys man, always something to say, the Town talk't of it as a sure & settled Affair. I can't say I think so and that I much doubt it, but assure you had Little Acquaintance with Mr. Morris and only slightly hinted it to Miss Polly; but how can you be Excused to Continue so long at Phila. I think I should have made a kind of Flying march of it if it had been only to have seen whether the Works were sufficient to withstand a Vigorous Attack, you a Soldier and a Lover. mind I have been arguing for my own Interest now for had you taken this method then I should have had the Pleasure of seeing you.
>
> I intend to set out tomorrow for New York where I will not be wanting to let Miss Polly know the sincere Regard a Friend of mine [Washington] has for her. and I am sure if she had my Eyes to see thro she would Prefer him to all others.[15]

It was reported that Washington did go to New York and he arrived on a winter's evening. It was late but he sought and was given an interview with Miss Mary. The English descendants of Mary Philipse claim that Washington did propose marriage and was turned down.

Mary later married Roger Morris in 1758 and since he supported the British when the Revolution began, Roger was forced to flee to England at the start of the Revolution. New York passed the Confiscation Act in 1779, and named landowners who acted in a way that was injurious to the state was guilty of treason. During the Revolution, only three women were named as traitors and Mary was one of them. At the end of the war Mary escaped to England.

Had Mary accepted George's proposal of marriage this might have been much different for the couple. Would George have been such an ardent supporter of the Revolution since he would be such a large landowner? How would Mary have been as the wife of the future president of the new country? It was probably no accident that George Washington chose to use Mary and Roger's house in New York as his headquarters between September 15 and October 20, 1776.

By now, George was not having very good luck with women. He had been long searching for an attractive woman who would have access to wealth. Although he was a handsome young man, he was not consider a good catch by the women he was interested in. During this time George only had a small farm along with a few slaves that he had earlier inherited from his father. He was a surveyor and an officer in the militia, neither were jobs that would bring in much money. Unfortunately, he had a champagne taste in women, but a soft drink budget.

—————

Sarah "Sally" Fairfax:

The name of Sally Fairfax did not really enter into Washington's history until 1886, when letters addressed to her by him were discovered and published. It excited much controversy, some horror, and just plain curiosity. Sally cannot be ignored in any story on George Washington because she had a profound influence on the formation of his character. She stirred feelings in his heart deeper than any other woman. His wandering heart finally settled on a woman that could never be his, because she was married to his best friend.

Washington's time with Sally was a period that alternated between joy and torment. She may have teased him over his inability to keep a sweetheart from marrying another man. When he was sad she might have flirted with him to raise his spirits. Most assuredly she enjoyed the attention she received from the young, attractive Washington. Her husband, George, was short and not nearly as handsome as the good-looking, tall, and muscular George Washington. Also, Sally was fond of dominating the men around her. Before she married she was the most sought after and grand belle in Virginia society. Washington was like a lump of clay in her hands, she could mold him into whatever she wanted, and George was only too happy to be a willing subject. Luckily she molded him into a better man.

Washington as a young man, from *Bibliotheca Washingtoniana, a Descriptive List of the Biographies and Biographical Sketches of George Washington.* Philadelphia, PA: Robert Lindsay, 1889.   Sally Fairfax as a young woman. Public domain.

George William Fairfax was a wealthy landowner and expert surveyor in Virginia. He became a good friend and mentor to George Washington, who was eight years younger. Washington was first introduce to the Fairfax family through Lawrence Washington who in 1743, married Anne, age fifteen, the sister of George Fairfax.

In 1748, George Fairfax married Sally Cary who was one of the most attractive women in Virginia and she was from a wealthy family. Sally soon met Washington, who being attracted to beautiful wealthy women, soon began to harbor secret feelings toward her. George would spend much of his time at the Fairfax home.

Over the years Washington and Sally performed together in amateur theatre, enjoyed dancing together at parties, and exchanging gossip about their friends. They enjoyed playing cards together and George like to listen to her speak French. Sally Fairfax was a woman of education and she inspired George to elevate himself to a higher social, cultural, and intellectual realm. This would prepare him for what was to come later in his life. She helped him with his writing and spelling, and helped to sharpen his manners in social and political situations.

Their relationship had its ups and downs most of the time. Washington would write to Sally while he was in the army he. In a letter in 1748, he wrote admitting writing to her several times and receiving no reply. Then he began flirting with his words, "I am almost discouraged from writing to you, as this is the fourth since I received any from yourself. I pass the time much more agreeably than I imagined I should, as there is a very agreeable young lady lives in the same house where I reside that in a great measure cheats sorrow and dejectedness, though not so as to draw my thoughts altogether from your parts."[16]

While Washington was in the British army in the 1750s he wrote to Sally suggesting that he had romantic feelings towards her. At times she would reply back that she might also have such feelings, or sometimes times if the letters became too romantic she would quit writing. Her off and on feelings toward Washington drew him even closer toward her. "Dear Madam, In order to engage your correspondence, I think it, expedient is incumbent on me to deserve it, which I shall endeavor to do, by embracing the earliest, and every opportunity of writing to you.[17]

First draft of letter to Sally Fairfax from Rupert Hughes, *George Washington The Human Being & the Hero*. New York, New York: William Morrow & Company, 1926.

The following is part of a letter written by Washington to Sally on September12, 1758. Apparently Sally sent him a letter after she had stopped writing to him for a short time. Washington replied to her letter [his spelling has been corrected to make it easier to read],

Yesterday I was honored with your short, but very agreeable favor of the first Instt. How joyfully I catch at the happy occasion of renewing a Correspondence which I fear was disrelished on your part.

If you allow that any honor can be derived from my opposition to our present System of management, you destroy the merit of it entirely in me by attributing my anxiety to the animating prospect of possessing Mrs. Custis. [Washington had been courting his future wife Martha since he met her the previous March.]

Tis true, I profess myself a Votary to Love—I acknowledge that a Lady is in the Case—and further I confess, that this Lady is known to you.—Yes Madam, as well as she is to one, who is too sensible of her Charms to deny the Power, whose Influence he feels and must ever Submit to. I feel the force of her amiable beauties in the recollection of a thousand tender passages that I could wish to obliterate, till I am bid to revive them.—but experience alas! sadly reminds me how Impossible this is.—and evinces an Opinion which I have long entertained, that there is a Destiny, which has the Sovereign control of our Actions—not to be resisted by the strongest efforts of Human Nature.

You have drawn me my dear Madam, or rather have I drawn myself, into an honest confession of a Simple Fact—misconstrue not my meaning—'tis obvious—doubt it not, nor expose it,—the World has no business to know the object of my Love, declared in this manner to—you when I want to conceal it—One thing, above all things in this World I wish to know, and only one person of your Acquaintance can solve me that, or guess my meaning.—but adieu to this, till happier times, if I ever shall see them.[18]

In this letter Washington wrote with passion that he did not use when he would write to Martha. It appeared that he told Sally that he was in in love and devoted to a lady known to her. Rather than come right out and name Sally as the one he loved, he chooses to hint that it might be her.

Less than two weeks after he sent Sally his passionate profession of love, an answer came back from Sally, but it has not been found. It was probably not the response that he wanted to hear. It was discrete and she refused to spell out any feeling she had for him. At this time he has met Martha, and the couple are engage to be married in a little over three months.

On September 25, 1758, George again wrote to Sally in response to her previous letter. In much of the letter he wrote about the military campaign he had been involved in. He feels that any romantic feelings the couple had for each other must remain their secret.

Dear Madam,

Do we still misunderstand the true meaning of each others Letters? I think it must appear so, tho I would feign hope the contrary as I cannot speak plainer without—but I'll say no more, and leave you to guess the rest.

I shoud th(ink) my time more agreable spent believe me, in playing a part in Cato with the Company you mention, & myself doubly happy in being the Juba to such a Marcia as you must make. [Their favorite play was Cato, which is about two lovers, Marcia and Juba. It takes place during the time of Caesar. Marcia was Cato's daughter and loves Juba a warrior. Cato refuses to approve of their love because Juba is beneath her socially.]

One thing more and then have done. you ask if I am not tired at the length of your Letter? No Madam I am not, nor never can be while the Lines are an Inch asunder to bring you in haste to the end of the Paper. You may be tired of mine by this. Adieu dear Madam, you possibly will hear something of me, or from me before we shall meet.[19]

This is as close to saying I love you as Washington would go [I profess myself a Votary to Love]. Sally never hinted that she would be willing to leave her husband. To do so would create a massive scandal, and a loss of friendship and possible lawsuit between her husband and Washington. It would also hurt the military career that Washington desired within the British army and affect his chances to achieve the wealth he sought. There was no possibility for divorce. In the English colonies only a special bill passed by Parliament in London could dissolve a marriage. An affair could lead to a court trial and an annulment in Virginia, but this was very rare.

At one point during the correspondence, Sally asked George to send his letter to her through another person. Even odder the other person was his younger brother. It is remarkable that her husband was not aware of this correspondence going on between the two. He was absent from home often since he was a colonel in the county militia and would be off recruiting men and training.

In 1773, Sally and her husband moved to England, and soon the Revolution broke out and they never returned to America. She never became Lady Fairfax. Unfortunately, George William Fairfax died in 1787, before he attained the title. Instead the title passed to Sally's sister, Elizabeth, who had married Sally's brother-in-law Bryan.

Sally received a letter dated Mount Vernon 16 May, 1798, one year before George Washington died. George and Martha wrote a joint letter to Sally, in which Washington, in his letter, reflected back on the couples' friendship. He began his letter with the assertion that five and twenty years "have nearly passed away since I have considered myself as the permanent resident at this place or have been in a situation to indulge myself in a familiar intercourse with my friends by letter or otherwise." He proceeded with a reference to existing events and closed the first paragraph of the letter with, "None of which events, however, nor all of them together, have been able to eradicate from my mind the recollections of those happy moments the happiest in my life, which I have enjoyed in your company." [20]

It appeared that Washington still had strong feelings for Sally and paid one final tribute to the woman who had provided such a strong influence on his life. She had taught him many things, especially how to act around and court a lady. She also prepared him to make a good marriage with Martha. Sally died in 1811, no family or friends were with her at the end, just her servants.

Martha Dandridge Custis Washington

"I live a very dull life . . . and I know nothing that passes in the town. I never go to any public place . . . indeed, I am more like a state prisoner than anything else." ----Martha in the early days as First Lady

⤚∞⧼⧽∞⤙

The Woman Behind the Man

Who was Martha?

Martha was the oldest daughter of John and Frances Dandridge. She was born on June 2, 1731, on a plantation near Williamsburg, Virginia. In keeping with the times, her education was almost negligible, except for learning domestic and social skills. Her letters lacked proper spelling and punctuation, later her spelling improved and sometimes she even had George write them. The following example of her poor spelling is from a letter to her sister Nancy Bassett,

> Mount Vernon Aug 28 1762 My dear Nancy, — I had the pleasure to receive your kind letter of the 25 of July just as I was setting out on a visit to Mr Washington in Westmoreland whare I spent a weak very agreabley I carred my little patt with me and left Jackey at home for a trial to see how well I coud stay without him though we ware gon but won fort-night I was quite impatiant to get home. If I at aney time heard the doggs barke or a noise out, I thought thair was a person sent for me.[1]

Historians have disagreed on Martha's looks. She did not have a portrait made until she was in her mid-twenties. She appeared to be an attractive, full figured woman who was barely five feet tall.

At the age of eighteen she married Daniel Parke Custis a rich landowner who was twenty years older. They had four children, two of whom survived to young adulthood and were alive when she married Washington. Her husband died in 1757, leaving Martha a very wealthy twenty-six year old widow with two children. Her inheritance included a large house, 17,000 acres, 300 slaves, other investments, and cash. Her total worth was in today's money would be around three million dollars.

Martha Dandridge Custis in 1757 at the age of 26. Public domain

After a proper mourning period, Martha had several men call on her, after all, she was very wealthy and young. During this time in Virginia, money was a significate item in considering marriage. Newspapers regularly stated the amount of a bride's net worth. One of the men that called on her was Charles Carter, who was also very wealthy. But Charles was an older widower and had many children. Martha had wanted to have more children and had money of her own so she did not consider him as marriage material.

Courtship of George and Martha:

When Washington was on his way to see the Virginia governor and a doctor in March of 1758, he stopped at the home of a friend for a quick visit. Also visiting at the time was the widow Martha Custis. Martha was not as attractive as Betsy Fauntleroy or Sally Fairfax. However, Martha's features did favor Mary Cary, the younger sister of Sally Fairfax, who Washington had been in love with. To make matters even better, Martha was also very wealthy, so she filled the double criteria Washington required for a wife.

Martha probably was attracted to the young Washington who appeared dashing in his colonial uniform, tall, and strong. Her previous husband was not near as good looking, rather pear shaped, and he was twenty years older than her. Also, Washington was a bachelor, he had acquired some land for a soldier, and he had been showing promise in Virginia society. Plus, Martha had a great amount of property and needed a manager for it.

After the couple met, Washington realized that Martha was not well-educated, nor eager to be, her spelling was even worse than his, but she could provide him with wealth and social standing. It must have appeared to Washington that his chances for finding someone better for a wife were not likely and he should move fast.

When Washington left Martha after their initial meeting on March 16, 1758, he noted in his account records that he left very generous tips [30 shillings] for Martha's house slaves. Washington probably did this to impress Martha, and it also left a favorable impression on the slaves. Years later one the slaves named Cully was interviewed, "And so, Cully, you remember when Mr. Washington came a-courtin' your mistress?" "Indeed I do, master," said Cully. "He was dar on'y fo' times afo' de weddin' for yo' see he was in de war all de time. We could'n keep our eyes offen him, he seem so gran'."[2]

Apparently Martha and George were attracted to each other, because on the way back from his trip, George called on her at her home in April, 1758. Tradition says that upon this occasion the lover was rowed across the river by a slave, who, when he was asked whether his mistress was at home, replied, "Yes, sah, I reckon you ' be the man what's 'spected," which proves that the fair widow was in readiness to receive her guest. The engagement evidently took place during this visit, as the lovers did not meet again until the time of their marriage.[3]

On May 4, George ordered a ring from Philadelphia and a suit of superfine broadcloth from London to fit a tall man. Martha also placed an order for wedding finery from London, and the shipment included brilliant purple slippers and a dress that was to be "grave but not extravagant nor to be mourning."[4]

When Martha was teased about her engagement, she explained, "I had to have a manager for my estate." This was not a very romantic thing to say, but when Washington was teased about the engagement, his reply was no better. A friend joked with George about the engagement and he replied, "You need not tease me about the beautiful widow. You know very well whom I love."[5] His love for Sally Fairfax was no secret to many of his friends.

On July 20, 1758, Washington was at Fort Cumberland on the Virginia frontier and he wrote the only remaining letter to Martha during their engagement that remains,

> My dear: We have begun our march for the Ohio. A courier is starting for Williamsburg, and I embrace the opportunity to send a few words to one whose life is now inseparable from mine. Since that happy hour when we made our pledges to each other, my thoughts have been continually going to you as another self. That an all powerful Providence may keep us both in safety is the prayer of your ever faithful and affectionate friend, Geo. Washington.[6]

A nice, friendly letter that closes with "your ever faithful and affectionate friend." It does not sound like a man in love and just recently engaged. It sounds more like a letter to a good friend. During this time Washington was still writing love letters to Sally Fairfax. Washington realized that his love for Sally was a fool's mission, and in a few months he and Martha would marry. Yet, he was still under the spell of Sally and he was not ready to end their relationship.

***

Marriage of George and Martha:

On January 6, 1759, George and Martha were married by David Mossum. The bride looked lovely in a heavy brocaded silk interwoven with silver threads; embroidered satin petticoat, high-heeled satin shoes with buckles of brilliants, point lace ruffles. Her ornaments were pearls, necklace, earrings and bracelets. The bridegroom appeared in citizen's dress of blue cloth, the coat lined with red silk, and ornamented with silver trimmings, and the waist coat of embroidered white satin. The shoe and knee buckles were of gold. His hair was powdered, and at his side hung a dress sword.[7]

When the last "I do," was whispered, George Washington, according to English common law, was the new owner of her Martha's property. This included a 17,000 acre plantation, almost 300 slaves, and two young children. Add to that what George brought to the marriage, forty-nine slaves and about five thousand acres of land-cleared and uncleared. His property had become badly run down through his absence during the three years of campaigns in the army. It had been often reported that Washington was one of the richest men in America. He became very wealthy after his marriage to Martha, but he probably did not rank in the top ten.

Washington now had achieved what he had been looking for, power, prestige, and wealth. He had married the richest, unattached woman in Virginia. Martha had at last married a young man and someone to run her large land holdings. It was a marriage for necessity for both, and if there was little love at first, they did grow to be fond and have great respect for each other. Unfortunately, they never had children together, probably due to the fact that George may have been sterile due to the smallpox treatment he receive years earlier. George once remarked that if Martha had died, he would remarry and then perhaps have children. Even though Martha had given birth to four children, he assumed they were barren due to her.

Washington's mother, Mary, was now fifty-two years old, surprisingly was very happy about the wedding. No doubt the hard to please woman probably found some flaws with Martha, but the new bride had achieved something she herself could not. Mary hated that Washington served in the army and often encourage him to quit the military, and George had resigned from the army a month before his wedding. Mary wrote to her brother, Joseph Ball in London, "There was no end to my troubles while George was in the army, but he has now given it up."[8]

Did George marry strictly for money or did he really love Martha?

Many people at the time and even years later thought it was a marriage for money. John Adams was a friend and admirer of Washington at times, but in one of his later harsh attacks on Washington, he declared that George Washington would never have amounted to much if he had not married Mrs. Custis' money.[9]

This author believes that their marriage began as one of convenience and necessity. They each knew going into it what they wanted and love was probably not a component at that time. Over time their respect for each other grew and love began to blossom. Over the years George still enjoyed talking and dancing with the ladies, but during all that time there was no one above Martha. Their marriage appeared to always have been a happy one, and both were dedicated to each other.

Martha would soon call George her "Old Man," a term still used in the South by wives in speaking of their husbands, and he called her "my dearest Patsy." Now married, George took charge of the property, her children, and even ordered much of Martha's own clothing. He once ordered, "…a Salmon-colored tabby of the enclosed pattern, with satin flowers, to be made into a sack. One pair of black, and one pair of white satin shoes, of the smallest."[10]

Married life:

After Washington brought his bride back to Mount Vernon, Sally and Martha became friends and spent many evenings at both George's home and at Sally's home. The women were equally secure in their life stations, Sally, with wealth and a future title, was a respectable married woman who was also secretly sure of Washington's passionate love. Martha, now Mrs. George Washington, was equally sure of Washington's devotion, for she had not only provided him with a fortune, but an already made family that he adored. So the two women were content in their friendship. Martha was perhaps aware of the past feelings her husband had for Sally, but the past remained in the past.

Once he married, Washington embraced the life of an English nobleman in dress and manner. He ordered the finest clothes from England, he imported household goods from London, he began to fill his library with books published in London, and he enjoyed fox hunting. This sport would be a natural for Washington because as Thomas Jefferson once said, "Washington was one the best horsemen of his age."[11] George was known to fox hunt up to seven hours a day.

Washington quickly began to remodel his home at Mount Vernon which would eventually double its size. In 1758, he raised the house to two and a half stories. Just before the Revolution in 1775, he added rooms to the north and south ends. His final expansion, some years later, increased his home to twenty-one rooms with an area of 11,028 square feet. Most of the work was done by slaves and artisans. He took great care and interest in every detail. Wallpaper made its appearance in Virginia about the middle of the eighteenth century and in 1757, George imported wallpaper for Mount Vernon.

Even when he was extremely busy trying to organize the American army in 1775, he was still taking an interest of the business at home. He had placed Lund Washington, his cousin, in charge of Mount Vernon during his absence. He would constantly write to Lund giving him instructions,

August 20, 1775, "I wish you would quicken Lanphire & Sears about the Dining Room Chimney Piece (to be executed as mentioned in one of my last Letters) as I could wish to have that end of the House compleatly finished before I return. I wish you had done the end of the New Kitchen next the Garden as also the old Kitchen with rusticated Boards; however, as it is not, I would have the Corners done so in the manner of our New Church. (those two especially which Fronts the Quarter.) What have you done with the Well? is that walled up?"[12]

After breakfast his custom was to ride around his plantation. On these morning rides he wore "plain dark clothes, a broad-brimmed white hat, and attached to his saddle-bow was an umbrella with a long staff." Toward the end of the morning he would return, and change his clothes. Then he ate a second breakfast, consisting of ham and eggs, or fresh fish, with corn-cakes, honey and tea. Dinner at Mount Vernon in colonial times was at two o'clock. After the Revolution it was changed to three o'clock. In the afternoon he would appear among the ladies and had tea on the verandah in one of the handsome suits which were made for him by his London tailor. His stockings were of silk, and his shoe-buckles of silver. His reddish-brown hair was powdered and tied in a queue. He was very happy to look and play the part of a country gentleman.

George and Martha seemed to think of marriage as a means of building alliances and consolidating a ruling aristocracy for the sprawling extent of America. He and Martha arranged sixteen marriages, including that between James Madison and Dolly Payne... maybe that is why Dolly saved his portrait when the British burned the White House in 1814.[13]

⚯

Raising step-children:

George Washington was always fond of children. Once when Gilbert Sullivan was painting a portrait of Washington, Jane, the daughter of Sullivan recalled, "One morning, while Washington was sitting for his picture, a little brother of mine ran into the room, when my father, thinking it would annoy the General, told him he must leave, but the General took him upon his knee, held him for some time, and had quite a little chat with him, and, in fact, they seemed to be pleased with each other. My brother remembered with pride, as long as he lived, that Washington had talked with him. Of course, this added to my father's regard for the General."[14]

Washington is called the father of our country, yet he was unable to have children of his own. After he married Martha, the couple had hopes of starting a family. Martha wrote to her sister on June 1, 1760, "The children are now very well and I think myself in a better state of health than

I have been in for a long time and don't doubt but I shall present you a fine healthy girl again when I come down in the Fall which is as soon as Mr. W.[15]

No more children came to Martha and when George wrote his will he said that there would be none, "My expectation of having issue had ceased."[16] He had suffered from a severe bout of the mumps as a young man and he had contracted smallpox and malaria simultaneously at nineteen Either of these events could have greatly decreased his chances of becoming a father. But that did not keep George for showing great love for his two step-children.

The artist Wilson Peale painted the portrait of Martha "Patsy" Parke Custis when she was sixteen in 1772. He thought she was so beautiful that he made a copy for himself and on the back wrote "A Virginia beauty." That same year he painted the portrait of John "Jacky" Parke Custis at the age of eighteen.

"Patsy" Parke Custis at the age of 16.　　　　John "Jacky" Parke Custis at the age of 18. Public domain

George felt that his role as stepfather to the children was to be generous and attentive to their needs. He recorded purchases of clothing, music lessons and even a pet parrot for Patsy. Every year, he ordered a new doll for her that was dressed according to the latest London fashions. If they needed to be lectured, he would take a moralizing position and try to counsel them with wisdom and affection.

Unfortunately, Patsy suffered from epilepsy that began when she was around six years old. In 1768, her seizures became more frequent, and in 1770 Washington kept a record of Patsy's seizures. He noted that between June 29 and September 22, 1770, she had a total of twenty-six seizures, with as many as two in one day. Over the years various treatments were tried, but to no avail. On June 19, 1773, at the age of seventeen, Patsy died at home after a seizure. George knelt at her dying bed, and with a passionate burst of tears prayed aloud that her life might be spared.[17]

With the death of Patsy all attention was centered on their son "Jacky," as he was known by the family. He was now nineteen and was a troubled, spoiled, and a lazy lad who took no interest in his education. When he was seventeen, Washington wrote of him to Rev. Jonathan Boucher, head of a famous school at Annapolis, "He has little or no knowledge of arithmetic, and is totally ignorant of the mathematics." He was sent to one school after another with his horse and Negro servant.

Early in 1774, to the displeasure of George and Martha Jacky married Eleanor Calvert, and soon he was almost bankrupted due to a poor business deal. In 1778, Jacky served in the Virginia House of Burgess and at times, as a civilian aid to his step-father. Washington once wrote to Jacky that even though he may not have much power in the House of Burgess, he should at least be punctual. During the war the two men wrote back and forth about buying and selling property, and many times Washington would offer advice to his step-son.

In 1781, Jacky insisted that he accompany George to Yorktown and while there he contracted camp fever and died on November 5, 1781. Washington promised the young widow that he would raise her children as if they were his own. Later the two youngest of Eleanor's children came to Mount Vernon to live with George and Martha. The two children were informally adopted by the couple. Eleanor, called Nelly, was about three years old and her brother George was six months old.

Two years later their mother, Eleanor, was remarried to Dr. David Stuart, and when Washington was asked about her getting married he wrote, "I never shall give advice to a woman who is setting out on a matrimonial voyage; first, because I could never advise one to marry without her own consent; and secondly, because I know it is to no purpose to advise her to refrain when she has obtained it."[18]

George and Martha Washington with their grandchildren, National Gallery of Art, Washington, D.C. Washington's slave, Billy is seen at the left. Public domain.

Raising grandchildren:

An interesting story occurred several years later when Nelly was in her early teens. She had several girls over to spend the night and for some reason they broke a house rule by appearing for dinner in their morning dresses. Martha, who was very proper, said nothing to the girls. During the meal a coach arrived bringing some distinguished guests, including some French officers of rank. The girls begged to be excused so they could run upstairs and dress properly to receive their company. Martha told them, "No, remain as you are, what is good enough for General Washington is good enough for any guest of his."[19]

Washington was very interested in his granddaughter Nelly. She was a beautiful young girl, a little wild according to Martha, and she had many young men seeking her hand in marriage. Nelly told George that all of the men pursuing her left her cold, and she was afraid that she would never marry. Washington took her dilemma serious and wrote to her on March 21, 1798,

> A hint here; Men and Women feel the same inclinations towards ⟨each other now that they always have done, and which they will continue to do until there is a new order of things.

> And you, as others have done, may find perhaps, that the passions of your sex are easier roused than allayed. Do not therefore boast too soon, nor too strongly, of your insensibility to, or resistance of its powers.

> Love is said to be an involuntary passion and it is therefore contended that it cannot be resisted. This is true, in part only; for like all things else when nourished and supplied plentifully with [aliment,] it is rapid in its progress; but let these be withdrawn and it may be stifled in its birth or much stunted in its growth.

> When the fire is beginning to kindle, and your heart growing warm, propound these questions to it. Who is this invader? Have I competent knowledge of him? Is he a man of good character? A man of sense? for be assured a sensible woman can never be happy with a fool. What has been his walk in life? Is he a gambler? a spendthrift, a drunkard? Is his fortune sufficient to maintain me in the manner I have been accustomed to live, and my sisters do live? and is he one to whom my friends can have no reasonable objections? If these interrogations can be satisfactorily answered there will remain but one more to be asked; that however is an important one. Have I sufficient ground to conclude that his affections are enjoyed by me? Without this, the heart of sensibility will struggle against a passion that is not reciprocated; delicacy, custom, or call it by what epithet you will having precluded all advances on your part, the declaration without the most indirect invitation on yours must proceed from the man to render it permanent & valuable. And nothing short of good sense, and an easy unaffected conduct can draw the line between prudery & coquetry; both of which are equally despised by men of understanding; and soon or late, will recoil upon the actor.

> Flirting is hardly a degree removed from the latter and both are punished by the counter game of men, who see this the case & act accordingly. In a word it would be no great departure from truth to say that it rarely happens otherwise, than that a thorough coquette dies in celibacy, as a punishment for her attempts [to] mislead others; by encouraging looks, words, or actions, given for no other purpose than to draw men on to make overtures that may be rejected.[20]

On February 22, 1799, Nelly married Washington's nephew, Lawrence Lewis and as a wedding gift Washington gave her 2,000 acres adjacent to Mount Vernon. There they built a home and raised eight children. On Nelly's wedding date, Washington made the following notation in his diary, "The Rev. Mr. Davis & Mr. George Calvert came to dinner & Miss Custis was married about Candle light to Mr. Law Lewis."[21]

George Washington Parke Custis, nicknamed "Washy," spent much of his youth with his grandparents, George and Martha. In the fall of 1796, he enrolled at the College of New Jersey (now called Princeton). There was concern that the boy, like his father, might not take his studies serious enough, so Washington decided to write to the boy some sound words of wisdom. Here are parts of the letter written on November 17, 1796,

> Yesterday's mail brought me your letter of the 12th instant, and under cover of this letter you will receive a ten-dollar bill, to purchase a gown, &c., if proper. But as the classes may be distinguished by a different insignia, I advise you not to provide these without first obtaining the approbation of your tutors; otherwise you may be distinguished more by folly, than by the dress.

> It affords me pleasure to hear that you are agreeably fixed; and I receive still more from the assurance you give of attending closely to your studies. It is you yourself who is to derive immediate benefit from these.

Your country may do it hereafter. The more knowledge you acquire, the greater will be the probability of your succeeding in both, and the greater will be your thirst for more.

I rejoice to hear you went through your examination with propriety, and have no doubt but that the president has placed you in the class which he conceived best adapted to the present state of your improvement. The more there are above you, the greater your exertions should be to ascend; but let your promotion result from your own application, and from intrinsic merit, not from the labors of others. The last would prove fallacious, and expose you to the reproach of the daw in borrowed feathers. *[This is a reference to "A Daw in borrowed Feathers" is a Greek fable. The daw or crow dresses in feathers of other birds before he competes against them. The story ends with the crow being exposed and shunned by the other birds. The lesson to learn is, borrowing finery items brings humiliation.]*

This would be inexcusable in you, because there is no occasion for it; forasmuch, as you need nothing but the exertion of the talents you possess, with proper directions, to acquire all that is necessary; and the hours allotted for study, if properly improved, will enable you to do this. Although the confinement may feel irksome at first, the advantages resulting from it, to a reflecting mind, will soon overcome it.

Endeavor to conciliate the good will of *all* your fellow-students, rendering them every act of kindness in your power. Be particularly obliging and attentive to your chamber-mate, Mr. Forsyth; *[John Forsyth had entered the College of New Jersey in 1795 and graduated in 1799. He was the son of Revolutionary War officer.]* who, from the account I have of him, is an admirable young man, and strongly impressed with the importance of a liberal and finished education. But above all, be obedient to your tutors, and in a particular manner respect the president of the seminary, who is both learned and good.

For any particular advantages you may derive from the attention and aid of Mr. Forsyth, I shall have a disposition to reward. One thing more and I will close this letter. Never let an indigent person ask, without receiving something, if you have the means; always recollecting in what light the widow's mite was viewed. *[from the bible, Mark 12:42-44]*

Your grandmother, sister, and all here are well, and feeling a strong interest in your welfare, join most cordially with me in every good wish for it. Affectionately, I am your sincere friend, g. Washington[22]

Washy later became a successful planter and builder in Virginia. In 1804 he married Mary Lee Fitzhugh and their surviving daughter married Robert E. Lee.

Military wife:

Martha joined her husband during the Revolution for all of the Continental Army's winter camps. Before the start of the Revolution she stayed close to home, but when it once started, she

would travel hundreds of dangerous and hard miles to be with him. At Valley Forge, Charles Willson Peale painted a miniature of Washington, for his usual fee of $56.00, and gave it to Martha. Colonel John Laurens saw the portrait and later wrote, "The defects of this portrait I think are, that the face is too long, and old age is too strongly marked in it."[23]

Charles Willson Peale painted a miniature of George Washington at Valley Forge. The Metropolitan Museum of Art.

There was a period during the siege of Boston in 1775-76, that Martha and George did not write to each other. The belief at the time was that the disease smallpox could be carried through letters, and George was fearful that a letter from her might carry the disease and then spread it to his army. When the threat passed during the winter of 1775, Martha, Jacky, and his wife Eleanor joined Washington at his first winter camp in Cambridge. It was a dangerous 600 mile trip and they ran the risk of being captured by British patrols, the roads were in horrible condition, and the weather was harsh. This was the farthest Martha had ever been from home.

This was Martha's first experience with war, and on December 30, 1775 she wrote to her friend Elizabeth Ramsay, "Some days we have a number of cannon and shells from Boston and Bunkers Hill, but it does not seem to surprise anyone but me; I confess I shudder every time I hear the sound of a gun." She later added, "...to me that never see any thing of war, the preparations, are very terable indeed, but I endever to keep my fears to myself as well as I can."[24] Some of the duties that Martha performed while in camp included copying letters for her husband, entertaining guests, making and encourage other women to make clothing for the soldiers, and helping with the sick soldiers. Martha was also seen as a positive influence on the morale of the troops. Her grandson, George Washington Parke Custis, pointed to her "kindness to the sick and wounded" as a reason her annual arrival in camp was "hailed as an event that would serve to dissipate the gloom of the winter quarters."[25]

Martha joined her husband at Valley Forge during the winter of 1777-78. General Knox on the night of February 22, sent a regimental band to play for the general on his birthday. Washington sent Martha out to the musicians to thank them and give them generous tips. She told them that the general had just gone to bed or he would have come in person.

These numerous visits by Martha provided George with comfort and a welcome distraction from his duties. General Nathanael Greene wrote to his wife on April 8, 1777, "Mrs Washington and Mrs Bland from Virginia are at Camp, happy with their better halves. Mrs Washington is excessive fond of the General and he of her. They are very happy in each other."[1] Martha Bland wrote to her sister from the Morristown camp on May 12 of that year that George's "Worthy Lady seems to be in perfect felicity while she is by the side of her Old Man as she calls him."[26]

Lady Washington:

George Washington was inaugurated on April 30, 1789, in New York City, and it would be nearly a month before Martha would join him. When she arrived in New York she was accompanied with her two grandchildren, Robert Lewis the President's nephew, and several personal slaves. The family first lived at #3 Cherry Street, and after finding it too small they moved to the Macomb House.

Martha offered warm hospitality to their numerous guests, but took little satisfaction in hosting "what didn't come from the heart," as she put it. She was not pleased with the restrictions placed on her life. She was referred to as "Lady Washington" as the term 'First Lady' came into vogue only after her death. In July 1790, artist John Trumbull gave Martha Washington a full-length portrait painting of General George Washington as a gift. It was later displayed in their home at Mount Vernon.

8

George Washington and Religion

"The mere politician, equally with the pious man, ought to respect and cherish religion and morality as the firmest props of the duties of men and citizens."---- George Washington

~∞⊙⊙∞~

Was Washington Religious?

Some earlier writers of Washington would focus on any account that portrayed him as religious, such as attending church every week, or praying daily. The purpose was to perpetuate the image of Washington as a devout and religious man. Whenever they encountered a writer or source that contradicted that image they would try and discredit the story or the person. At times a person would make claims about Washington being religious that even Washington himself showed to be false. For example, his pastor Rev. Lee Massey wrote that he was constant in attending church. However, in Washington's personal diaries he wrote that he did not regularly attended services at home and in the year 1760 he went sixteen times, and in 1768 he went fourteen.[1]

As the years passed, biographers of Washington began to portray him as a man that believed in religion, but it was not the central focus of his life as it was earlier depicted. Historians agreed that he believed in God, but how religious was he and what were his religious views? Most of the other founding fathers at this time were noted about writing about their religious beliefs. Washington, however, rarely discussed his personal religious views.

A member of the church:

It is known that he was baptized, as it was recorded by his mother in the family Bible. Washington's parents were members of the Church of England, which was almost the only denomination of Christians then known in Virginia. We know that he attended the Anglican Church during his life. In fact, he attended several churches and even served as a vestryman and warden for over fifteen years. In speeches and personal correspondence he would sometimes refer to "Providence", a term used for God, heaven, or blessings. He rarely mentioned Christ in his writings, and he usually referred to God as "the great disposer of human events," On July 9, 1776, Washington issued a General Order which in part read, "The blessing and protection of Heaven are at all times necessary but especially so in times of public distress and danger—The General hopes and trusts, that every officer and man, will endeavor so to live, and act, as becomes a Christian Soldier defending the dearest Rights and Liberties of his country."[2]

~⊙⊙~

God takes a side:

"God is on our side," said General Washington when he was told that the British troops at Lexington, April 19, 1775, had fired on and killed several of the Americans. He then replied: "I grieve for the death of my countrymen; but rejoice that the British are still determined to keep God on our side. The smiles of Heaven can never be expected on a nation that disregards the eternal rules of order and right, which Heaven itself has ordained."[3]

Yes, George Washington was a religious man, but with some limitations. Martha furnished much of the religion for the family, as was often the norm at that time. It was reported that his great Bible looked as if it had rarely been opened. As president he encouraged his countrymen to attend church, yet he was very lax in his attendance. At times he served as a vestryman and church warden, but he would leave services instead of taking communion. He opposed his soldiers gambling or swearing on moral grounds, yet he enjoyed placing wagers and would at times swear at his men.

Religious tolerance

There can be no doubt that religious intolerance was not a part of Washington's character. When the New England troops intended to celebrate Guy Fawkes day as usual, the General Orders declared that "…as the Commander in chief has been apprised of a design, formed for the observance of that ridiculous and childish custom of burning the effigy of the Pope, he cannot help expressing his surprise, that there should be officers and soldiers in this army so void of common sense, as not to see the impropriety of such a step." [Guy Fawkes Day is celebrated in the United Kingdom on November 5. On November 5, 1605, Fawkes and his supporters, a radical Catholic group, attempted to assassinate King James I by blowing up Parliament. The plot failed and the conspirators were put to death. It is celebrated by the English by burning effigies, bonfires, and fireworks.]

When trying to secure some servants he wrote that, "…if they are good workmen, they may be from Asia, Africa, or Europe; they may be Mahometans, Jews, or Christians of any sect, or they may be Atheists." When the bill taxing all the people of Virginia to support the Episcopal Church (his own) was under discussion, he threw his weight against it.[4]

In a letter on August 15, 1787 to the Marquis de Lafayette he addressed religious toleration, "I am not less ardent in my wish that you may succeed in your plan of toleration in religious matters. Being no bigot myself to any mode of worship."[5]

Going to church:

His adopted son said, "Washington was a member in full communion of the Protestant Episcopal Church."[6] As a young soldier and planter before his marriage, he rarely attended church. Once married he joined two parishes in Truro and Fairfax. This was because his estate was so large it was located in two parishes. During this time he became much more active in church affairs. The custom of the day was to purchase a pew in church, so he paid 36.10 pounds for one at Fairfax. It was, up until that time, the largest price paid by any parishioner.

During much of his life, Washington spent a lot of time on the road. During this time he attended many different denominations including, Presbyterians, Quakers, Congregationalists,

Roman Catholic, Baptists, and Dutch Reformed. According to his diary he usually attended church an average of once a month. He liked to use Sunday for his letter writing day and receiving guests.

Washington the godfather:

In 1747, at the age of fifteen years, young Washington was godfather to a baptized child. In 1748, at sixteen, he was godfather to his niece, Frances Lewis. In 1751, at nineteen, to his nephew, Fielding Lewis, his sister's first child. In 1760, at twenty-eight, he again became godfather for another nephew, Charles Lewis.

Washington the mason

When George Washington joined the Masons it was a rite of passage and civic responsibility. On November 4, 1752, at the age of twenty he joined the Freemasons in the Lodge at Fredericksburg, Virginia. When he became a member he paid a fee in the amount of two pounds and three shillings.[7] During various times in his life, he corresponded with the organization, but the lodge's records show Washington attending no further meetings after January 4, 1755.

Washington as a freemason, Library of Congress.

Did he kneel in prayer?

As mentioned earlier, it was important to the myth of Washington to portray him praying on his knees. The story of his praying at Valley Forge is still believed even today by many people. In one early biography of Washington it was reported that Robert Lewis, nephew of Washington, saw him in the morning and evening in his library kneeling with an open Bible. Lewis later claimed he only saw this once, however, the biographer made it appear that it was an almost daily occurrence. Washington, as noted before, did not like kneeling in or out of church. It was recorded that, "Mrs. Washington knelt during the prayers; he always stood, as was the custom at that time."[8]

Did he receive communion?

The record of Washington receiving communion is spotty. Some writers reported that Washington received communion most every Sunday, but ministers at four of the churches that he attended wrote that he regularly left services before communion. His granddaughter Nelly wrote, "On communion Sundays he left the church with me, after the blessing, and returned home, and we sent the carriage back for my grandmother."[9]

Nelly also said that at times he took communion before the Revolution, but did not after the war. There is evidence from his financial papers that he supplied wine for the communion service at Pohick Church before he left for the war.

When Washington was President, he was once chastised from the pulpit for regularly leaving before communion service in Philadelphia, although according to Nelly most people did. Concerned about his reputation, he told the minister that he was sorry for setting such a bad example and would not do it again. Afterwards he remarked, that he would no longer annoy Dr. Abercrombie by his presence. After that he did not attend services on Sundays when communion was offered, which at that time was only 3 or 4 times a year rather than every Sunday. This was a shock to the church goers in Philadelphia, because they just assumed he was a very religious man.

It was the custom in some of the colonial churches to administer communion only at Christmas, Easter, and Whitsuntide [the seventh Sunday after Easter, which commemorated the descent of the Holy Spirit upon the Disciples of Christ], and it was not an uncommon practice for some communicants to receive only once a year. Martha continued to take communion.

Religion and the President:

He believed while President, it was necessary that he should use much caution in whatever came from him touching on theological subjects. He felt he should also guard against favoring one denomination over another. As President in 1789 and 1790, he usually attended St. Paul's Chapel and Trinity Church on Manhattan. When the capital was located in Philadelphia he attended church at St. Peter's and Christ Church. After he became President, he exchanged greetings with 22 leading religious groups and made a practice of attending the church services of a variety of denominations.

Washington considered his time during the week belonged to public business, and therefore, was obliged to attend to private matters on Sunday. While he was at Mount Vernon he would spend most Sundays catching up on his correspondence and receiving guests. According to his grandson he had a different Sunday routine as President, "On Sundays, unless the weather was uncommonly severe, the President and Mrs. Washington attended divine services, and in the evenings the President read to Mrs. Washington, in her chamber, a sermon, or some portion from the Sacred Writings. No visitors, with the exception of Mr. Speaker Trumbull, were admitted to the president's house on Sundays."[10] If he did go to church that often perhaps it was because he was more in the public eye and he felt the need to set an example.

Religion and the military:

The common soldier was more interested about his everyday life, rather than the abstract cause for the fighting. Since the soldiers faced death from either battle or disease, they kept routine religious rituals, maintain closed relationships with their chaplains, and were exceptionally tolerant toward other religious beliefs.

During the French and Indian War (1754-1763), young George Washington and other officers led the men in church services because there were no army chaplains. Once the Revolution began, General Washington and his commanders knew that clergymen provided comfort and encouragement to the common soldier. This was especially true in the early years of the war when the cause looked hopeless. These men of the cloth could make the difference between defeat and victory. Their presence could encourage the soldiers to stay the course and not give up hope of an eventual victory.

In July of 1776, the Continental Congress voted to pay the chaplains thirty-three and a third dollars per month and to give them the rank and rations of an army colonel. They each were assigned to a regiment and many bore arms and joined in the fighting. General Washington required, when possible, the soldiers attend Sunday service each week. On July 9, 1776, Washington issued a General Order that stated,

> The honorable Continental Congress having been pleased to allow a chaplain to each regiment, with the pay of thirty-three dollars and one third per month, the colonels or commanding officers of each regiment are directed to procure chaplains accordingly, persons of good characters and exemplary lives, and to see that all inferior officers and soldiers pay them a suitable respect. The General hopes and trusts, that every officer, and man, will endeavour so to live, and act, as becomes a Christian Soldier defending the dearest Rights and Liberties of his country.[11]

Prayer and thanksgiving:

Washington encouraged the declarations of days of prayer and fasting as a means of seeking divine assistance in dangerous situations. He also supported the proclamation of days of Thanksgiving to praise God for His help. On March 6, 1776, at Cambridge, General Washington issued the following order,

> Thursday, the 7th instant, being set apart by the honorable the Legislature of this Province as a day of fasting, prayer, and humiliation, "to implore the Lord and Giver of all victory to pardon our manifold sins and wickedness, and that it would please Him to bless the Continental arms with His divine favor and protection," all officers and soldiers are strictly enjoined to pay all due reverence and attention on that day to the sacred duties to the Lord of hosts for His mercies already received, and for those blessings which our holiness and uprightness of life can alone encourage us to hope through His mercy to 0btain.[12]

In a General Order dated May 2, 1778, Washington stated, "...that divine Service be performed every Sunday at 11 o Clock in those Brigades to which there are Chaplains—those which have none to attend the places of worship nearest to them—It is expected that Officers of all Ranks will by their attendance set an Example to their men."[13]

Washington and his troops also offered thanks to God for the favorable events and successes of the war. For instance, immediately following the decisive American victory at the

Battle of Yorktown, the final battle of the Revolution in 1781, Washington again recommended that his men attend a church service and reminded them to offer gratitude for God's assistance. He also directed his army chaplains to "render thanks to Almighty God for all his mercies, to thank God for granting victory to the Americans." Evidently, throughout the war, in both low and high moments, Washington acknowledged the important role of Providence in the outcome of the war.

General orders on proper behavior

Washington was certainly no stranger to betting on cards or horses, drinking, and he would break into some very salty language when angry. However, he frowned upon the men under his command to engage in any of those behaviors. Washington thought the troops should exemplify good moral conduct in order to best represent the American cause in the eyes of God and the people, upon whose support they depended. When he addressed the troops' conduct, he forbid cursing, swearing, offensive oaths, profanity, blaspheming, gambling, and drunkenness. He essentially banned any conduct that he thought might offend God or the colonists. In June, 1756, while at Fort Cumberland, he issued the following order,

> Colonel Washington has observed that the men of his regiment are very profane and reprobate. He takes this opportunity to inform them of his great displeasure at such practices, and assures them, that, if they do not leave them off, they shall be severely punished. The officers are desired, if they hear any man swear, or make use of an oath or execration, to order the offender twenty-five lashes immediately, without a court-martial. For the second offense, he will be more severely punished.[14]

Washington's General Orders on August 3, 1776, was one of several issued about swearing during the Revolution,

> The General is sorry to be informed that the foolish, and wicked practice, of profane cursing and swearing (a Vice heretofore little known in an American Army) is growing into fashion; he hopes the officers will, by example, as well as influence, endeavour to check it, and that both they, and the men will reflect, that we can have little hopes of the blessing of Heaven on our Arms, if we insult it by our impiety, and folly.[15]

Washington also ordered that any soldier found drunk would receive one hundred lashes, without benefit of a court-martial. Dueling was popular in those days, and to challenge another, or to accept the same from another, the general also discouraged. Washington never challenged or accepted a challenge for a duel, and earnestly discouraged others from the practice.

In a letter to his nephew Bushrod Washington he wrote, "The last thing I shall mention is first of importance and that is, to avoid Gaming—This is a vice which is productive of every possible evil--- equally injurious to the Morals & health of its votaries—It is the child of Avarice—the brother of inequity—& father of Mischief—It has been the Ruin of many worthy familys—the loss of many a mans honor—& the cause of Suicide.[16]

9

George Washington: Teeth, Illness, and Death

"I am just going! Have me decently buried; and do not let my body be put into the vault less than three days after I am dead." Then, "Do you understand me? . . . Tis well!"---last words of George Washington

❧❦❧

Bad Teeth

Sitting for portraits:

Washington did not like to sit for a portrait painting, but at times would agree to pose, usually at the urging of Martha. Many times Washington would urge the painter to speed up the process so he could deal with more important matters. The ill-fitting dentures that Washington wore were part of the reason he dislike sittings. The dentures made it difficult to smile and sometimes he could barely close his lips. As a result, he usually had a stern look on his face with his lips pressed tightly together.

He agreed to sit and pose for Gilbert Stuart on four separate occasions. At one sitting Stuart was trying to get the stoic general to relax so he said to Washington, "Now, sir, you must let me forget that you are General Washington and that I am Stuart the painter." "Mr. Stuart," Washington replied politely, "need never feel the need of forgetting who he is, or who General Washington is."[1]

Another time Stuart tried to get a spark of life on Washington's face with an old joke. He told the President how James II, on a journey through England to gain popularity, arrived in a town where the Mayor, who was a baker, was so frightened that he forgot his speech of welcome and stood there stammering. A friend jogged the Mayors elbow and whispered: "Hold up your head and look like a man." When Stuart told how the flustered baker had repeated this statement to the King, Washington's stern face unbelievably broke into a smile. But before Stuart could lift his brush, the smile was gone.[2]

⚓

Washington's teeth:

George Mercer, who had served with Washington in the Virginia militia, said in 1760, that when Washington's mouth was open it showed some "defective teeth." As early as 1754, Washington had one of his teeth extracted by a Doctor Watson for five shillings. After that time, a toothache, followed by an extraction, became an almost a yearly event. One of Washington's diary entry states, "indisposed with an aching tooth, and swelled and inflamed gum." There would be many more entries made like that over the years. Martha Washington also had problems with her dentures, which resulted in her urging her children and grandchildren to take care of their teeth.

Washington didn't purposely neglect his teeth, but dental hygiene wasn't known or practiced by most people. In some groups, taking care of your teeth made you appear to be effeminate or vain. Washington later believed in order to portray the image of a leader he must have teeth. So he endured painful tooth loss and wearing painful dentures.

By 1789, Washington was using false teeth, and he lost his last tooth in 1795. His final tooth was given to his dentist, John Greenwood as a gift. The dentist preserved the tooth in a gold locket he wore on his watch fob.

At first, these substitute teeth were very badly fitted, and when Stuart painted his famous picture of Washington he tried to remedy the malformation the dentures gave the mouth by placing cotton padding under the lips. The result made what looked bad even worse and gave that otherwise fine portrait a feature that was poor and unlike Washington. For this reason alone the miniature painted by James Sharples, which in all else, approximates so closely to Stuart's masterpiece, is preferable.[3]

Left: This portrait is a copy painted in 1803 by Stuart based on his own uncompleted work. Public domain

Right: Portrait of George Washington c. 1796, by James Sharples. Public domain

Were his teeth made of wood?

Washington did not have wooden teeth. Had this been true it would have been an even more horrible experience than what he did endure. They would have certainly splintered and they could have warped and easily gotten out of shape. How then did the myth get started that they were made of wood? Historian and forensic dentist have proposed that the ivory and bone that his teeth were made of had hairline fractures in them. Washington was very fond of dark Madeira wine, which over time would have stained his false teeth. The tiny fractures in the bone or ivory would darken even more than the rest of the tooth. This would give the lines the appearance of the grain in a piece of wood.

Washington's dentures:

In his lifetime, it was believed that Washington had four sets of dentures. By 1781, he began wearing partial dentures. His dentures may have been a combination of ivory from an elephant, walrus, hippopotamus, and teeth from a horse, donkey, cow, or elephant. These animal teeth would have been filed down to fit his mouth size. His dentures may well have been some of his own pulled teeth because in a letter to Lund Washington he wrote, "In a drawer in the Locker of the Desk which stands in my study you will find two small (fore) teeth; which I beg of you to wrap up carefully, and send enclosed in your next letter to me. I am positive I left them there, or in the secret drawer in the locker of the same desk," he added.[4]

Only one set of Washington's dentures have survived and they are on exhibit at Mount Vernon. The upper row of teeth consist of horse and donkeys' teeth, and the lower row are a mix of cow's teeth, elephant and walrus ivory, with a few human teeth. The teeth were set into lead frames with a wire running through a hole drilled in each tooth that held it in the base. To join the top and bottom dentures, there were two very tight silver springs. The springs forced the upper denture to rise with his mouth, and allowed him to open and close it.

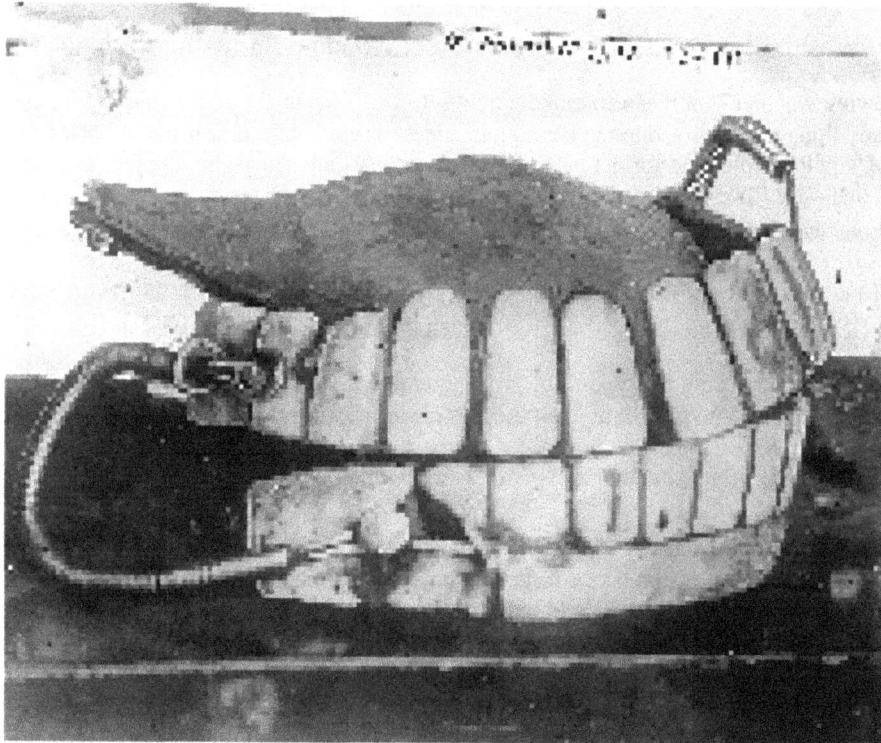

George Washington's teeth. Library of Congress

Keeping his mouth closed was a problem for Washington. He had to apply pressure to the springs and clench his teeth to keep his mouth closed. Since he had to grit his teeth much of the time his dentures hurt considerably while he wore them. When you look at some of his portraits you can see how uncomfortable and painful it was for him to keep his mouth closed.

Both full and partial dentures required maintenance and attention:

During the last ten years of Washington's life he wrote to Dr. Greenwood about the problems he had with his teeth, repairs needed, and ordering new teeth for his dentures. Below are parts of several of the letters sent to his dentist over the years.

> Your letter of the 6th and the box which accompanied it came safe to hand. The contents of the latter were perfectly agreeable to me, and will, I am persuaded, answer the end proposed very well. Enclosed I send you Twenty dollars in payment for them and the repairs of the old ones, and, etc. Dr. Greenwood bought human teeth for a Guinea each and it appears that Washington had purchased some of the teeth.[5]

In the next letter, sent in January 1797, Washington complained of problems associated with his dentures and some repairs needed,

> The teeth herewith enclosed have, by degrees, worked loose and, at length, two or three of them have given way altogether. I send them to you to be repaired. I would thank yo⟨u⟩ for, returning them as soon as possible for although I now make use of anoth⟨er⟩ sett, they are both uneasy in the mouth and bulge my lips out in such a manner as to make them appear considerably swelled. Send with the teeth, springs about a foot in length, but not cut; and about double that length of a tough gold wire, of the size you see with the teeth, for fastening the springs.[6]

Just days later, Washington again wrote to Dr. Greenwood about teeth problems,

> Not knowing whether you mean to make a new sett, or to repair the old, I must again caution you against adding any thing that will widen the bars on the sides, or extend them in front at bottom—They are already too wide, and too projecting for the parts they rest upon; which causes both upper, & under lip to bulge out, as if swelled—By filing these parts away (to remedy that evil) it has been one cause of the teeth giving way, having been weakened thereby.[7]

In the last surviving letter from Dr. Greenwood, Washington was given some instructions on taking care of his dentures. Note that the doctor's spelling is even worse than Washington's,

> Acid is Used in Coulering every kind of Ivory. therefore it is very pernicious to the teeth. I Advice you to Either take them out After dinner and put them in cleain water and put in another scett or Cleain them with a brush and som Chalk scraped fine. it will Absorbe the Acid which Collects from the mouth and preserve them longer—I have found another and better way of useing the sealing wax when holes is eaten in the teeth by acid &c.
>
> First Observe and dry the teeth. then take a peice of Wax and Cut it into As small peices as you think will fill up the hole. then take a large nail or any other peice of Iron and heat it hot into the fier. then put your peice of wax into the hole and melt it by meanes of introduceing the Point of the Nail to it. I have tried it and found it to Consoladate and do better then the other way and if done proper it will resist the saliva. it will be handyer for you to take hold of the Nail with small plyers than with a tongs thus the wax must be very small not bigger than this. if your teeth Grows black take some chalk and a Pine or Ceder stick. it will rub it of. If you whant your teeth more yellower soake them in Broath or pot li:quer but not in tea or Acid. Porter is a Good thing to Coulor them and will not hurt but preserve them but it must not be in the least pricked.
>
> You will find I have Altered the upper teeth you sent me from Philadelphia[.] leaveing the enamel on the teeth dont preserve them any longer then if it was of. it onely holds the Color better. but to preserve them they must be very Often Changed and Cleained for whatever atackes them must be repelled as Often or it will gain Ground and destroy the works—the two setts I repaired is done on a different plan then when they are done when made intirely new for the teeth are screwed on the barrs insted of haveing the barrs Cast red hot on them which is the reason I beleive the[y] destroy or desolve so soone near to the barrs.[8]

Did Washington use slave teeth in his dentures?

We know that George Washington did purchase teeth from an enslaved person or persons at Mount Vernon. The record of the transition was entered twice in his financials records. It was recorded in 1784 by Lund Washington, who was the plantation manager, "Cash paid on Acct of Genrl. Washington. To pd Negroes for 9 teeth on acct of the French Dentis Doctr Lemay."[9]

When this transaction took place, French dentist Jean Pierre Le Moyer was staying in the area around Mount Vernon and he was the recipient of the teeth that were purchased. Since he had been advertising in local newspapers of his availability to perform tooth transplants, he would need a stock of teeth to perform this service. This would indicate that the teeth purchased were not for Washington's personal use.

Some people who wish to discredit George Washington claim that he purchased the teeth and used them in his dentures. There are no facts to back this claim. If Washington purchased the teeth for himself, there would have been no reason to make the journal entry with that information. It simply would have read, "purchased teeth" and with the amount shown. This was how entries were recorded when Washington purchased, for example, corn from enslaved people. The entry would read, "corn for six shillings". There is no proof that he had slave teeth inserted into any of his dentures.

How a teeth cleaning may have helped to lead to the surrender of Cornwallis:

In Washington's diaries he constantly complains about lost teeth, pain, ill-fitting dentures, and broken parts in his dentures. His account records shows numerous entries of money being sent to dentists for toothbrushes, teeth scrappers, cleaning products, and medication for toothaches.

On May 29, 1781 Washington wrote a letter to Dr. Baker requesting cleaning utensils for his false teeth, "Sir, A day or two ago I requested Col. Harrison to apply to you for a pair of Pincers to fasten the wire of my teeth. I hope you furnished him with them. I now wish you would send me one of your scrapers as my teeth stand in need of cleaning, and I have little prospect of being in Philadelphia. Soon. It will come very safe by the Post and in return, the money shall be sent so soon as I know the cost of it."[10]

Unfortunately, the letter was captured by the British and never reached Dr. Baker. Washington was upset that the letter fell into British hands, because he liked to keep it secret about his teeth problems. Washington stated in the letter that he did not plan to be in Philadelphia anytime soon. This simple sentence convinced British General Clinton that Washington's troops, as well as the French troops camped around New York City, would not be moving south to threaten the army of General Cornwallis at Yorktown. What Clinton did not know was that Washington had already decided to march to Yorktown. Once at Yorktown, the Americans surrounded Cornwallis forcing him to surrender in October of 1781.

How did the dental problems affect Washington?

Washington's dental problems, according to some historians, impacted the shape of his face and may have contributed to his quiet, somber demeanor. Since opening his mouth relaxed the pressure on the springs connecting the upper and lower dentures, it could cause them to slip out. So, if he was among a group of people and gave off a hearty laugh it could cause the dentures to go flying out. Also, Washington was not comfortable with public speaking because of his teeth problems. During his time at the Constitutional Convention he addressed the assembly only once.

His teeth also affected what foods he could eat. He was forced to eat soft foods when possible and he had to be careful when he chewed. His granddaughter Nelly said that his favorite breakfast was mushy "hoecakes swimming in butter and honey."[11]

Numerous Illnesses

Washington was frequently plagued with illness throughout his life. Fortunately for the country, during the time of the Revolution he appeared to be exempt from illness. Once he retired from the military, some of his earlier sicknesses returned.

It is not known exactly what childhood diseases he had, but it appears that he may have contracted measles at an early age. When he married, Martha was stricken with measles and George took care of her without contracting the disease. His first known illness occurred in 1748, in which he complained of ague and fever. Ague is a severe fever accompanied with chills, shivering, and sweating. Since he lived in the south he became infected with malaria. He was prescribed quinine so much due to repeated attacks of malaria, which he suffered a marked hearing loss and was nearly deaf by the time he left the presidency.

Over the years, Washington contracted and survived: diphtheria, tuberculosis, smallpox, dysentery, malaria, quinsy, anthrax, skin cancer, typhoid fever, and pneumonia. It was on his trip to Barbados with his brother that he contracted smallpox, malaria and had a brush with tuberculosis. After he returned to Virginia he was soon taken with a violent pleurisy which quickly sapped his strength.

From the age of seventeen until his last few years of life, Washington had recurring attacks of malaria. This disease was common to the southern coastal states, and a treatment for it had been discovered in the previous century. For some unknown reason, Washington did not receive this treatment until 1784.

On the frontier 1752-1758:

In 1755, during Braddock's march, Washington served as an aid to the British General Braddock and he had to be left behind on the expedition due to a case of dysentery. Washington wrote in his diary, "immediately upon our leaving the camp at George's Creek, on the 14th, . . . I was seized with violent fevers and pains in my head, which continued without intermission ' till the 23d following, when I was relieved, by the General's absolutely ordering the physicians to give me Dr. James' powders."[12] This was a popular medicine at the time for fevers, and was later cited as an example of medical quackery.

When Washington recovered, and after riding painfully in a wagon, he caught up with the army near Fort Duquesne on July 8. The next day he was so ill that he had to tie pillows to his saddle in order to ride his horse.[13] Later that day, the British engaged the enemy in a battle in which Washington was one of the few British officers to survive.

After the battle he led the army in a retreat and was able to ride forty miles through the night to summon reinforcements. He later said that the ride left him "in a manner wholly unfit for the execution of the duty."[14] When he returned home to Mount Vernon he was very weak and feeble, and his attacks of dysentery and fever continued for the rest of the year.

While he was in service on the Virginia frontier towards the end of 1757, he again had a violent attack of dysentery, accompanied by fever and pleurisy which forced him to leave the army and return to Mount Vernon to recuperate. After three months at home, he still found no relief from the illness. He decided to go to Williamsburg to consult the best doctor there and it was on this journey that he met his future wife, Martha. Less severe attacks continued.

After the frontier 1759-1774:

In 1761 Washington was attacked with a disease known in Virginia at that time as the "river fever." Today we call it malaria. Hoping to cure it, he went over the mountains to the Warm Springs, being "much overcome with the fatigue of the ride and weather together."[15]

Washington's visit to Warm Springs in Virginia did improve his health. He wrote to Rev. Charles Green, his rector of his home parish of Truro, describing his visit, "We found of both sexes about 2⟨5⟩0 People at this place, full of all manner of diseases & Complaints; some of which are much benefitted, while others find no relief from the Water's—two or three Doctors are here, but whether attending as Physicians or to Drink the Water I know not."[16] Over the years, Washington made numerous trips to the springs to improve his health.

After writing from Warm Springs in 1761, a relapse brought him "…very near my last gasp. The indisposition ... increased upon me, and I fell into a very low and dangerous state. I once thought the grim king would certainly master my utmost efforts, and that I must sink, in spite of a noble struggle, but thank God, I have now got the better of the disorder, and shall soon be restored, I hope, to perfect health again."[17] Washington's health improved and he did not mention any further serious health problems until after the Revolution.

During the Revolution 1775-1783:

Luckily for the country, George Washington's health was comparatively good throughout the Revolutionary War. Smallpox was a major threat during the first half of the war, but Washington was immune. He did suffer from several attacks of dysentery during the war. In the spring of 1779, while at Morristown, New Jersey, he developed a severe abscess of the tonsils. He wrote that he was so weak and feverish that he feared that he might die. He left instructions that General Nathanael Greene was to take over the army if he died.

Retirement from the army 1783-1789:

In 1786 he wrote in a letter to a friend, "I write to you with a very aching head and disordered frame. . . . Saturday last, by an imprudent act, I brought on an ague and fever on Sunday, which returned with violence Tuesday and Thursday, and, if Dr. Craik's efforts are ineffectual I shall have them again this day."[18] He was given several doses of bark as treatment. The bark was from the cinchona tree and was used to treat fevers.

In 1787, he developed a new health issue, a rheumatic complaint which he had for more than six months. He complained that at times he could only raise his hand or turn in bed with great difficulty. When he finally recovered, he wrote to a friend that he was still very feeble.

Presidency 1789-1797:

During his Presidency, Washington had several dangerous illnesses. The earliest one began on his tour of New England in 1789, when he was detained an extended amount of time due to mismanagement at a reception at Cambridge. The weather was terrible and Washington soon took cold. For the next several days there was an outbreak of influenza in Boston and the surrounding area. The outbreak soon became known as the Washington Influenza.

The President again took sick six months later in New York. It began as a bad cold and became so severe that the doctor referred to it as, "a case of anthrax, so malignant as for several days to threaten mortification."[19] One of the doctors predicted that Washington might soon die from this illness. For several weeks he could not carry out his duties as President.

That summer of 1789, Washington developed a high fever and his head hurt so much that the slightest noise became painful. His secretary had the street around his house roped off so that the noisy carriages and carts could not pass by and disturb him. In addition, straw was place on sidewalks to reduce the sound made by people walking.

Washington then developed an irritation on his left buttock that started out as a small saddle-sore and soon became as infected boil. The doctors reported to the press that the injury was on his upper thigh, so that his "Presidential dignity" could be preserved. Soon a large tumor appeared with it and along with the fever it developed into a life threatening situation. The tumor was reported to be the size of two fists and had to be removed.

A father and son team of doctors went to Washington's bedroom on June 17, 1789 to perform surgery on the tumor. As they began to cut away the mass there seem no end to it as more and more tissue was removed. The President was given no anesthesia, yet he never flinched or made the slightest sound. The older doctor told his son, "Cut away, deeper, deeper still." The man knew that they must not leave any of the infected tissue. As the son continued cutting his father said, "Don't be afraid," and referring to Washington, "You see how well he bears it!"[20]

The surgery proved to be successful, and by the end of June, Washington's fever broke and his appetite returned to normal. However, he was not able to sit or sleep normally for several weeks as his right side was tender and numb. During July, Washington was able to ease back into his official duties as President. People around his residence could see doctors with grave faces going in and out of the house for many days. To prevent any false rumors from spreading about his health, he had a mattress placed in his carriage so he could lie on it and people could see that he was still alive and somewhat active.

During his convalescence the President wrote to a correspondent, "I have the pleasure to inform you, that my health is restored, but a feebleness still hangs upon me, and I am much incommoded by the incision, which was made in a very large and painful tumor on the protuberance of my thigh. This prevents me from walking or sitting. However, the physicians assure me that it has had a happy effect in removing my fever, and will tend very much to the establishment of my general health; it is in a fair way of healing, and time and patience only are wanting to remove this evil. I am able to take exercise in my coach, by having it so contrived as to extend myself the full length of it."[21] Washington also started seeing visitors to show people that he was not bed ridden and was still functioning.

During his presidency, Washington's hearing began to fail him. One man who attended one of Washington's dinners in 1789 wrote, "He seemed in more good humor than I ever saw him, though he was so deaf that I believe he heard little of the conversation." Three years later the President was reported as saying to Jefferson that he was "sensible, too, of a decay of his hearing, perhaps his other faculties might fall off and he not be sensible of it."[22]

During a visit to Mount Vernon in 1794, Washington wrenched his back while trying to save himself and his horse from falling among the rocks at the Lower Falls of the Potomac River. The injury prevented him from riding again for several weeks. During this same year, Doctor Tate operated on Washington for cancer. It was likely a form of melanoma and Washington urged the doctor to cut even deeper into his body to fully remove it and hopefully prevent its return.

***

Retirement 1797-1799:

After he retired in 1798, Washington came down with a fever which he did not treat until it became so bad that he finally had to call for medicine. Once again he took doses of bark and soon the fever left him, but not before he had loss twenty pounds. The next year he became fatally ill.

Washington was superstitious, and just before his death he had a dream which convinced him that his earthly days were numbered. Before this dream he had hoped to pass many more happy and serene years at Mount Vernon. He repeated his dream to Martha. "A great light shone around him and her in the summer house, and amidst the light was the figure of an angel. His wife turned pale and began to vanish slowly from him and he was left alone." When repeating this dream to his wife she remarked, "Dreams go by contrary, you know, I may soon leave you, instead of your leaving me."[23]

Final illness:

Washington's final illness began December 12, 1799, with a severe cold taken while riding about his plantation to inspect some of his more distant farms. The weather changed and rain, hail, and snow began falling with a cold wind. When he returned home after four or five hours, his heavy coat had kept his body dry, but his head and neck was wet with snow. The next day Washington complained of a sore throat, and even though it was still snowing he went out for the afternoon to mark some trees that needed to be cut down. He developed a hoarseness that increased in the evening, and as usual, he declined to take anything for it.

At two o'clock the following morning, he was seized with a severe ague, but would not let Martha call for a servant. That morning the personal secretary to Washington, Tobias Lear, sent for Doctor Craik and Rawlins who was the overseer. Rawlins bled Washington removing half a pint of blood. Washington then tried to gargle a mixture of molasses, vinegar, and butter, but he could not swallow and almost suffocated.

Doctor Craik and two other doctors, Dr. Elisha C. Dick and Dr. Gustavus Richard Brown, arrived and ordered three more bleedings, in which a total of about thirty-two ounces of blood (the average human has 160 ounces) were removed from an already sick George Washington. Martha tried to stop the doctors from taking more blood, but Washington insisted that they do. After the last bleeding, Washington was sensing that he was going to die and gave some directions concerning his will and said, "I find I am going, as it was the debt which we must all pay."[24] Washington had written two wills, and at this time he asked Martha to bring both to him. He read over both documents and had one thrown into the fire.

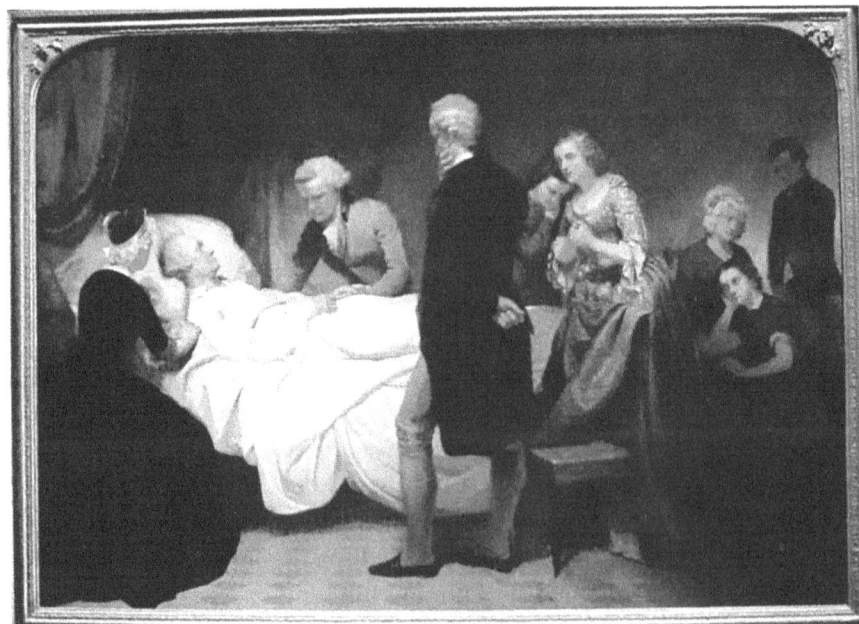

George Washington on his Deathbed, by Junius Brutus Stearns, 1851. Public domain

From this time on a friend mentioned, "he appeared to be in great pain and distress." Washington remarked, "Doctor, I die hard, but I am not afraid to go. I believed from my first attack that I should not survive it." A little later he said, "I feel myself going. I thank you for your attention, you had better not take any more trouble about me, but let me go off quietly." The last words he said were, "Tis well."[25]

George Washington died on December 14, 1799, and because of the number of servants present, the blacks outnumbered the whites in his room. A servant removed the miniature portrait of Martha that he had worn around his neck for the past forty years. According to his wishes he was not buried until three days later. Many people during this time were afraid of a premature burial.

Then the bizarre happened:

During this period of time, it was not unusual to hear of cases in which a person thought to be dead came back to life. One friend of Washington wanted to help the process of "resuscitation" after he died. Doctor William Thornton, a longtime friend of Washington, was invited to Mount Vernon to help the President while he was on his deathbed. Unfortunately, the doctor arrived after the former president had died. The doctor was heartbroken that his friend had died, but he had a plan to bring him back to life.

The weather was very cold and Washington's body remained in a frozen state. The plan was for Thornton to thaw him out in cold water and wrap him in blankets to raise the body temperature. Next, infuse the lifeless body with lamb's blood which would activate the blood vessels. Then, open up the passage to the lungs by performing a tracheostomy to produce an artificial respiration. Thornton belief that this combination of heat, air, and blood would bring George Washington back to life, even though rigor mortis had set in. All Thornton needed was permission to start the process.

The decision was left up to Martha, who thought it over and decided against it. Years later Doctor Thornton wrote that he had no doubt that the procedure would have brought the great man back to life.

William Thornton was an American physician, inventor, painter and architect who designed the United States Capitol. Public domain

After Washington's death:

After George Washington's death, Martha burned every letter that she had ever received from him, with the exception of three or four, that escaped apparently by accident. No one has ever explained the motive behind this letter burning. Did she not want to share their intimate moments? Did the letters not show their relationship the way she wanted the public to see it? Did she feel that the letters were hers only, and no one else had a right to read them? Did George ask her to burn them? She never gave her reasons.

Many people at the time burned the letters of their spouse. For example, Hamilton's and Madison's wives burned their letters. They felt that their private life should be kept private. Some wives like Abigail Adams, saved the letters she sent to and received from John. Both of them loved politics and wanted to preserve the letters for posterity.

Only one of Martha's letters to George has survived. She wrote it in 1767, while he was in Williamsburg attending a session of the House of Burgesses. It also shows that Martha was a very poor speller,

> My Dearest
>
> It was with very great pleasure I see in your letter th⟨at⟩ you got safely down we are all very well at this time but it still ⟨is⟩ rainney and wett I am sorry you will not be at home soon as I expe⟨ct⟩ed you I had reather my sister woud not come up so soon, as May woud be much plasenter time than april we wrote to you las⟨t⟩ post as I have nothing new to tell you I must conclude my self your most. Affcetionate   Martha Washington[26]

Martha died in an upper chamber of Mount Vernon in May, 1802, never again sleeping in the great chamber which she and Washington occupied and in which he died. To the end of her life, Martha saved a piece of her wedding dress, and the white gloves her husband had worn to the ceremony.

Washington's Bedroom in which he died. This is said to be the bed that was in the room at the time of his death. From: Lear, Tobias, *Letters and Recollections of George Washington* by Tobias Lear, 1906, page 35.

10

Washington the Planter

"Agriculture has ever been the most favorite amusement of my life."----George Washington

❧⊗❧⊗❧

Establishing His Plantation

Buying land:

Over the years, Washington made many business investments, particularly in land. In 1784, he became a partner in land purchases in New York that cost him 1,875 pounds and years later it was sold for a nice profit. In 1790, he had inside information that the nation's new capital was being moved from New York to Philadelphia so he purchased land in that city hoping to turn a quick profit. Unfortunately neither the move nor the profit happen.

He continued to buy and sell land for years, and by the time of his death his holdings, excluding Martha's real estate and Mount Vernon property, amounted to 51,395 acres, exclusive of town property. One person remarked, "General Washington was, perhaps, the greatest landholder in America."[1]

For much of his life, Washington's property rarely produced much of a profit due to his large expenses. During the Revolution, his income fell causing him to sell property to meet his expenses. Even though Washington had large and valuable land holdings, he was cash poor much of the time.

⸻

Mount Vernon:

In 1758, George Washington resigned his command from the militia and looked forward to returning to civilian life. Agriculture was his favorite employment, and in the early years of his marriage he mainly studied agriculture. It was not until later that he began to read widely on other subjects. To acquire and communicate practical knowledge, he corresponded with the celebrated Arthur Young, an English agriculturist, and with many other agricultural gentlemen in the colonies. He also took copious notes relative to his own experiments, the state of the seasons, the nature of soils [of which he was an excellent judge], and the effects of different kinds of manure on the various crops.

For example, Washington had a huge box with ten compartments in which he placed soils from different parts of his plantation. In each compartment he planted, at the same depth, grains with different fertilizers. He then water them the same, and exposed them to the equal sunlight. He could then determine which type of fertilizer was best for a particular grain.

With the death of Anne Fairfax, the former wife of Lawrence Washington, in 1761, he gained complete control of Mount Vernon and soon began enlarging the estate. From 1759, until the start of the Revolution, George Washington operated Mount Vernon as five separate farms. During this time, he lived the aristocratic life of a Virginia planter.

He loved Mount Vernon for the rest of his life, and showed his feelings for his estate when he wrote, "No estate in United America, is more pleasantly situated than this. It lies in a high, dry and healthy country, three hundred miles by water from the sea, and, as you will see by the plan, on one of the finest rivers in the world."[2]

His day books, ledgers, and letter books were all kept by himself, and it appeared that he did not resort to the aid of a clerk or secretary for this work. He usually drew up his own contracts, deeds, and other papers, requiring legal knowledge and accuracy. It was a rule with him, in private as well as public transactions, not to rely on others for what he could do himself.

Before the Revolution, the main crop of a Virginia planter, particularly in the lower counties, was tobacco. Washington exported this crop to London for market, making the shipments in his own name, putting the tobacco on board vessels, and sending them down the Potomac River. He gradually switched to wheat and corn that he could market in the American colonies, and by 1765, Washington stopped planting soil-depleting tobacco on his plantation.

He also built a profitable fishing business on his property that aided in his quest to avoid being in debt to British merchants who entangled many area planters. The bulk of labor on his land was done by his own slaves and those he controlled through his marriage to Martha.

Dividing his property:

Because his estate was so large, he divided the property into five farms: Mansion House, Dogue Run, Muddy Hole, River, and Union. Mansion House Farm included the main house and the surrounding area. The farm had no crops but consisted of gardens, woods, tree groves, and meadows. Dogue Run Farm was two miles southwest of the Mansion House. In 1786, there were thirty-nine enslaved people living on that farm and the number had grown to forty-five by 1799.

Muddy Hole Farm was about 476 acres of clay land located in the northeast corner of the plantation. According to Washington's diary, hemp was grown there and later it became part of the crop rotation system he employed. River Farm was the northern most of the five farms. Washington did not live on or work the land there, instead he decided to rent it. It was first rented in 1761 to Samuel Johnson who planted tobacco on it. Years later, Washington gave the land to Tobias Lear and his new bride who was Martha's niece and the widow of George's nephew.

Union Farm was composed of two smaller farms that contained a seven-field crop system. The two farms were under one manager and in 1788, a large barn was built on the property. It contained twenty stalls for cattle, and on one side of the building was a browsing area for sheep. Another section of the barn had additional stalls for cattle and horses. By 1799, a slaves list showed seventy-five slaves living at that farm. All of the family groups at Union Farm seem to be headed by women with about 1/3 of them being single.

Each of the farms had an overseer that managed the property and operated it as a separate plantation. On every Saturday afternoon reports were given to Washington by all of his overseers, and he recorded the data in books kept for the purpose, and these accounts were so planned as to show how every laborers time had been employed during the whole week, what crops had been planted or gathered, what increase or loss of stock had occurred, and every other detail of farm work.

A separate account was kept of each farm, and whenever there was a surplus of any product an account was opened to cover it. Thus in various years there were accounts raised dealing with cattle, hay, flour, flax, cord-wood, shoats, fish, whiskey, pork, etc. His secretary, Shaw, once told a visitor that the "books were as regular as any merchant whatever."[3]

During Washington's long absences from Mount Vernon his chief overseer sent him these reports, as well as writing to him. The manager received in return, long letters of instruction, sometimes to the length of sixteen pages, which showed Washington's familiarity with every acre of the estate and the character of every laborer.

Once Washington took command of the Continental Army, he was away from Mount Vernon from May 1775 until the summer of 1781. He placed his distant cousin Lund Washington in charge of running the estate for him during this period. There was considerable correspondence between the two men during the war especially since at that time, Lund was supervising renovations of the manor house and slave quarters. Below are examples of the letters Washington wrote to Lund,

November 26, 1775, "I observe you mention something, in respect to the removal of my valuable Furniture, but where can you carry it? or what will be done with it? I wish the Wine could be secured, & the Rum in the Barn Sold—the last I should think might easily be done, & to a good Acct as the Importation will be stopped—If you are obligd to give Credit for this, or any thing else, be sure of your Men—I had rather take much less than be obliged to enter into letigeous disputes.

Let the Hospitality of the House, with respect to the Poor, be kept up; Let no one go hungry away— if any of these kind of People should be in want of Corn supply their necessities, provided it does not incourage them in Idleness; and I have no objection to your giving my money in Charity to the amount of Forty or Fifty pounds a year, when you think it well bestowd. What I mean by having no objection, is, that it is my desire that it should be done—you are to consider that neither myself, or wife are now in the way to do these good Offices. In all other respects I recommend it to you, and have no doubt of your observing, the greatest economy and frugality; as I suppose you know, that I do not get a farthing for my Services here, more than my Expences; it becomes necessary therefore for me to be saving at home."[4]

August 19, 1776, "Before I conclude I must beg of you to hasten Lanphire about the addition to the No. End of the House, otherwise you will have it open I fear in the cold & wet Weather, and the Brick work to do at an improper Season, neither of which shall I be at all desirous of."[5]

Crops:

George Washington was not the typical planter because most plantations during this time produced only tobacco, while he attempted to grow other crops. He realized that growing only tobacco had two draw-backs. First, growing only this particular crop ruined the soil. Secondly, growing just one crop made him totally dependent on the London based merchants who bought the crop in massive quantities. Washington decided that he needed the security of growing several crops, rather than just depending on one. Over the years, he experimented with 60 other crops including cotton and silk.

The diet of Washington's household contained a range of sources for protein, while the typical family in the area mainly consumed a large amount of beef. He began to experiment with other crops such as wheat, hemp, and corn. He also started trying new irrigation techniques and crop rotation. None of these innovations made him a wealthy man, however it did keep him out of debt and enabled him to enjoy a comfortable lifestyle. He did better than his neighbor Thomas Jefferson who basically bankrupted his estate by the end of his life.

Farm Management:

Most of the plantation owners were content to leave the care of their land and their slaves to overseers, so they could engage their time taking part in entertaining, sports, or politics. This type of management did not suit George Washington. He had a love of work and did not want to spend money on something he could do for himself. As a military man, he was used to hardship, being busy, and looking after details. On a typical day, he rose early usually before light when the days were short. He enjoyed a light breakfast at seven in the summer and at eight in winter, and after breakfast he was in the saddle visiting the different parts of his estate, and looking after any improvements.[6]

Dinner followed at two o'clock, after which he had an early tea. When living at home, he was often in bed by nine o'clock. These were regular, old fashioned hours, and the life which he led enabled him to accomplish a vast amount of work. At times, Washington could even be found working with his men, which was a rare thing for a Virginia planter to do.

He wrote out all his letters and orders, entered every item in his daybook and ledger, and was scrupulously exact about every penny that went in or out of his accounts. He did not guess how he stood at any time, but he knew precisely how last year's crop compared with this year's, how many head of cattle he had, how many acres he had planted with a given crop, what wood he had cut, and what goods he had ordered from London.

Washington had been appointed by the court guardian of his wife's two children, who had inherited property from their father. Because of this, he kept all their accounts separate, with the same minute care, for he believe a trust to be sacred. Twice a year he sent to his agent in London a list of such articles as he needed. These items included plows, hoes, spades, and other agricultural implements, drugs, groceries of various sorts, and clothes both for his family and slaves. The orders sometimes would also include books, busts, ornaments, household furniture, and linen.[7]

Washington watched the market closely, and knew just what the varying prices of his crops were, and what he might expect for any other goods which he sent to be sold. He was determined that everything from his plantation should be of value and should receive its full price. He gained so high a reputation for honesty that it was said that any barrel of flour that bore the brand of George Washington, Mount Vernon, was exempted from the customary inspection in the West Indian ports.[8]

When the war finally ended in 1783, Washington returned to Mount Vernon and for the next few years he spent much of his time improving the landscape of the plantation. He continued to do this during his presidency, as during those eight years, he spent a total of 434 days at Mount

Vernon. When he returned home for one last time he worked on repairs to the buildings, gardening and socializing with his numerous friends.

Crop rotation

When Washington became a planter, the system of agriculture at the time in Virginia was as follows: First, A piece of land was cleared and under constant cultivation. Next, tobacco, and Indian corn (plants that were very exhausting on the soil) were planted until the soil would no longer yield a crop. Then a second piece of land was cleared and the cycle would repeat itself over and over again.

Once the land was ruined, the farmer often did not have the skill to recover the land, so he would either raise something of poor quality and be hurt financially, or move to another location to farm. Washington converted to the rotation of crops and he drew tables that sometimes covered five years, so that the quality of each crop would not vary as his fields changed. Under this system he grew large crops of flax, hay, clover, buckwheat, turnips, and potatoes. By moving away from tobacco his labor cost was less, less attention was required of him, and his fields and profits improved.

Manufacturing:

By 1768, he was manufacturing cloth needed on his plantation. In that year, his weavers produced eight hundred and fifteen and three-quarter yards of linen, three hundred and sixty five and one-quarter yards of wool, one hundred and forty-four yards of linsey, and forty yards of cotton, for a total of thirteen hundred and sixty-five and one-half yards. Labor used for all that work consisted of one man and five Negro girls. Looms on the plantation turned all that woven material into a variety of cloths. He also derived income from a gristmill which produced cornmeal and flour for export, and it also ground neighbors' grain for fees.

Fishery:

One of the large industries of the plantation was its fishery. Washington wrote, "This river is well supplied with various kinds of fish at all seasons of the year, and in the spring, with the greatest profusion of shad, herrings, bass, carp, perch, sturgeon, &c."[9] Workers would catch the fish, salt it down, and in most cases, it was a meat substitute for the food the slaves ate. In good years there was not only enough for the consumption on the plantation, but it was sold in the area.

Making whisky:

Distilling became particularly profitable at Mount Vernon. Washington's whiskey was made from, "Rye chiefly and Indian corn in a certain proportion." This used much of the estate's product of those two grains, so at times quantities were purchased elsewhere. In 1798, the most successful year, the profit from the distillery was three hundred and forty-four pounds twelve shillings and seven and three-quarter pence, with a stock carried over of seven hundred and fifty-five and one-quarter gallons. Cider too was produced in large quantities.[10]

Mount Vernon became one of the new nation's largest distillers of whiskey in the country. According to a visitor to the plantation, it distilled 12,000 gallons a year. In 1799, Washington wrote to his nephew. "Two hundred gallons of Whiskey will be ready this day for your call, and the sooner it is taken the better, as the demand for this article (in these parts) is brisk."[11] Washington even tried growing his own grapes for wine. However, during the experiment, he was called upon to lead the army in the Revolution and he never again tried to make his own wine.

Washington and animals, the mule:

Washington saw the value the mule provided the farmer, and he began to create the mule stock that later became important to agriculture in the south for many decades. In 1785, the King of Spain sent President Washington two pure Andalusian jackasses as a gift. There was no hidden meaning with the gift, the King had heard of Washington's interest in farm animals. Unfortunately, one of the animals died at sea. The surviving mule was tall, about five feet, and Washington called it his royal gift.

Washington purchased around thirty mares in Pennsylvania for breeding with his gift animal. The jack was mated with animals from Washington's stock as well as females from other plantations in the area. On one trip, Washington earned nearly $700. in stud fees. People would come as far as fifty miles just to see George Washington's jackass. (You can insert your own joke here.)

He wrote amusing letters to Lafayette and others about the jack's indifference to the charms of the mares, and his lazy way of going about his primary business, "The Jack which I have already received from Spain, in appearance is fine; but his late royal master, tho' past his grand climacteric, cannot be less moved by female allurements than he is, or when prompted, can proceed with more deliberation & majestic solemnity to the work of procreation."[12] Washington also wrote to a nephew about the breeding problem of his new mule, "If Royal Gift will administer, he shall be at the service of your Mares, but at present he seems too full of Royalty, to have anything to do with a plebeian Race."[13]

This breeding soon introduced a new line of mules in the United States. The old line of American mules were too small to pull heavy farm equipment, while the new line were stronger, and sure footed for the farm and hill country.

Hunting dogs:

George Washington loved fox hunting, so it was no surprise that he loved dogs and wanted to breed the perfect foxhound. Because of this, some have called Washington the father of the American Foxhound. The breeding began when Washington acquired regular hounds from

Philadelphia, two slow pace hounds from England, and French hounds which were a gift from Lafayette. Washington bred the three breeds and developed the American Foxhound.

He eventually had thirty-six of the pups and gave them not so manly names such as Sweet Lips, True Love, Dutchess, Singer, Music, and Countess. In 1794, when he had a serious fall involving his horse, he quit foxhunting and eventually gave away his dogs.

⁓⁓⁕⁓⁓

Horses:

A stud service was maintained at Mount Vernon. At times, an ad ran in Virginia newspapers that the stud horses Sampson, Magnolia, Leonidas, or Traveler were available for such service. In addition to the stud, there were, in 1793, fifty-four draught horses on the estate. Washington was fond of horseraces and became a breeder of his own racehorses.

⁓⁓⁕⁓⁓

Cattle and sheep:

In 1793, there were a total of 317 head of cattle, including a number of oxen. A dairy was operated separate from the farms and in addition to milk, they produced some butter. Washington also bred sheep that provided over five pounds of wool each. The flock, in 1793, consisted of 634 animals which yielded 1,457 pounds of fleece.

⁓⁓⁕⁓⁓

Workers on the farm:

In addition to the slaves, which will be mentioned later, Washington employed indentured servants and some hired laborers on his plantation. The hired workers included blacksmiths, carpenters, brick makers, masons, shoemakers, and weavers. There were also numerous gardeners and a staff that worked at the water mill. Several coopers made the barrels that were used to pack goods taken to market.

Washington had decided that he no longer wanted to buy goods from England or anywhere else, rather he wanted Mount Vernon to be a self-efficient estate. He could now raise his own food, make his own clothing, and remodel his home with materials found on his own land.

⁓⁓⁕⁓⁓

Protecting his property:

At times poachers would sneak into Mount Vernon. The following is an amusing story of one such uninvited guest. In canvas-back duck season, Washington was out with his fowling-piece early and stayed late. The story is told that he had been much annoyed by a lawless fellow who came without permission to shoot on the estate. He crossed over from the Maryland shore, and hid his boat in one of the creeks. One day Washington heard the report of a gun, and guessing it to be that of this man, who had more than once been warned to leave, he jumped on his horse and rode in the direction of the sound. He pushed his way through the bushes just as the intruder, who had seen him approach, was pushing his boat off. The trespasser raised his gun, and aimed it at Washington, who spurred his horse at once into the water and seized the boat before the man knew what was happening. Then Washington, who had powerful arms, seized the fellow and gave him a sound thrashing, and was never troubled by him again.[14]

"Washington as Farmer at Mount Vernon", 1851, part of a series on George Washington by Junius Brutus Stearns. Located at the Virginia Museum of Fine Arts. Public domain.

11

George Washington and Slavery

"I can only say that there is not a man living who wishes more sincerely than I do to see a plan adopted for the abolition of slavery."----George Washington April 12, 1786.

~∞⊙⑥⊙∞~

George Washington's Role in Slavery

How did Washington feel about slavery?

In colonial America slaves were sold the way one would nowadays sell a used car. The owner would clean up the car, try to conceal any faults it may have, put a price tag on it, and emphasize the good points about it. The buyer would examine the car carefully and then try to haggle over the price. Slaves in the 1700s were sold in such the same way as we now sell cars.

When Washington sent a slave named Tom to the West Indies to be sold, he wrote the following to the captain of the ship, "This fellow is both a rogue and a runaway (tho he was by no means remarkable for the former, and never practiced the latter till of late) I shall not pretend to deny. But that he is exceedingly healthy, strong, and good at the hoe . . . which gives me reason to hope that he may with your good management sell well, if kept clean and trim'd up a little when offered for sale."[1]

Washington up with slavery as an inherited institution throughout the colonies. He was no more racist than most Americans of his time. At the age of eleven he inherited ten slaves from his father's will. He looked upon his slaves as property and took care of them in the usual ways. He did not ordinarily have them whipped when they resisted their condition, but he sometimes sold those he could not control or had them shipped off to the West Indies.

Washington's patience and tolerance proved of value to him as the commander of the American Army, but these virtues often did not extend to slaves. He recognized early in the war that he and others like himself, slaves owners, stood on ironic ground. They claimed liberty for themselves and all the rights of free men, yet they held thousands of black people in slavery.

The year Washington married Martha he brought thirteen slaves with him to add to the slaves that came to him with his marriage. In his first fifteen years as a planter, he bought and sold slaves with a clear conscience. Sending off a shipment to the islands, he told his Caribbean agent to buy "Negroes if choice ones could be had for under 40 pounds Sterling." And "if not then buy rum and sugar."[2]

The ownership of slaves in Virginia was considered to be a practical necessity to the Virginia planter. It would be nearly impossible to cultivate the large land holdings without them. In time, some of the plantation owners grew to detest slavery so much that they gave up their plantations. Arthur Lee sailed to England to live, claiming that he could not bear to own slaves or even live where there were slaves.

In 1774, Washington's neighbor and friend George Mason wrote the Fairfax Resolves, in which he condemned the trade of slaves in the resolves. There was however, no resolve in the document that called for an end to slavery. Washington signed the resolves and played a part in getting them approved by the county.

Washington never really spoke out against slavery publicly, but he later arrived at the decision that it was morally wrong according to ideas of the Revolution. It was a private decision that he gave much thought to. Much of his criticism of slavery was not based on morality, however rather the institution was becoming inefficient because of the lazy and lack of work among the workers. His views likely were not supported by many of his neighbors and possibly not even by Martha.

Washington's treatment of his slaves:

Mount Vernon, at its height, was composed of eight thousand acres that were divided into five farms. [He would eventually own a total of more than 70,000 acres.] They were: Mansion House, where the Washington family lived, Dogue Run, Muddy Hole, and River. Each farm had a small village for the slaves, which contained both African born slaves and those born in the colonies. The population of Mount Vernon consisted of slaves (the vast majority of people), hired workers that were white and their families, and the smallest group, Washington's family.

About ninety slaves were assigned to the Mansion House. They supplied the labor to keep the plantation running, and consisted of servants, semi-skilled tradesmen, field workers, and drivers for the various wagons and carts. The other slave villages were of various sizes and consisted mainly of field hands.

Of Washington's general treatment of the serving class a few facts can be uncovered. He told one of his overseers, that "to treat them civilly is no more than what all men are entitled to, but my advice to you is, to keep them at a proper distance; for they will grow upon familiarity, in proportion as you will sink in authority if you do not." To a housekeeper he promised "a warm, decent and comfortable room to herself, to lodge in, and will eat of the victuals of our Table, but not sit at it, or at any time with us be her appearance what it may; for if this was once admitted no line satisfactory to either party, perhaps could be drawn thereafter."[3]

One historian noted that Washington did not take any special pains to develop the mental and moral nature of "my people" as he referred to his slaves. Many planters of the period made their slaves go to church on Sundays and tried to encourage chastity and marriage among them.[4]

The lives of the slaves at Mount Vernon were fairly typical of the lives of slaves that lived on the large plantations in Virginia in the 1700s. It's very possible that Washington's slaves had more freedom over some parts of their lives than they would have encountered on other plantations. When the Mount Vernon slaves had time off from their hard work they were allowed to earn small amounts of money to better their lives. Sometimes Washington would purchase food items from his slaves or slaves from another plantation. This would include chickens, eggs, and garden items such as melons, cucumbers and honey. One of Washington's slaves sold a broom that he had made for sixpence. Sometimes slaves could sell items door to door in the area or at the Sunday market in town.

On occasions, slaves might receive a reward for finding and returning a lost article, or they might receive a tip for special services rendered. For example, when George Washington left the home of a friend he might leave a tip for the slaves that may had performed extra duties in caring for him.

Washington did grant his slaves some time and freedom to pursue their own personal interests. On evenings, Sundays and special holidays, they were allowed to engage with their families and others in various activities that benefited them and not their masters. However, Washington like all slave owners, could change his mind at any time about allowing certain liberties. A holiday could be cancel without notice, a marriage could end without the consent of the husband or wife, no special trips could be made, or a person could be sold for any reason. Washington, on occasion, sold slaves when they attempted to run away because to him this was an unforgettable form of theft of his valuable property.

Washington required his slaves to work hard and long from sun up to sun down six days a week. During free time they had to attend to their own needs, such as their own animals, garden crops, keeping house, and getting enough rest as to remain productive. He regularly delivered weekly to every working slave; two or three pounds of pork, salt herrings, often badly cured, and a small portion of India corn.

But for the time he seemed to have treated his slaves fairly well, not exactly as one treats human beings, but as one treats a stable of valuable horses. He established a small hospital at Mount Vernon for them, and he paid a doctor named John Laurie a salary of fifteen pounds a year to take care of them. There are many instances in his diary of the doctor's attention to sick Negroes.

Late in the summer of 1761, four of his valuable slaves escaped, so he wrote out a long detailed description for inclusion in Virginia and Maryland newspapers and with a hefty offer of 40 shilling reward for their capture. Below is a copy of the ad,

Fairfax County (Virginia) August 11, 1761.
Ran away from a Plantation of the Subscriber's, on Dogue Run in Fiarfax, on Sunday the 9th Instant, the following Negroes, viz.
　　Peros[?], 35 or 40 Years of Age, a well-set Fellow, of about 5 feet 8 Inches high, yellowish Complexion, with a very full round Face, and full black Beard, his Speech is something slow and broken, but not in so great a Degree as to render him remarkable. He had on when he went away, a dark colour'd Cloth Coat, a white Linen Waist-coat, white Breeches and white Stockings.
　　Jack, 30 Years (or thereabouts) old, a slim, black, well made Fellow, of near 6 Feet high, a small Face, with Cuts down each Cheek, being his Country Marks, his Feet are large (or long) for he requires a great Shoe: The Cloathing he went off in cannot be well ascertained, but it is thought in his common working Dress, such as Cotton Waistcoat (of which he had a new One) and Breeches, and Osnabrig Shirt.
　　Neptune, aged 25 or 30, well set, and of about 5 Feet 8 or 9 Inches high, thin jaw'd, his Teeth stragling and fil'd sharp, his Back, if rightly remember'd, has many small Marks or Dots running from both Shoulders down to his Waistband, and his Head was close shaved: Had on a Cotton Waistcoat, black or dark colour'd Breeches, and an Osnabrig Shirt.
　　Cupid, 23 or 25 Years old, a black well made Fellow, 5 Feet 8 or 9 Inches high, round and full faced, with broad Teeth before, the Skin of his Face is coarse, and inclined to be pimpley, he has no other distinguishable Mark that can be recollected: he carried with him his common working Cloaths, and an old Osnabrig Coat made Frockwise.
　　The two last of these Negroes were bought from an African Ship in August 1759, and talk very broken and unintelligible English. the second one, Jack, is Countryman to those, and speaks pretty good English, having been several Years in the Country. The other Peros [?], speaks much better than either, indeed has little of his Country Dialect left, and is esteemed a sensible judicious Negro.

As they went off without the least Suspicion, Provocation, or Difference with any Body, or the least angry Word or Abuse from their Overseers, 'tis supposed they will hardly lurk about in the Neighborhood, but steer some direct Course (which cannot even be guessed at) in Hopes of an Escape. Or, perhaps, as the Negro Peros [?] has lived many Years about Williamsburg, and King William County, and Jack in Middlesex, they may possibly bend their Course to one of those Places.

Whoever apprehends the said Negroes, so that the Subscriber may readily get them, shall have, if taken up in this County, Forty Shillings Reward, beside what the Law allows; and if at any greater Distance, or out of the Colony, a proportionable Recompence paid them, by

George Washington[5]

Overseers and whipping slaves:

Various sources give different views of how George Washington treated his slaves. Richard Parkinson was an agriculture writer who came to American in 1798 and spent some time at Mount Vernon. He reported, "It was the sense of all his [Washington] neighbors that he treated his slaves with more severity than any other man."[6]

Yet, another visitor traveling in American wrote that Virginians typically treated their slaves harshly providing them with "only bread, water and blows," while Washington treated his slaves, "far more humanely than do his fellow citizens of Virginia."[7]

In a letter to Arthur Young in 1792, Washington wrote, "With the farmer who has not more than two or three Negros, little difference is made in the manner of living between the master & the man; but far otherwise is the case with those who are owned in great numbers by the wealthy; who are not always as kind, and as attentive to their wants & usage as they ought to be."[8]

There is no record of George Washington personally whipping his slaves, however his slaves were whipped on occasion by his overseers. This punishment was usually given after repeated disobedience. He paid overseers good wages and one, John Alton, worked for him for 30 years until his death in 1785. These overseers screened his view of any harsh treatment that the slaves received, so Washington was possibly not aware of most whippings, but at times he did support them.

While Washington was President, Anthony Whitting was placed in charge of Mount Vernon replacing Lund Washington who was in ill health. In a letter dated January 16, 1783, Whitting gave Washington a lengthy account of what was going on at Mount Vernon. He mentioned that he had to take a hickory switch to Charlotte, a seamstress slave at the Mansion house, and give her a "good whipping" because she had been impudent. Charlotte was angry about the beating and told Whitting that she had not been whipped in fourteen years and she threaten to tell Mrs. Washington when she returned home. Whitting added in the letter to Washington, "I fully expect I shall have to Give her some More of it before She will behave herself for I am determined to lower her Spirit or Skin her Back."[9] [Charlotte was one of the slaves in the bedroom when Washington died.]

Washington wrote back a few days later and voiced his support of Whitting's actions toward Charlotte, "Your treatment of Charlotte was very proper—and if she, or any other—of the Servants will not do their duty by fair means—or are impertinent, correction (as the only alternative) must be administered."[10]

114

However, at times he would stop a whipping from taking place. On one occasion he came unexpectedly upon a white overseer giving a slave a thrashing. The sight enraged Washington, and he fell into one of his furious tempers. He seized his horse-whip and approached the overseer, his eyes blazing. The overseer, realizing that he was about to take the Negro's place as an object of castigation, kept walking backward and saying, "Remember your character, General-remember your character!" Washington remembered his character and rode off with a few words of rebuke.[11]

It was very likely that he was supportive of a slave being whipped if they ran away. Washington would sometimes feel hurt if a slave tried to escape to freedom. He believed that he provide the person in bondage with a good life, and they were treated fairly. He felt they should be grateful for what he had done for them. However, if the slave ran away again he would have the final say if a slave was sold away from his family and sent to the West Indies.

There were times that Washington may have neglected the needs of his slaves, or someone did not remind him on time of their needs. On more than one occasion, the overseer had to remind Washington that blankets had not been provided for some of the slaves and that some of the children were almost without clothing as winter was approaching. Many times the overseers did not call a doctor if the slaves were sick, once one slave was forced to work even though he had the measles and was vomiting. Washington was possibly not aware of these oversights.

As Washington neared the end of his life he looked back on his days of owning slaves and wrote, "The unfortunate condition of the persons, whose labour in part I employed, has been the only unavoidable subject of regret. To make the Adults among them as easy & as comfortable in their circumstances as their actual state of ignorance & improvidence would admit; & to lay a foundation to prepare the rising generation for a destiny different from that in which they born; afforded some satisfaction to my mind, & could not I hoped be displeasing to the justice of the Creator."[12]

White slaves:

Washington did buy white slaves now and then. They were either indentured servants or convicts which usually worked with the carpenters and other skilled workmen. On March 14, 1774, William McGachen purchased some new workers for 110 pounds sterling. He wrote to Washington of his purchase,

> I received your very agreeable favour by Mr Crawford I have done my self the pleasure to give him every assistance in my power and has purchased for you Four men convicts four Indented servants for three years and a man & his wife for four years, the price Is I think rather high but as they are country likely people and you at present wanted them Mr Crawford said he imagined you would be well satisfied with our Bargain I have agreed to pay £110 Sterling for them the first of next may which I hope you will be pleased with should you want any more there is a ship expected this month with country convicts.[13]

The convict slaves would also try to escape for freedom whenever they got the chance. On April 24, 1775, Colonel Washington, from Fairfax County, advertised, offering forty dollars reward for the capture and return of two convict men-servants, warning all vessels against receiving them.[14]

Washington's position on African Americans in the military:

The enlistment of African Americans whether free or slave, was a question Washington had occasionally faced since first taking command. Free black men were already a part of the provisional army or militia that awaited him at Cambridge in 1775. But should African Americans be part of a national army the founding fathers intended to form? Washington's initial answer was no. In 1775, recruiting officers for the Continental Army were ordered not to enlist "any stroller, negro or vagabond."[15] Black men already serving in the Continental Army could stay.

The American commander felt it was necessary to issue orders several times about the enlistment of black soldiers in the army, "Negroes, boys unsuitable to bear arms, nor old men" were to be enlisted.[16] On October 31, he charged his quartermaster to provide clothing to all who reenlist except, "negroes…which the Congress do not incline to enlist again."[17] And on November 12, general orders were issued, "Neither negroes, boys unable to bear arms, nor old men unfit to endure the fatigues of the campaign, are to be enlisted."[18]

Slave owners, especially in the south, were concerned that training and arming black men could lead to a black uprising. A group of Carolina slave owners stated, "There must be great caution used [allowing blacks into the military] lest our slaves when armed might become our master."[19] Washington was a southern slave owner who needed the support of the southern states. The rebel army had no chance against the British if they lost support of the south. African American soldiers were no longer needed….until they later were.

Leaders in the south urged the general to discharge all Negroes, free or slave, from the army at once. But by the year's end, with new recruits urgently needed and numbers of free blacks wanting to serve, Washington changed his mind in a landmark general order authorizing their enlistment. Washington issued the following order on December 30, 1775, "As the General is informed, that Numbers of Free Negroes are desirous of enlisting, he gives leave to the recruiting Officers, to entertain them, and promises to lay the matter before the Congress, who he doubts not will approve of it"[20]

Washington then wrote to the President of Congress, John Hancock about his order to enlist free black men that had already served,

> It has been represented to me that the free negroes who have Served in this Army, are very much disatisfied at being discarded—as it is to be apprehended, that they may Seek employ in the ministerial Army—I have presumed to depart from the Resolution respecting them, & have given Licence for their being enlisted, if this is disapproved of by Congress, I will put a Stop to it.[21]

In 1776, Congress agreed with Washington and authorized the re-enlistment of free Black men who had already served. In 1777, things began were not going well for the American Army. They had suffered huge losses, desertions, and recruitment had begun to dwindle as morale sank. They lengthened the service time to one year for the Continental Army, which also slowed the signing of new recruits. To meet the crisis, Congress called for eighty-eight new battalions from the colonies. Despite paying bonuses and bounties to new recruits, men were slow to enlist.

Many of the colonies, particularly those in the north, had trouble filling their quotas. In addition to drafting men, they soon began to recruit black men. Some slave owners were given the option of freeing their slaves and sending them in place of members of their family. Slaves were guaranteed their freedom in exchange for service in the army. New England had the smallest black population of any region, and yet they provided the majority of black recruits. The southern colonies, with the exception of Maryland, still refused to send black men to fight.

In January 1777, Washington retracted his earlier order which barred all free blacks from serving. His change in orders may also have been influenced by his abolitionist aids: Marquis de Lafayette, John Laurens, and Alexander Hamilton. In addition, it had not gone unnoticed by Washington that early in the war, northern black soldiers had fought bravely. In January 1778, Washington promptly approved Brigadier General James Mitchell Varnum's request to be authorized to raise "a Battalion of Negroes" from his native Rhode Island.

At the time of the Revolutionary War, about 20% of the Colonial population of 2.5 million was black and the total number of black men who fought for the Americans was estimated to be over 5,000. By 1779 15% of the army was black. These men served in an integrated army, which would be the last one until the Korean War. Henry Laurens wrote to Washington on March 16, 1779, that if he had 3,000 black men under arms, he could drive the British from Georgia. Descendants of slaves and former slaves were now allowed to come to the rescue of the country that had held them in bondage.

Washington's interactions with black men during the war:

If Washington shared the prejudices of his class and region, he was not completely close-minded. Before leaving Boston he invited Phillis Wheatley, the young and already celebrated African writer who had honored him with a poem, to visit his headquarters.

During the war, Washington had a slave name William (Billy) Lee who he had purchased in 1768 for sixty-eight pounds and fifteen shillings. He accompanied Washington on foot or horseback at all times and would brush the general's hair and tie in in a queue every morning. Washington had noted in his will that Lee would receive immediate freedom or he could remain at Mount Vernon upon the general's death. He was also given $30.00 a year for the rest of his life.

Prims Hall was born to a slave on February 29, 1756 in Boston, and at the age of nineteen he enlisted in the American army. In 1781, Primus became a steward to Quartermaster Colonel Thomas Pickering.

When Washington visited the camp of Colonel Pickering he sometimes felt the need for exercise. Primus would get a rope and fastened one end to a stake about breast high, and he would hold the other end taut at his chest several feet away. Washington then would run and jump over the rope again and again until he grew tired. Whenever Washington visited the camp, he would say, "Come, Primus, I am in need of exercise."

Another story occurred late one night when Washington was at the camp of Colonel Pickering. Primus found some straw and a blanket and made Washington a bed. After the General had fallen asleep Primus sat on a box or stool and leaned his head into his hands to sleep. Primus had given the General the last of the straw and the last blanket for his bedding.

Washington awoke during the night and saw Primus asleep sitting on the stool and he realized that he had been given the last of the bedding. He woke Primus up and insisted that Primus join him in his bed since there was enough room for two people. It was not uncommon during that period for travelers to share the same bed at inns when space was limited or share on the ground during cold weather.[22]

—·····❖·····—

Washington's view on slavery after the Revolution:

During his life, Washington's views about slavery slowly evolved. This change came about due to economic reasons and the American Revolution. The movement for emancipation had already begun to stir in Virginia as well as elsewhere. In time it influenced Washington, to the point that he was ashamed of keeping slaves and longed to be rid of them. By an odd coincidence, slave labor in tobacco fields grew less profitable as wheat began at last to earn the favor of the Virginians. This became especially apparent to Washington when he decided to stop growing tobacco and replaced it with various other crops. The new crops were less labor-intensive than tobacco; hence, his estate had a surplus of slaves. But Washington refused to break up families for sale. Washington began to hire skilled indentured servants from Europe to train the jobless slaves for service on and off the estate.

In his early years at Mount Vernon, Washington did not see his slaves as equal to white people. As he became exposed to people who felt differently about slavery, he began to question those beliefs. For example Lafayette, for whom Washington had great respect, spent many years trying to convince Washington to free his slaves and discussed with him various ways to do so. He sent this letter to Washington on February 5, 1783,

> Now, My dear General, that You are Going to Enjoy some Ease and Quiet, Permit me to propose a plan to you Which Might Become Greatly Beneficial to the Black part of Mankind—Let us Unite in Purchasing a small Estate Where We May try the Experiment to free the Negroes, and Use them only as tenants—Such an Example as Yours Might Render it a General Practice, and if We succeed in America, I Will chearfully devote a part of My time to Render the Method fascionable in the West indias—if it Be a Wild scheme, I Had Rather Be Mad that Way, than to Be thought Wise on the other tack.[23]

Washington's reply to Lafayette's proposal of freedom for the slaves was not rejected, nor embraced, as evident of the letter sent back to the Frenchman on April 5, 1783,

> The scheme my dear Marqs which you propose as a precedent, to encourage the emancipation of the black people of this country from the Bondage in wch they are held, is a striking evidence of the benevolence of your Heart. I shall be happy to join you in so laudable a work; but will defer going into a detail of the business, 'till I have the pleasure of seeing you.[24]

On September 8, 1786, Washington wrote from Mount Vernon to an early advocate of anti-slavery, Governor John Francis Mercer of Maryland, "I never mean, unless some particular circumstances should compel me to it, to possess another slave by purchase, it being among my first wishes to see some plan adopted by which slavery in this country may be abolished by law."[25]

Throughout the 1780s and 1790s, Washington stated privately that he no longer wanted to be a slave owner, that he did not want to buy and sell slaves or separate enslaved families, and that he supported a plan for gradual abolition of slavery in the United States. Yet, Washington did not always act on his antislavery principles.

Anti-slave societies began to appear in the south and former influential slave holders like Benjamin Franklin joined their cause. George Washington, like other leaders of the time, thought

118

that the liberal principals of the Revolution would eventually destroy the institution of slavery. However by the end of the revolutionary period there were more slaves in the country than in 1760.

Slavery had come up time and time again in the Constitutional Convention of 1787. Washington, was chosen president of the convention, and the delegates were soon deadlocked on the question of slavery. Georgia and the two Carolinas said they would not join the union if slavery was not allowed. Washington would not support anything that jeopardize the proceedings, so in order to preserve the Union, he supported a twenty-year moratorium on any further congressional debate over slavery. As a result, the delegates decided to kick the can of slavery down the road for another generation to solve the problem. By doing this however, the convention was able to proceed onward to establish a new government.

In his later years, Washington had the problem of having more slaves than he needed. On August 17, 1799, Washington wrote his nephew Robert Lewis in regards to slavery, "To sell the overplus I cannot because I am prejudiced against this kind of traffic in the human species, to hire them out is almost as bad, because they cannot be disposed of in families to any advantage and to divide families I have an aversion."[26]

Slaves in the President's house:

When he became president, Washington brought a number of slaves up from Mount Vernon to act as servants around the Presidential mansion in Philadelphia. He soon learned that, according to a judicial decision in Pennsylvania, slaves brought into the state were to be considered freed if they lived in the state for six months, so Washington had to make sure that they left for Mount Vernon before the six months was up, and another group took their place.

Washington's favorite chef:

Hercules Posey was a slave and the chief cook at Mount Vernon. President Washington was not happy with the cook at his presidential residence, so in 1790, he brought Hercules to Philadelphia. Hercules ruled his kitchen with an iron hand. Punishment might be administered if there was a spot of dirt on the dinner table or if the utensils did not shine like polished silver. Since the president was fond of him, Hercules received special privileges and was allowed to sell leftovers from the kitchen. He spent the extra money on clothing and luxuries and soon gain the reputation as a "dandy."

President Washington assumed that the slaves were well aware of the law in Pennsylvania about being free after six months of living there. In his second term, he accused Hercules of plotting to escape. This was odd because Washington gave Hercules and other slaves some limited freedoms and they could have escaped at any time. Soon Washington's suspicions would prove to be true.

When Washington left to retire to Mount Vernon at the end of his second term, Hercules ran away instead of going back with Washington. However, some historian reported that Hercules did return to Mount Vernon, but later ran off because he and some other slaves were put to work with the bricklayers and gardeners.

This information was based on some new documents that claimed Hercules may have been left behind at Mount Vernon when the President and his wife returned to Philadelphia in December 1796. It is suggested that in February some of the servants, including Hercules, were assigned as laborers to work in the yard. Records show that Hercules was reported missing on February 22, 1797, the President's birthday. Whichever account is true, it is a fact that Hercules did run off, and it was suspected that he ended up in New York City.

Washington was angry and hurt that Hercules had fled the "privileged life" that he had provided for the chef. The distraught Washington wrote to his friend George Lewis on November 13, 1797, "The running off of my Cook, has been a most inconvenient thing to this family; and what renders it more disagreeable, is, that I had resolved never to become the master of another Slave by *purchase;* but this resolution I fear I must break."[27]

He did try to find the missing man but to no avail. By the provisions in Washington's will in 1801, Hercules was legally freed and no long a fugitive.

Martha's escaped slave:

In Washington's final year of his presidency, Martha's personal slave, twenty-two year old Oney Judge, successfully escaped to Portsmouth, New Hampshire. Several months after her escape, Washington unsuccessfully attempted to have her kidnaped and forcibly returned to Mount Vernon. He wrote to his Secretary of Treasury, Oliver Wolcott for assistance in returning the slave,

> Enclosed is the name, and description of the Girl I mentioned to you last night. She has been the particular attendent on Mrs Washington since she was ten years old; and was handy & useful to her, being a perfect Mistress of her needle.[1]
>
> We have heard that she was seen in New York by some one who knew her, directly after she went off. And since by Miss Langden, in Portsmouth; who meeting her one day in the Street, & knowing her, was about to stop and speak to her, but she brushed quickly by, to avoid it.
>
> I am sorry to give you, or any one else trouble on such a trifling occasion—but the ingratitude of the girl, who was brought up & treated more like a child than a Servant (& Mrs Washington's desire to recover her) ought not to escape with impunity if it can be avoided.[28]

Oney later said that the reasons she ran off was that if she went back to Mount Vernon with the family she would never get her freedom. She said the other reason she ran away was because she overheard that she would be given to Martha's granddaughter Eliza Parke Custis Law, who had a reputation for a fiery temper. Oney was determined never to be the slave of that woman. She remained a free woman until her death in 1848.

Runaway Advertisement for Oney Judge, enslaved servant in George Washington's presidential household. *The Pennsylvania Gazette*, Philadelphia, Pennsylvania, May 24, 1796

Did Washington free his slaves upon his death?

The short answer is yes and no. A clause in Washington's will directed that "Upon the decease of my wife it is my will and desire that all the slaves which I hold in my own right shall receive their freedom. Emancipate them during her life, would, tho earnestly wished by me, be attended with such insuperable difficulties, on account of their intermixture of marriages."[29]

Because his and Martha's slaves had intermarried, he stated that only upon the death of his wife would all the slaves be freed. He also forbid the sale, or transportation out of the state, of any of the slaves for any reason. Washington did not want any of the slave families broken up and taken away from each other.

Then he added an additional clause when they became free, "And whereas among those who will receive freedom according to this devise there may be some who from old age, or bodily infirmities & others who on account of their infancy, that will be unable to support themselves, it is my will and desire that all who come under the first and second description shall be comfortably clothed and fed by my heirs while they live and that such of the latter description as have no parents living, or if living are unable or unwilling to provide for them, shall be bound by the Court until they shall arrive at the age of twenty five years. The negroes thus bound are (by their masters and mistresses) to be taught to read and write and to be brought up to some useful occupation."[30]

The only slave freed by Washington:

In his will he did grant his personal slave William [Billy] Lee immediate freedom and $30.00 each year for the rest of his life. He said that if William did not want to be free and remain, then all his needs were to be taken care of in addition to the yearly $30. He granted this to Billy for his faithful service during the war.[31]

So when someone writes that Washington freed his slaves when he died it should be noted that he actually freed only one. The rest of the slaves would have to wait until his wife died. Some historians believe that Washington wanted to do more for the slaves at Mount Vernon but may have been held back by Martha and the Custis estate. At the time of George's death Martha was left with over 300 slaves.

What became of the slaves after the death of Washington?

Martha did not share her husband's attitude toward slaves. She never struggled with the moral dilemma about human bondage in a free society as her husband did. She viewed the slaves as children that were lazy and not very trustworthy.

She did, however, on January 1, 1801, free her husband's slaves before her death. She did not do this because of an epiphany toward slavery, rather it was out of fear for her life. After all, the slaves knew that according to George's will, they would be free after the death of Martha. Martha realized that they would certainly have a motive to cause a premature end to her life. After a series of very suspicious fires at Mount Vernon years after George's death, Martha thought it best to free George's slaves early.

The remaining slaves with the exception of one did not actually belong to Martha. They belonged to the Custis heirs of her first husband and could not be freed by her. When Martha died they were divided among the grandchildren. This division of families took children away from their parents which would have disappointed George. The one slave Martha did own, Elish, could have been legally freed by Martha, instead she awarded the slave to her grandson George Washington Parke Custis.

Washington's relationship with Native Americans:

He maintained a somewhat complicated relationship with Native Americans over the years. During Washington's early life, the native people were important players between the French and English rulers in the New World. Each side sought the support of the various Indian tribes in their struggle over control of the territory.

During those years, Washington fought against some of the tribes, served alongside some of them, and at times negotiated for the rights to buy their land for his personal use. This interaction with the Native warriors led to an appreciation of their fighting ability and tactics. This knowledge became useful later when he commanded the Americans against the British during the Revolution.

Once the war was over, the Indians became more of a liability than an asset to the new American Republic. Washington and other leaders began to believe that the Indians must either assimilate into the American society of be eliminated. The Indians now stood in the way of American expansion and the war against the Native Americans became a necessity.

On July 21, 1791, President Washington wrote to David Humphreys, who was appointed minister to Portugal, "For some time past the western frontiers have been alarmed by depredations committed by some hostile tribes of Indians. I cannot see much prospect of living in tranquility with the Indians, so long as the spirit of land jobbing prevails, and our frontier settlers entertain the opinion, that there is not the same crime in killing an Indian, as in killing a white man."[32]

12

George Washington Begins His Military Career 1752-1757

"The right wing, where I stood, was exposed to and received all the enemy's fire ... I heard the bullets whistle, and, believe me, there is something charming in the sound."----George Washington in a letter, July 18, 1755.

~∞◎◎∞~

1752

Background:

George Washington's military experience began in 1752, when he was appointed a major and commander of four militia districts in Virginia. This was probably due to the Lieutenant Governor being friends with both Washington's brother Lawrence and Lord William Fairfax, the father of George's mentor and husband of Sally Fairfax. During this time the British and French were in competition for control of the Ohio Valley.

1753

When Washington rode out of Williamsburg, October 1, 1753, he took with him his Dutch fencing teacher and mercenary, Jacob Van Braam, who pretended to understand French well enough to serve as an interpreter. Governor Dinwiddie sent George to demand that the French forces leave the land that the British had claimed. Washington, who at the age of twenty-one had not achieved anything of distinction, had requested the honor of carrying this demand to the French.

On this mission he had to pay a visit to the local Native American royalty to make peace. He visited with Queen Aliquippa, an Indian majesty, who had expressed concerns to George that she had been slighted. So, Washington recorded, "I made her a present of a match…coat and a bottle of rum; which the latter was thought much the best present of the two."[1] This gesture and probably some soothing words restored warmth to her majesty's feelings. Also during this time he met with other Native American leaders.

Toward the end of 1753, Washington had met with the French leader and delivered to him the British demand to vacate the land. He refused and gave Washington a sealed letter to take back to Governor Dinwiddie. After 77 days in the field, Washington returned back to Williamsburg to deliver the secret letter which basically said that the French had no intention of leaving. As a reward for his participation in this mission, Washington was commissioned a Lieutenant Colonel in the newly created Virginia Regiment.

~⋯⋯†⋯⋯~

1754

George Washington helps to start the French and Indian War:

Governor Dinwiddie ordered Washington to enlist two hundred men, train them, equip them, and then go out and "finish and compleat in the best Manner and as soon as You possibly can, the Fort w'ch I expect is there already begun by the Ohio Comp'a. You are to act on the Defensive, but in Case any Attempts are made to obstruct the Works or interrupt our Settlem'ts by any Persons whatsoever You are make Prisoners of or kill and destroy them."[2]

This would prove to be a terrible blunder by the governor. He was almost giving a green light to Washington to start a war if necessary, as well as assigning this task to a military greenhorn. Washington had never drilled a soldier, or been drilled in a company. His military knowledge came from information from private tutors. As a result, confusion, disaster, and disgrace would be Washington's companion on this adventure.

Washington learned that his pay was to be $3.50 a day, which was only about half that paid to the same rank of officers with a royal commission. He considered this an insult and started to refuse the commission but was encouraged by Lord Fairfax to accept it.

In April Washington was ordered to confront the French troops at the Forks of the Ohio. As he arrived at his destination, he learned that the French had about 1,000 men and were constructing Fort Duquesne. That May he established a defensive position at Great Meadows and found that the French had a camp just seven miles away. Washington discovered that their camp contained only about fifty men, so he decided to take the offensive.

On May 28, 1754, Washington took a small force of sixty-two troops and Indian allies to ambush the French. This surprise skirmish during peacetime became known as the Battle of Jumonville Glen. The battle lasted about fifteen minutes, and what really happen there was a subject of controversy and debate. The dead were left on the field or in shallow graves to be later found by the French. The bottom line was that the French commander was killed, and most of his men either killed or captured. Washington wrote about the battle to his brother, "I can with truth assure you, I heard bullets whistle and believe me, there was something charming in the sound."[3]

Apparently, the proud brother passed the letter around, because in time the contents reached the ears of King George II of England. His comment toward Washington's bravado was, "He would not say so, if he had been used to hear many."[4]

Governor Dinwiddie congratulated Washington on his victory. Unfortunately, this "victory" helped to ignite the French and Indian War in North America, which was a part of the larger Seven Years War that would last until 1763.

―――――――

Washington is captured and makes a large blunder:

One of the French soldiers escaped from the Battle of Jumonville (named for the French commander Joseph Coulon de Jumonville) and gave an account in which the Indians with Washington's force killed and wounded French soldiers and scalped them. This information stirred hatred and motivated the French, especially the brother of Jumonville, the slain French commander, to get revenge against Washington. Following the battle Washington and his men returned to Great Meadows and built a fort they named Fort Necessity.

On the morning of July 3, 1754, 600 French troops and Indians, led by the brother of Jumonville, attacked the uncompleted Fort Necessity. Washington was forced to surrender and the terms of surrender were put in writing. If only this document and had not been in writing and signed by Washington. The paper was written in French, which Washington did not understand and his translator, Van Braam, was very poor at translating French. Washington signed a surrender that indicated twice that the French had not attacked the English, were at peace with them, and the French commander Jumonville was assassinated by Washington. This surrender document was an admission by Washington of starting this encounter. Van Braam, Washington's so-called interpreter, translated the French word for "assassinated" as "causing the death of," which was a whole different meaning. Once signed, Washington was released along with his men and they returned to Virginia.

In the aftermath, Dinwiddie reorganized the Virginia Regiment into separate companies that had no ranks above captain, Because this would have required Washington to step down from colonel to a captain, he resigned from the militia.

The earliest authenticated portrait of George Washington shows him wearing his colonel's uniform of the Virginia Regiment from the French and Indian War. The portrait was painted about 12 years after Washington's service in that war. Public domain.

1755

Washington is a volunteer aid in the British Army:

In early 1755, a real British Army led by General Edward Braddock was sent to Virginia to deal with the French. When Washington heard of the British offensive against the French, he became interested in offering his services to General Braddock. The general was aware of Washington's familiarity with the area and the maps he had made. He was also aware that Washington was interested in serving in the army. After Washington had written to Braddock, congratulating him on his arrival, he received a reply in a letter on March 5th.

> The General, having been inform'd that you exprest some desire to make the Campaigne, but that you declin'd it upon the disagreeableness that you thought might arise from the Regulation of Command, has order'd me to acquaint you that he will be very glad of your Company in his Family, by which all Inconveniencies of that kind will be obviated. I shall think myself very happy to form an acquaintance with a person so universally esteem'd.[5]

It was likely that either Sally or George Fairfax wrote to General Braddock about Washington's earlier treatment in the militia and his desire to still serve in the army. Washington accepted the invitation and joined the British army as an aid de camp to the general. Officially Washington was a volunteer with a rank of captain, but he hoped this would present an opportunity to later become commissioned as a British officer. Many British officers during this time gained their rank by paying for it and would then rise quickly in rank because of being from a powerful family. Washington had neither money nor the backing of a prominent family. Because of this, and also being a colonial, his chances of acquiring and rising in rank were very slim. Washington wrote to his younger brother John,

> I am treated with freedom not inconsistent with respect, by the General and his family; I have no doubt, therefore, but I shall spend my time more agreeably than profitably, during the campaign, as I conceive a little experience will be my chief reward.[6]

Washington becomes a hero....well, sort of:

Washington had entered the campaign in high spirits, regretting only that there was no prospect of fighting. He was much younger than Braddock, and he had one year of war compared to over forty for the general. At times Washington gave advice to Braddock that almost amounted to orders. Yet the two men seemed to get along quite well.

General Braddock led about 1,500 troops to Fort Duquesne to confront the French. In June Washington became very ill with dysentery that had spread in the camp. He had a high fever, severe headache, dehydration, and suffered from a round of sunstroke. By June 23 he was too weak to sit on a horse and had to ride in the supply wagon. He later ended up in a make-shift hospital to recover. In early July he was still weak, but recovered enough to rejoin Braddock.

On July 8, 1755, Colonel Washington, in a covered wagon because he was still ill, overtook General Braddock on the eve of the memorable Monongahela engagement with the French. Washington wrote, "My illness was too violent to suffer me to ride, therefore I was indebted to a covered wagon for some part of my transportation, but even in this, I could not continue far, for the jolting was so great."[7]

Washington tried to warn General Braddock about the flaw in his battle plan. For example, the French and Indians fought differently than the open field attack the British used. The Virginia troops adopted the Indian style of fighting, which was that each man was for himself and fought behind a tree, rock, or some type of cover. This was prohibited by General Braddock, who formed his men into platoons and columns, as if they were maneuvering on an open plain.

The next day the British were attacked by the French and their Indian allies hiding in trees and behind logs. Some later reports said that the attack was an ambush, but it was not. The initial engagement began when the Indians were trying to set an ambush. The skirmish began early in the morning and by the end of the day, of the eighty-six commissioned British officers, sixty-three were killed or disabled, four hundred and thirty-seven soldiers were killed, and almost as many wounded. General Braddock was severely wounded and died five days later. Washington attended to the general until the end, and then he arranged for the funeral service the following morning.

Washington had no official position in the chain of command, but due to a lack of surviving officers, he was able to keep order and form a rear guard so the remaining force could retreat that evening. During the skirmish Washington's coat received four bullet holes in it, and he had two horses killed under him. Providence was doubtless aided in his rescue by the fact that before the battle he had changed his brilliant coat for a neutral-toned hunting shirt. During the fight a British officer later reported, "Washington behaved with the greatest courage and resolution."[8]

His conduct under fire helped to restore some of his reputation that was tarnished during the Battle of Fort Necessity incident. He later was called the Hero of Monongahela and received numerous toasts overs his actions at the skirmish. To his credit, Washington never said or pretended that he took command in the retreat.

George Washington at the Battle of the Monongahela. The painting appears to make Washington taking command after the General Braddock is wounded. Library of Congress.

Many histories written about George Washington created the impression that he alone saved the remains of the British army. In fact, he really had no authority to command anyone, and much of the praise should have been shared with the surviving British and Virginia officers. Ironically, the other officer that helped Washington organize the retreat was Lieutenant Colonel Thomas Gage. The two men would later oppose each other at the start of the Revolution. As a reward for his bravery, Washington won his rank of colonel back, and the command of the Virginia militia forces that were charged with defending the colony's frontier.

Many years later a surviving Indian chief that faced George Washington at the skirmish relayed an interesting observation of Washington during the battle, "Our rifles were leveled, rifles which, but for him, knew not how to miss. Twas all in vain, a power, mightier far than we, shielded him from harm. He cannot die in battle."[9]

1756

Strict discipline under Colonel Washington:

Washington, once again a colonel in the Virginia militia, now had 1,000 men under his command. At this time, Virginia's draft laws were unfair toward the poor, and the men that were caught in it were resentful about serving. Desertion and the lack of discipline became a problem within the militia. As a result, Washington was forced to impose strict British discipline so far as the laws of Virginia allowed.

He ordered brutal floggings for desertion, drunkenness, swearing, looting, and more. All troops were required to line up and watch the floggings, which sometimes brought tears to the eyes of the onlookers. When desertions continued, he requested from the Virginia Assembly the use of the death penalty. All of these changes in discipline were approved by the Virginia government. During this period, Washington still entertained hopes that he would somehow be awarded that coveted British commission with a rank of Colonel or higher.

Washington and scalping:

The Indians and French were deep inside the territory, and there was enough to do to just push them back across the boundaries. The Virginia frontier had become a dangerous place with constant looting, burnings, and killings. The Virginia government suggested that a string of forts be built to provide protection. Washington was opposed to this, because it would require excessive amounts of manpower. Instead, he urged enlisting friendly Indians to help police the border. He sent this suggestion in a letter to the Virginia government with the scalp of a French officer.

The French officer, Monsieur Douville, was overtaken by some of Washington's soldiers on the frontier, and in the letter Washington wrote about the scalp, "I hope, although it is not an Indian's, they will meet with an adequate reward at least, as the monsieur's is of much more consequence. The whole party jointly claim the reward, no person pretending solely to assume the merit."[10]

Taking scalps was nothing new to the colonies, and whether white or red they meant very little to the people. In Massachusetts in the 1600s, some colonists had earned good money for the little skulls of Indian children and had brought them in some meal sacks like cabbages. In August, 1755, Virginia had made the standard offer of £10 for every male Indian scalp over twelve years old. In April 1757, the price was raised to £15, with a bonus of £1 for every further scalp taken by the same scalper in the next two years. Maryland increased the price up to £50. Scalps were worth more than any other form of fur and worth more than gold.[11]

It was unfortunate about what happened to Douville, because even though his men were burning and killing, they were under special orders. They were instructed to prevent the Indians that fought with them from committing any cruelties to anyone that fell into their hands, which included scalping. So, what happen was Washington approved the scalping the young officer who had orders to prevent scalping. But scalping was part of frontier life.

1757

Puritans attack the command of Washington:

Washington and his men came under a new attack from a very unlikely source. Even with the strict discipline that Washington insisted upon, Puritan factions of the population accused the militia of gross immorality, intoxication and general corruption. Washington was also criticized by Governor Dinwiddie, which led to more rules on discipline. It was ordered that any soldier that quarreled or fought should receive 500 lashes and if drunk 100 lashes, all without the benefit of a court-martial.

These criticisms, and the continued attacks by the French and Indians, once again had Washington thinking of resigning his commission. During this time he also received little support from Governor Dinwiddie, and there were constant problems in maintaining an effective militia. Washington was becoming increasingly unpopular with many of the troops and some of the politicians.

Later in the year, Washington once again began to suffer from attacks of malaria and dysentery. In addition to these complaints, his teeth also began to create problems. He was suffering from pyorrhea, and the only treatment available was to continue extracting the teeth when they became too loose for comfort.

1758

Washington becomes disillusioned with the military:

Washington's Virginia militia was assigned to a British expedition commanded by General John Forbes, to capture Fort Duquesne controlled by the French. Washington did not agree with Forbes' tactics or the chosen route to the fort. Nevertheless, Washington was assigned to lead one of the assault brigades that would assault the fort. Before the attack, the expedition learned that the French had abandoned the fort, and there was an incident involving friendly fire resulting in the death of fourteen men with twenty-six wounded.

It became apparent during this time that the prize he coveted from the British would not be forthcoming. For several years he desired to receive a British army commission at the rank he wanted, and now it became obvious that it would not be granted. Washington realized that the British had no respect for the colonials or their abilities. In addition, the Virginia House of Burgesses would not provide the needed money or provisions to maintain an effective militia. Even the people that the militia were protecting no longer offered support. All of this, combined with health problems brought on by attacks of dysentery, caused Washington to believe he had no choice but to once again resign and return to private life. At the age of twenty-seven George Washington was now through with the military life.

What Washington learned would help win the American Revolution:

During his brief time in the military, Washington won one minor skirmish and lost all other battles. He failed to protect the Virginia frontier, he had lost a fort, he had many of his men killed, he helped start a world-wide war, and he never received the promotion he sought after. He was not only disgusted with the British but with himself. Life in the military had cost him money and respect of some people, his farm had been neglected, and his health was poor.

Little did he realize that he had learned some valuable lessons that would later help him to defeat the most powerful army in the world, and achieve independence for his country. He had gained insight into British tactics and the strengths and weaknesses of the British army, as well as knowledge of overall strategy, logistics, and problems of organization. He saw the weakness of depending on local militias and a need for a trained and disciplined professional army.

For the next sixteen years, Washington would enjoy his life as a married man with a family, a planter, and a politician. Little did he know that although he was through with the military, the military was not through with him.

13

George Washington the Politician

"Every post is honorable in which a man can serve his country."....George Washington

~∞◯◉◯∞~

1755 Election

Washington learns a lesson:

George Washington first ran for election for the Virginia House of Burgesses at the age of twenty-three. Each county elected two burgesses among the white male landowners and they were required to vote or pay a fine of two hundred pounds of tobacco. The members served until the body was dissolved by the governor or until seven years had passed, whichever came first.

The elections were decided by voice vote. Each voter was required to approach a table that had seated there the county sheriff, a clerk, and a representative of each candidate. The voter would verbally give his vote to the group and the winner was decided, not by majority, but by who got the most votes.

In Washington's first election in 1755, he received forty votes. Thomas Swearingen received 270 votes and second place whet to Hugh West with 271 votes. Washington's poor showing was due to no organization and no money spent. Washington was devastated because during this time he had been refused by the women that he loved (see chapter 6) and now the voters had likewise rejected him. The only silver lining to the election was that Washington was not present for the election, because he was off in the army on the frontier.

The rural voters had rejected Washington because at one time he had called them corrupt traitors. This was prompted when the horse traders had sent a poor quality of horses to be used by General Braddock's army, of which Washington was a member. The saloon voters were against him because they remembered that Washington had punished drunken soldiers and he fought against houses that sold liquor. The moral group of voters turned against Washington because they blamed him for the drunkenness and immorality of his groups. It was a miracle that Washington received the forty votes.

Colonel Adam Stephen, one of the few supporters of Washington, wrote to him on December 23, 1755 and stated that the defeat was an insult and suggested revenge. "Such a Spirit of Revenge and Indignation prevailed here, upon hearing you were insulted at the Fairfax Election, that we all were ready and violent to run and tear Your Enemies to pieces."[1]

~∞◯◉◯∞~

Washington has a new strategy to win the election:

In the summer of 1757, a new election was called. Washington's supporters wanted him to take a leave of absence from the army on the frontier and campaign for office. Washington knew he was not a good speaker, so he declined and placed his friends in charge of getting him elected. This time Washington's election team campaigned English style, which meant much eating and drinking for the voters at the expense of the candidate. Napoleon once said that an army marches on its stomach, and now Washington's supporters believed that elections are won through the stomach.

Colonel James Wood, Washington's campaign manager, offered twenty-eight gallons of rum, fifty gallons of rum punch, thirty-four of wine, forty-six of beer, and two of cider for the county's 794 voters. In addition to the alcohol, a large amount of food was also made available to the qualified voters. This time 310 voters were sober enough to give Washington the victory. The second member chosen with 240 votes was Colonel Thomas Bryan Martin.

Washington, upon hearing of his election to the House of Burgesses, wrote to Colonel James Wood: "I am extremely thankful to you and my other friends for entertaining the Freeholders in my name. I hope no Exception was taken to any that voted against me, but all were alike treated and all had enough. It is what I much desired. My only fear is that you spent with too sparing a hand."[2]

The astonishing victory by Washington did not go unnoticed by other members of the House, and they soon passed a law which stated that a candidate would be disqualified if, before the election, a voter was given any gift, or entertainment by the candidate in order to get elected. The law was later disregarded by Washington and others who ran against him.

———

Washington is on top of the world:

Things were looking up for George. On February 22, 1759 he was serving in the Virginia House of Burgesses, plus he had recently married a wealthy woman. At the first meeting in the House, Speaker of the House John Robinson had the members vote to give Washington a thanks for his military service. Washington rose to make a small speech of gratitude, but he began to blush and stammer. The speaker relieved Washington of his embarrassment by saying, "Sit down, Mr. Washington, your modesty equals your valor, and that surpasses the power of any language that I possess."[3]

His election to the House came at just the right time, as Washington was tired of the military life. He wanted to enjoy his new family, start a life in politics, and expand Mount Vernon. This many have been one of the happiest periods in Washington's life.

———

His first appointment on a committee:

There had been many new delegates voted into the House. A large group of the aristocrats had been voted out and replaced by delegates who were rough, poorly dressed, and at times raw in their behavior. A rule was quickly put through the House banning the chewing of tobacco while the speaker was in the chair. In addition, no member could spit on the floor at any time.

Washington, being a new member, was given an appointment to an important committee that was fitting for his experience. He and several other men were given the task to draw up a law that would forbid hogs to run wild in Winchester. Hogs were an important member of the Virginia society, the punishment for stealing one was death. There is no record how Washington handled this important assignment.

Additional elections:

Washington continued to get re-elected to the house in 1761 and 1765. In the 1768 election his election expenses included large quantities of strong beer, ale, and food. There was money even set aside to pay a fiddler, Mr. John Muri, at the victory party. During this time, the terms did not last the full seven years because the House was dissolved by the governor several times, causing new elections to occur.

George gives advice to others that serve:

Washington spent fifteen years serving in the House of Burgess, and when his nephew was elected, he sent these words of advice to the new politician, "The only advice I will offer; if you have a mind to command the attention of the House, is to speak seldom but on important subjects, except such as particularly relate to your constituents; and, in the former case, make yourself perfect master of the subject. Never exceed a decent warmth, and submit your sentiments with diffidence. A dictatorial style, though it may carry conviction, is always accompanied with disgust."[4]

Where Did Washington Stand on Independence?

Did he always favor independence for America?

In March, 1765, the Stamp Act was passed by the English Parliament that required that many printed materials be printed on paper from London that had an embossed revenue stamp. The act was passed to pay for the British military troops stationed in the colonies after the French and Indian War.

Washington was in the House of Burgesses when it became a subject of discussion. Many members like the fiery Patrick Henry spoke out against it. Washington took no prominent part of the public outrage against the act, but likely was privately against it. After all, being a big supporter of card playing with guests at Mount Vernon, the Stamp Act put a 10 shilling tax on each deck of cards.

At this time, Washington was not a revolutionist, revolutionary thoughts were far beyond him and would not catch up with him for another ten years. During those ten years his name rarely surfaced during this period that some men were speaking out against Britain. Washington, not noted for his intellectual powers, moved with extreme caution in discussions involving politics. During the early years he was not pro-British as some historians tried to portray him, he showed his anti-British feelings as early as 1760.

He did not share the lofty ideals of Thomas Jefferson in regard to freedom from British rule. Washington was happy with the social structure of Virginia, however he did hope to get out from under dependence of the British government which was three thousand miles away. He was an aristocratic Virginia land owner that who later fought for independence. As the call for a revolution began to grow from 1765 to 1775, Washington was more concerned with Mount Vernon, his family, and acquiring more land. These ten years were calm years, and the only tranquil years he was ever to have.

On December 16, 1773, the Boston Tea Party, a political and business protest, took place in Boston. Like most Virginians, Washington denounced the dumping of British tea in the harbor by the Sons of Liberty as an act of vandalism.

In 1774, to punish Massachusetts for the Boston Tea Party, the British Parliament passed a series of punitive laws, called the Intolerable Acts. They hoped that these laws would isolate the rebels in Massachusetts from the rest of the colonies. Their plan backfired and people who were once moderates began to speak out against the British government actions. The Virginia legislature began to challenge and oppose what England was doing. Washington was against these acts, however he was not speaking out for independence.

Washington wrote to Robert McKenzie, a British officer and friend, on October 9, 1774, "I was involuntarily lead into a short discussion of this subject by your remarks on the conduct of the Boston people; & your opinion of their wishes to set up for independency. I am well satisfyed, as I can be of my existence, that no such thing is desired by any thinking man in all North America; on the contrary, that it is the ardent wish of the warmest advocates for liberty, that peace & tranquility, upon Constitutional grounds, may be restored, & the horrors of civil discord prevented."[5]

Even in the fall of 1775, months after Bunker Hill and now in command of the American Army, Washington was still opposed to independence. Rather than being a revolutionist like Samuel Adams or Patrick Henry, Washington was more of a reformer. He wanted to change the role that the British played in America, without cutting the ties between the two nations.

On Monday, September 5, 1774 delegates from all the colonies, except Georgia, were sent to Carpenter's Hall in Philadelphia in response over growing tensions between the colonies and Great Britain. (Georgia did not send delegates because they were facing a possible war with neighboring Indian tribes and they did not want to jeopardize British assistance.) Almost every significe political figure of the American Revolution was present including George Washington. No record of the discussions and speeches that were made exists during the fifty-one days they were in session.

This meeting became known as the First Continental Congress. Washington rarely spoke out during the meeting, however it was evident to many there that Washington tried to bring friendship and harmony to the group. When one member was asked whom he considered the greatest man in Congress, he replied, "If you mean the man who knows the most and has the best judgment, Colonel Washington of Virginia is unquestionably the greatest man on that floor."[6]

It is important to understand why Washington did not immediately jump on the "independence now" bandwagon. He thought of the other colonies, not so much as all parts of one great country on this side of the ocean, rather as each separately a part of the British Empire. Most of all, he was a Virginian, and he was interested in how events would affect his colony.

News of Lexington and Concord:

Washington was at Mount Vernon, preparing to leave for Philadelphia as a delegate to the Second Continental Congress, when he received the news of the fighting at Lexington and Concord on April 19, 1775. Unlike men such as Samuel Adams, Washington was not pleased with the events. He was unhappy that the British in the colonies had drawn their sword against the mother country.. Washington was leaning toward the members of Congress that wanted self-government and colonial rights, and he still hoped that reconciliation could be reached.

Due to his limited military experience, Washington was appointed chairman of several committees for military affairs. Most of the rules and regulations for the army and the measures for the defense were devised by him.

In May, 1775, at the Continental Congress the news of Lexington and Concern was still fresh in the minds of each member. The American militia, 15,000 strong had surrounded the British Army at Boston, some Royal Governors had run away, and the colonies had to look after themselves. Congress took charge of the militia encircling Boston and these citizen soldiers needed a leader. Whom should be?

14

George Washington Takes Command

"War is when the government tells you who the bad guy is, revolution is when you decide that for
yourself."
......Ben
Franklin

∽⧢⧢∽

Congress Selects a Military Leader

How and why was Washington chosen?

After the Battle of Lexington and Concord the American militia, nearly 15,000 strong, surrounded the British Army in Boston. The lines of the American forces extended from shore to shore, but they were too far away to threaten the British. Facing them was the British army of 6,500 troops, who were commanded by General Thomas Gage.

Regional newspapers called the army outside of Boston the Grand American Army. It consisted of militiamen, who would return home after a few weeks, and enlistees whose service would be up at year's end. Congress was meeting in Philadelphia in the spring of 1775, and they realized that they needed an organized army with an appointed commander. On June 14, 1775 a resolution was passed by the Second Continental Congress forming the Continental Army.

The army was a mainly a New England army and the colonies were widely separated, which meant that they rarely acted together on most issues. Would it be better if a New England man commanded the new army? Some Americans feared that an army in New England, under the command of someone from that region, could exert power over the colonies in the south. To avoid having the wrong army under the wrong leadership, many believed that the army and its officers should be taken from all over the colonies. Congress faced a major question….who to appoint as the commander of this new army? There was concern that the current army might dissolve if its present commander, General Artemas Ward, a New Englander from Massachusetts, was replaced, and especially if the replacement was from outside of New England. Congress needed a man who could unify the factions in this untrained army, organize and supply the army, and then defeat the British, the most powerful nation in the world.

George Washington was a member of Congress and at the meetings he informed Congress that he was available for the job, by being the only man on the floor of Congress in a military uniform. John Adams wrote to his wife on May 29, 1775, "Coll. Washington appears at Congress in his Uniform and, by his great Experience and Abilities in military Matters, is of much service to Us."[1] Earlier Washington had declared in the Virginia House of Burgesses that he was willing to raise a thousand men and march them at his own expense to the relief of Boston.

Washington had retired from the military in 1758, yet he now chose to attend Congress in a splendid blue and buff military uniform. He sat there day after day in uniform and in silence. Visitors to the Congress would sometimes ask who was the tall gentleman in uniform? The members knew that Washington had more military experience than any other American born soldier. They also knew that he had never led more than 300 men into battle, he had little practical experience in commanding, and he had not won any major engagement.

John Adams had first met George Washington in 1774 when they served as delegates in the First Continental Congress. They had several meals together with Adams doing the talking, which he enjoyed, and Washington doing the listening, which he enjoyed. The two developed respect of each other that would not weaken until Washington became president.

Adams knew that if the colonies were going to declare their independence from England, they would need to have the support of the southern colonies. By appointing a commander from Virginia, John and others hoped to gather support from the south for the current siege of Boston. Virginia was the largest, most populated, and most powerful colony and critical to the coalition. Who else but Washington could be chosen? What could better show unity than having a New England politician nominate a Virginia man to lead the army?

John Adams explained to his cousin and fellow revolutionary, Samuel Adams, "It is just because he is from Virginia, and aristocratic and wealthy, that I propose to nominate him. There is nothing that the revolutionary movement needs quite as much as it needs aristocracy and wealth; and above all it needs Virginia and the South."[2]

Were others even considered to lead the American Army?

On June 15, John Adams moved that Congress appoint a general to command it. There were several candidates that were discussed to lead the new army. The present commander, General Artemas Ward, was the favorite among many members of Congress. Then there was John Hancock, the President of the Continental Congress. He already had a gorgeous custom made uniform made should he be chosen. Hancock had no love for the British, since they had several charges against him for smuggling. Other men that were considered were Horatio Gates, Charles Lee, Richard Montgomery, and Israel Putman. Thirty-nine year old Patrick Henry, a delegate to the First and Second Continental Congress, was also put into the mix.

During the meeting John Adams declared that he had but one gentleman in mind for commander of the army, "very well known to all of us, a gentleman whose skill and experience as an officer, whose independent fortune, great talents and excellent universal character, would command the approbation of all America, and unite the cordial exertions of all the Colonies better than any other person in the Union."[3] John Hancock began to smile because he thought his name was about to leave the lips of John Adam.

Hancock's smile quickly vanished as Adams placed the name of George Washington in nomination. Adams later wrote, "I have never seen anyone's expression change as quickly as Hancock's that day."[4] Washington sat nearby listening to John Adams talk. He had heard rumors that he might be nominated for the job, and when he heard his name he was apparently startled, for he rose hurriedly and left the room and ran into the library room.

—·····⁂····—

Was Washington really surprise that he got the job?

He probably had a good idea that it was coming his way. After all, wearing his uniform every day to Congress was no accident. Also, he had earlier asked Edmund Pendleton to draw up his will, and in his letters to Martha he had stopped mentioning the month he would be coming home.

On the day of his election as delegate to the Continental Congress, George Washington wrote, "Dear brother Jack: It is my full intention to devote my life and fortune to the cause we are engaged in, if needful!"[5] It sounded as if Washington was hoping for a military appointment.

—·····⁂····—

Did Washington get the job right away?

The appointment of commander was debated in secret deliberation for two days. There were some that questioned the selection of Washington, not based on his ability, but the impact his selection might have on the army outside Boston. One of the men opposed to Washington's nomination was Edmund Pendleton of Virginia. They worried that the army might break apart if their current commander General Ward was not chosen. There was also the fear that the army would not follow a leader from a southern colony.

The delegates wanted to obtain a unanimity, and most of the voices in Congress were clearly in favor of Washington. The question was deferred until next day so they could discuss it in secret. Nothing else was talked of as the men met in groups and small circles. Members in dissent were persuaded to withdraw their opposition, so that unity could be shown. On June 19, 1775, the Second Continental Congress commissioned George Washington, at the age of forty-three, to command the new American Army. Charles Thompson, Secretary of Congress, sent a messenger to summon Washington, who humbly accepted the next day.

When Washington assumed command of the American Army he knew the penalty for failure. If captured, he would not be just a prisoner of war, but treated as a traitor and hanged for high treason. His head then would be cut off and his corpse would be cut into four parts and sent to the four corners of the country. All his land and money would be confiscated. His wife would also be killed if convicted of treason. If not, she and her children would be forever forbidden to own or purchase property. Washington knew that failure was truly not an option.

Washington, now General Washington, rose in his place to thank the Congress for the honor conferred upon him, and to his words of acceptance, he added, "I beg it to be remembered by every gentleman in the room that I this day declare with the utmost sincerity I do not think myself equal to the command I am honored with."[6]

—·····⁂····—

How Confident was Washington in His Ability to Command?

Be careful what you wish for:

Washington wanted a military appointment and now he had it. He would need to convince uneducated and unsophisticated men that accepting his commands would be in their best interest. He had to raise, train, feed, clothe, and equip an army. Then he had to find a way to defeat the British army, considered to be the world's greatest fighting force.

Washington quickly began to have doubts about his ability to fill this important position. He could not turn it down without being considered a coward or afraid of the risk. Publicly Washington showed confidence and determination, however, privately Washington sounded unsure of his ability and was fearful of failure. He realized that he lacked experience and knowledge in commanding a large group of men, and failure would have far reaching consequences on his life. He both wanted and did not want to serve in the army as its commander.

On June 18, 1775 Washington wrote to Martha about his reservations of taking command of the army,

> It has been determined in Congress, that the whole Army raised for the defense of the American Cause shall be put under my care, and that it is necessary for me to proceed immediately to Boston to take upon me the Command of it. You may believe me my dear Patsy, when I assure you, in the most solemn manner, that, so far from seeking this appointment I have used every endeavor in my power to avoid it, not only from my unwillingness to part with you and the Family, but from a consciousness of its being a trust too great for my Capacity and that I should enjoy more real happiness and felicity in one month with you, at home, than I have the most distant prospect of reaping abroad, if my stay was to be Seven times Seven years. But, as it has been a kind of destiny that has thrown me upon this Service, I shall hope that my undertaking of it, is designed to answer some good purpose—You might, and I suppose did perceive, from the Tenor of my letters, that I was apprehensive I could not avoid this appointment, as I did not even pretend ⟨t⟩o intimate when I should return1—that was the case—it was utterly out of my power to refuse this appointment without exposing my Character to such censures as would have reflected dishonor upon myself, and given pain to my friends— this I am sure could not, and ought not to be pleasing to you, & must have lessened me considerably in my own esteem.[7]

Martha was aware that her husband's new job carried a risk. One relative wanted to remind her of what could happen if he was defeated by the British. Martha also received a letter from another relative telling her that it was folly for her husband to be drawn into action with the riotous rebels. The relatives reminded Martha that if the rebellion failed, he would be arrested as a traitor to the King and probably hanged or beheaded. Martha replied that George always did what was right.

On June 19, Washington wrote to his stepson, John (Jack) Parke Custis, voicing the same concerns about his leadership that he said to Martha. He was relieved that John and his family would stay at Mount Vernon and watch over their mother,

> I have been called upon by the unanimous voice of the Colonies to take the command of the Continental Army—It is an honour I neither sought after, or was by any means fond of accepting, from a consciousness of my own inexperience, and inability to discharge the duties of so important a Trust. However, as the partiallity of the Congress have placed me in this distinguished point of view, I can make them no other return but what will flow from close attention, and an upright Intention. for the rest I can say nothing—my great

concern upon this occasion, is the thoughts of leaving your Mother under the uneasiness which I know this affair will throw her into; I therefore hope, expect, & indeed have no doubt, of your using every means in your power to keep up her Spirits, by doing every thing in your power, to promote her quiet—I have I must confess very uneasy feelings on her acct, but as it has been a kind of unavoidable necessity which has led me into this appointment, I shall more readily hope, that success will attend it, & crown our Meetings with happiness.

At any time, I hope it is unnecessary for me to say, that I am always pleased with yours & Nelly's abidance at Mount Vernon, much less upon this occasion, when I think it absolutely necessary for the peace & satisfaction of your Mother.[8]

Years later Doctor Benjamin Rush wrote that Patrick Henry told him that he (Henry) was with George Washington and the general expressed a lack of confidence in his ability to lead the army, "Remember, Mr. Henry, what I now tell you; From the day I enter upon command of the American armies, I date my fall, and the ruin of my reputation."[9]

In a letter on June 21, 1775 to Burwell Basset, the husband of Martha's sister, Washington again voiced concern about his appointment, "God grant therefore that my acceptance of it may be attended with some good to the common cause & without Injury (from want of knowledge) to my own reputation."[10]

In a letter from George Washington to his brother John A. Washington, June 20, 1775 he once again cast doubts on his abilities. He vowed to do the best he could, and if he failed then the fault would lie with those who appointed him,

That I may discharge the Trust to the Satisfaction of my Imployer, is my first wish--that I shall aim to do it, there remains as little doubt of. How far I may succeed is another point--but this I am sure of, that in the worst event I shall have the consolation of knowing (if I act to the best of my judgment) that the blame ought to lodge upon the appointers, not the appointed.[11]

The thoughts of inadequacy would continue to plague Washington for the remainder of the year. He later wrote a friend, "I have often thought how much happier I should have been if, instead of accepting a command under such circumstances, I had taken my musket on my shoulders and entered the ranks, or if I could have justified the measure to posterity, and my own conscience, had retired to the back country and lived in a wigwam."[12]

As late as July 1775, Washington still doubted his ability to lead as he stated in a letter to Martha on July 20th, "Lest some unlucky event should happen unfavorable to my reputation, I beg it may be remembered by every gentleman in the room, that I this day declare with the utmost sincerity I do not think myself equal to the command I am honored with."[13]

On July 30th, Washington expressed his optimism about the chances of the Americans against the British. He wrote to his brother Samuel about the British victory at Bunker Hill, "…a few more such victories will destroy their army and put an end to the present contest."[14]

Although the British were victorious at Bunker Hill, they left the field with one-third of their men killed or wounded. General Henry Clinton wrote in his diary about the victory, "A few more such victories would have shortly put an end to British dominion in America."[15] General Nathanael Greene, on the other hand said, "I wish we could sell them another hill at the same price."[16] The American hopefulness after Bunker Hill would soon fade.

How Much is a Good Leader Worth?

How was Washington to be paid?

Once Washington was selected to lead the new army, Congress had to decide what they would pay him. Congress set the pay for privates at a little over $6.00 per month, officers $20 and higher depending upon their rank. George Washington was offered $500 a month. Since Congress was not allowed to tax the people, they had to get creative in raising money. Paying the soldiers would be a major problem for the duration of the war.

Washington did not want anyone to think he might profit from the war, so he refused to be paid. Instead, he said he would keep an account of what he spent and charge that to Congress. Since he would be spending his own money while away from Mount Vernon and not making any, he needed to be sure to keep his expenses in check. While away from his plantation, he appointed his distant cousin Lund to take care of his property. He wrote to Lund November 26, 1775, "In all other respects I recommend it to you, and have no doubt of your observing, the greatest economy and frugality; as I suppose you know, that I do not get a farthing for my Services here, more than my Expences; it becomes necessary therefore for me to be saving at home."[17]

Did charging just his expenses save Congress money?

George Washington resigned his command in December 1783. In all, he served as commander of the army from June, 1775, to June, 1783, and at $500 a month he would have been paid a total of $48,000.

After eight plus years he turned in his personal expense account to Congress which was a bill for $160,074. His total expenses, which included his personal expense account and money spent on the members of his headquarters, or his military family as he called them, came to a whopping $449,261.51.

Washington was an aristocratic land owner and he was used to the finer things, even in war. The final bill included such personal items as a saddle and case. Washington wrote an accounting entry on June 22, 1775, "To cash paid for Sadlery, a Letter Case, Maps, Glasses, &c &c &c. for the use of my Command... $831.45." From July 21-22 1775 he bought "a pig, a number of ducks, 1 dozen pigeons, veal, 1 dozen squash, 2 dozen eggs, hurtleberries, biscuit and a cork cask."[18]

Washington's expenses for July 4, 1776 included a broom (which cost 6 pence) as well as mutton, veal, beef, cabbage, beets, beans, potatoes, and lobster. He also paid for the mending of his "Chariot" a type of carriage. From September 1775 to March 1776 Washington spent over $6,000 on alcohol to entertain various visitors. After the war Congress approved his expenses.

Some could think that he may have cheated the public because of such a large bill, but they should consider the following. When George left Mount Vernon to assume control of the army he would not return to his home until the summer of 1781. When he finally returned to his plantation he found it suffering from years of neglect. For eight years, day and night he was in danger, at times starving, and in unimagined anguish at seeing so many of his men suffer and die. Yet, he performed the impossible by keeping the army together and was able to achieve victory against the most powerful nation in the world. What price tag would you put on such an accomplishment and the freedom of a nation?

Washington leaves to take command:

When Washington assumed command of the army, he had to join them at once. There was no time for a quick trip home to tell his family good-by. He had to leave immediately, not knowing when or if he would ever see them again. This is one of the few surviving love letters between George and Martha. It was written on June 23, 1775 as George was leaving Philadelphia to take command of the army in Boston.

> My dearest,
>
> As I am within a few Minutes of leaving this City, I could not think of departing from it without dropping you a line; especially as I do not know whether it may be in my power to write again till I get to the Camp at Boston—I go fully trusting in that Providence, which has been more bountiful to me than I deserve, & in full confidence of a happy meeting with you sometime in the Fall—I have not time to add more, as I am surrounded with Company to take leave of me—I retain an unalterable affection for you, which neither time or distance can change, my best love to Jack & Nelly, & regard for the rest of the Family concludes me with the utmost truth & sincerety Yr entire Go: Washington.[19]

This letter showed a side of George and Martha's relationship rarely seen in his other letters to Martha. He indicated his feelings for his step-son Jack and his wife Nelly. He expressed his love for his wife and family as he traveled into battle.

The group that went with Washington to Boston included Generals Horatio Gates and Charles Lee. Both men would be remembered for opposing Washington during his command and later disgracing themselves. All along the route people turned out to see the man who was going to save the country. At New Haven, college students welcomed Washington with a small band. One member was a freshman who later would become famous. The young man was Noah Webster of dictionary fame.

When Washington reached Cambridge on Sunday July 2, 1775 he first stayed at the house of the Harvard president, then later took up residence at the mansion of John Vassal, a loyalist who had fled to the British in Boston for protection. In 1843, he house would be given to Henry Wadsworth Longfellow and his bride as a president. It was at that home he wrote *Paul Revere's Ride*.

Washington Meets His New Army

First impressions of his new army:

When Washington first joined his new army he wheeled his horse, drew his sword, and waved it in a saluting manner to the assembled men. When he gazed at his army he was

145

disappointed and shocked. What he saw resembled a mob of men, not an army. General Sullivan remarked that Washington was so struck that he did not utter a word for a half hour. The men from Virginia wore Indian leggings and other garments of backwoodsmen and pioneers, looking as if they were out on a hunting expedition. As for the rest of the men, they looked like a group of farmers and shopkeepers wearing everything except uniforms. To make matters worse the men considered Washington to be an outsider. After all, he was a wealthy land owner from Virginia, and most of them were working class men from New England.

The troops were a mixture of men and boys with little or no military training. Some had served in the French and Indian War that was fought years earlier. For most of the men, their only experience with a musket consisted of hunting animals for food. They came from various small towns across the area, and they did not agree on the same rules of conduct. Their officers were selected by vote and were usually the leading citizens of the town. The army was supplemented by local militias, who would usually serve for a short time and then go back home.

Washington's army lived in makeshift huts, their uniforms were whatever they had worn from home, and their weapons consisted of their family muskets. Most of the men were more worried about their crops at home than they were about fighting the British. Washington was shocked that the enlisted men and their officers treated each other as equals. He even saw officers shaving the enlisted men. In addition, he found some of the men engaging in conversations with the British across the lines.

In August 1775, General Washington complained to Lund Washington, his cousin and manager of Mount Vernon, that his officers were "the most indifferent kind of People I ever saw." Several had already been reprimanded for cowardice and theft. And so, despite believing the enlisted men to be potentially effective fighters, he also found them "an exceeding dirty & nasty people."[20]

Washington immediately became worried that the British would find out how disorganized the army was and how little supplies they had. He discovered that the amount of powder in camp and the surrounding area amounted to about nine rounds per man. To try to hide the problem of the powder shortage from potential spies that might be in the area, Washington had barrels of sand with powder covering in the top, placed in the power magazine. He quickly urged Congress to send supplies at once. They were not aware of the sad state of the new army, in fact they urged Washington to begin a bombardment of Boston. The only problem was that the new army had no cannons.

The one bright spot Washington saw was in the camp of the Rhode Island troops. Under the leadership of the Quaker General Nathanael Greene, the camp was well organized. This was the only group of real soldiers who were properly uniformed and equipped with arms, tents, and other supplies. The tents were pitched in the English style, soldiers were well drilled and prepared, and there was an air of discipline and subordination among the troops.

When introduced to Washington, Greene made a soldier-like address, welcoming him to the camp. Greene's appearance and manner made an instant impression upon Washington. Greene would continue to impress his commander, and a few years later, Washington said that if anything should happen to him, Greene should take charge of the American Army.

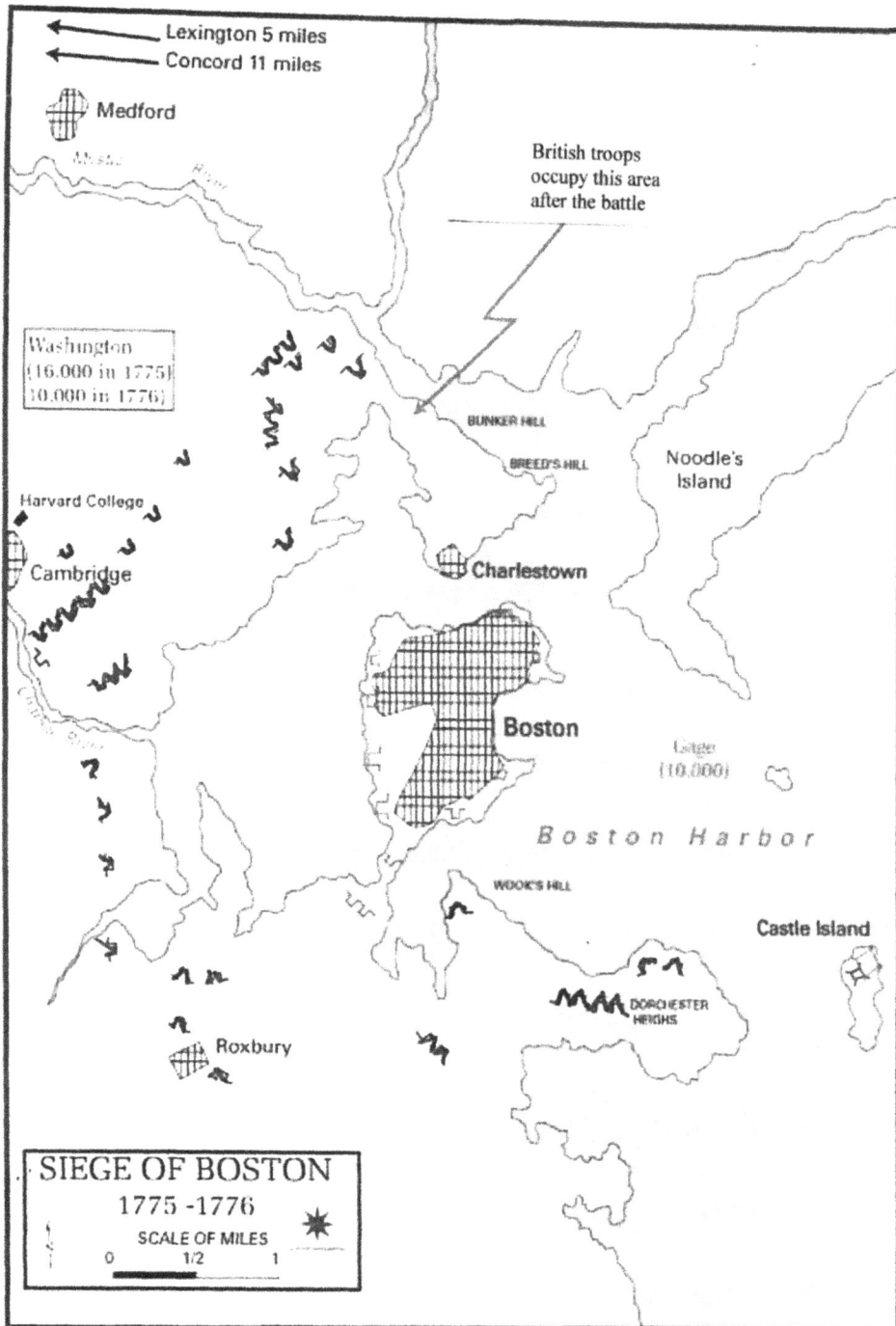

Map of Boston 1775, United States Military Academy

Problems with the Troops

Washington sees a total lack of discipline:

Washington found these raw recruits to be men of many minds. There was no discipline, and each man appeared to think of himself as a law unto his own. Instead of being at a battle, they appeared to be taking part in a club outing or a party. They felt that no one had any authority over them, and they could do as they wished. Some of the men thought they had some political influence, so they would come and go as they wanted. They even made a practice of leaving their post before being relieved. Even though powder was very scarce, groups of soldiers would often fire their guns because they enjoyed the sound, or they took shots at the British who were usually out of range.

Due to a lack of discipline, hygiene was neglected. The camps smelled of excrement, and the men were not especially clean. Soldiers were known to urinate and defecate in the areas surrounding their camps. New England men were even averse to washing their own clothes, because they considered it to be woman's work. If their wives or any camp followers were not around, then their clothing went unwashed.

Soldiers without discipline do not build adequate latrines, practice proper sanitation, or protect their drinking water from contamination. Nor did the officers recognize the importance of camp hygiene. As a result, diarrhea and dysentery were common in camps which greatly reduced the effectiveness of the colonial troops.

The officers were no better than the men they commanded, they hesitated to give orders that might not find favor within the ranks. Officers were quarrelling over rank and many began resigning. Washington saw officers and other soldiers mingling, as if there was no distinction between the two. Many of the officers were friends and neighbors of the men under their command. This made it difficult to issue orders or receive any respect.

A visitor to the camp related a dialogue which he heard between a captain and one of the privates under him. "Bill," said the captain, "go and bring a pail of water for the men." "I sha'n't. It's your turn now," said Bill. "Captain, I got it last time."[21]

Another story surfaced in regard to General Putman. The general was inspecting the defenses being built when he came upon a soldier working. Putman asked the soldier to remove a large stone in the path. The soldier protested and informed the general that he was a corporal. Putman apologized, got off his horse and removed the rock himself.

When discipline was enforced, disgruntled soldiers went home in large numbers and there was a wave of court-martials. A number of officers were reduced in rank. Thirty and forty lashes for insubordination became a regular punishment for various infractions. To Washington's chagrin, one of the few southern units in his Army, a company of Virginia riflemen, rebelled against discipline and had to be surrounded and disarmed.

One of Washington's biggest problems was finding officers to lead the men. He wanted leaders that would enforce the needed discipline to build an effective army. The current officers were at times no more responsible than the troops they commanded. Considering the disorder and confusion in the army, Washington was alarmed when he heard that, at times officers would run during battle, and sometimes disobey orders from their superiors.

Washington orders the men to get along:

When Washington took command the troops considered themselves to be members of their individual colonies and not Americans. In order to get the men to think of themselves in different terms he ordered them to forget regional differences and to get along. He issued the following general order on August 1, 1776,

It is with great concern, the General understands, that Jealousies &c: are arisen among the troops from the different Provinces, of reflections frequently thrown out,1 which can only tend to irritate each other, and injure the noble cause in which we are engaged, and which we ought to support with one hand and one heart. The General most earnestly entreats the officers, and soldiers, to consider the consequences; that they can no way assist our cruel enemies more effectually, than making division among ourselves; That the Honor and Success of the army, and the safety of our bleeding Country, depends upon harmony and good agreement with each other.

If there are any officers, or soldiers, so lost to virtue and a love of their Country as to continue in such practices after this order; The General assures them, and is directed by Congress to declare, to the whole Army, that such persons shall be severely punished and dismissed the service with disgrace.[22]

Washington begins discipline and punishment:

Washington wrote, "Discipline is the soul of an army. It makes small numbers formidable; procures success to the weak and esteem to all."[23] On his first day of arrival Washington began to issue general orders on establishing order and obedience. To disobey the orders invited swift and harsh punishment. To misbehaving soldiers Washington showed little mercy. In his first service back in Virginia, he had deserters and plunderers flogged, and threatened that if he could "lay hands" on one particular culprit, "I would try the effect of 1000 lashes." At another time he had a Gallows nearly 40 feet high erected, which had terrified the rest exceedingly.[24]

Washington established a system of punishments and some were rather quaint. For example, one of them was called "riding the wooden horse." The soldier was tied straddled on the sharp edge of a board, or some peaked device. He was raised about six feet off the ground, and weights were put on his feet. It could be quite painful, but the weights were never heavy enough to split the person in two. Most of the men would faint in a few minutes, however, the more experienced offender might last for an hour.

Walking the gauntlet was another punishment that some men enjoyed participating in, as long as they were not the offender. Soldiers were lined up in two rows facing each other, and the man to be punished was to move slowly between the men. As he moved along, the men would beat him with straps or switches. To prevent the man from running through the gauntlet, a sergeant walked in front of him with a bayonet to his chest.

The most common punishment was flogging. The victim removed his shirt and then his hands were tied over his head to a post. Next, he was lashed on his bare back with a drummer keeping time of the lashes. Thirty-nine were considered a severe punishment, but sometimes up to two hundred could be given. Usually when the larger amount was given, they were administered over several days and with a doctor present. After all, these men were civilized and not sadistic. The punishments were usually given in front of the rest of the men which would hopefully act as a deterrent to bad behavior.

Here are some examples of the offenses and punishments; John Reynolds was given 100 lashes for striking an officer, John Cline was given 200 for stealing a horse and trying to desert, and a man named Lewis was given only sixty lashes for threatening several officers. Young boys could also be held accountable this way. Young James Whaling tried to run away, but because of his youth he was only given thirty lashes.

The following was taken from the pension application of James Chich (S10440) and it describes the punishment of a young man, "One young man was heard by Col. Tolls to say that his time was out and he would go home. Tolls had him put under guard and the next day for his offence he received 25 lashes, four muskets was stacked up with bayonets locked in each other, the young man was tied and hitched to the bayonets, the men were drawn up in a circle to see him whipped—after this although many of us thought we had a right to go home nothing more was said."

These were free men who received these punishments, not like European soldiers who were usually forced into the army against their will. To use this punishment in the American Army was not effective as some of the officers thought it would be. Washington and other southern officers were accustomed to using this punishment on slaves and others engaged in manual labor, so they were more in favor of it than officers from the northern colonies. Washington also called for punishment for other undesirable behaviors such as cursing and drunkenness.[25] Michael Nash was given fifty lashes for being drunk.

On October 2, 1775, Washington issued the following order: Any officer, non-commissioned officer, or soldier who shall hereafter be detected playing at toss-up, pitch, and hustle, or any other games of chance, in or near the camp or village bordering on the encampments, shall without delay be confined and punished for disobedience of orders.[26] This did not include any games that were considers sports or recreation.

On February 26, 1776, in a council of war at Cambridge, it was decided that the troops would march upon the enemy, on the anniversary of the Boston massacre. Also on that day, Washington issued the following order, "All officers, non-commissioned officers, and soldiers are positively forbid playing at cards and other games of chance. In this time of, public distress men may find enough to do in the service of their God and their country without abandoning themselves to vice and immorality."[27]

Washington Has Second Thoughts

During the first year Washington remained discouraged:

Many of the soldiers were militiamen. They typically served until the emergency was over, which at most times was a term of several days. Most were farmers and shop keepers that were more concerned about what was happening at home than the British they faced. The majority were under the age of thirty-five and a large percent were even teenagers. Since there was no fighting and there were things to do at home, many of the men simply walked away and went home. Some returned when the chores at home were completed.

Washington became concerned with men leaving camp with the enemy so close. Men enrolled for short terms believed they had a legal right to leave camp when these expired, regardless of how close the enemy might be. Soldiers in the army had enlisted for a longer term, and their commitment ran out at the end of the year. Washington faced the possibility that at the end of 1775 he would have practically no army left to command.

Washington wrote his cousin Lund on September 30, 1776 about his displeasure with the lack of discipline, length of service, and poor battlefield performance of the American militia under his command.

> This time last year I pointed out the evil consequences of short enlistments, the expenses of militia, and the little dependence that was placed in them. I assured [Congress] that the longer they delayed raising a standing army, the more difficult and chargeable would they find it to get one, and that, at the same time that the militia would answer no valuable purpose, the frequent calling them in would be attended with an expense, that they could have no conception of. Whether, as I have said before, the unfortunate hope of reconciliation was the cause, or the fear of a standing army prevailed, I will not undertake to say; but the policy was to engage men for twelve months only. The consequence of which, you have had great bodies of militia in pay that never were in camp; you have had immense quantities of provisions drawn by men that never rendered you one hour's service (at least usefully), and this in the most profuse and wasteful way.
>
> I am with a variety of perplexing circumstances—disturbed at the conduct of the militia, whose behavior and want of discipline has done great injury to the other troops, who never had officers, except in a few instances, worth the bread they eat.[28]

Enlistments into the new army went on at a slow pace. This, along with the lack of discipline of the troops, and the shortage of supplies kept Washington's anxiety levels high. He constantly was told that he would get his recruits and that supplies would be sent, but they were empty promises. Politics continued to play an important part in the selection of officers which also discouraged Washington. Many of the officers were given their rank based on who their friends were or how important they were.

Washington complained, "The different States [were], without regard to the qualifications of an officer, quarrelling about the appointments, and nominating such as are not fit to be shoeblacks, from the attachments of this or that member of Assembly." As a result, he wrote of New England, "Their officers are generally of the lowest class of the people and, instead of setting a good example to their men, are leading them into every kind of mischief, one species of which is plundering the inhabitants, under the pretence of their being Tories."[29]

Washington also was alarmed that the troops that surrounded Boston, were stealing from farmers in the surrounding area. Then to make the supply shortage even worse, Washington wrote to Congress that the New Jersey militia not only deserted, but took much of the supplies for the army with them. He was disturbed that Congress's dependence upon the militia to fight the British would totally ruin the American cause. Washington found that the militia was not dependable, which was a problem that he would face during the entire war. At this time there was much opposition to forming a standing army by many in Congress. They knew that in the past standing armies threaten the liberty of the people. Also, they did not want to pay the taxes that would be required to maintain it.

Luckily for the American army, the well-trained British army in Boston was smaller. It had been purposefully kept small since 1688, in order to keep the King from using it against Parliament. The Americans estimated the British force facing them to be around 11,500 [a little high, it was closer to around 7,000]. The American commanders felt that they would need at least 22,000 men to have a successful attack. Since they only had around less than 14,000 fit for duty, an attack was not feasible at the present. Washington had a little time to instill some discipline in his troops, which were described by British General John Burgoyne as a "rabble in arms," and a "preposterous parade."[30]

How Did Washington Feel About Independence Now?

Did Washington favor independence once he took command of the Army?

After the dust had settled at Lexington and Concord and time had passed, the reality of what was happening began to settle in on most of the people. Leaders like Samuel Adams and Patrick Henry were still pushing for independence, however the average colonist was beginning to have second thoughts. Sure, they wanted more voice in their own affairs, but they were not convinced that a break from England was necessary. After all, they still considered themselves Englishmen and the British Empire offered them protection in a hostile world. Many colonist began to think that the colonies had gone too far in their resistance. The legislatures of North Carolina, New York, Pennsylvania and Maryland passed resolutions against separation.

As late as October 1775, Washington, while in command of the American Army, was still opposed to independence. He was in favor of changes in the relationship between the two countries, but he did not want a break from the mother country. He believe they were still British subjects and this war was not about independence, but about defending rights. He stated in a letter to General John Thomas on July 23, 1775, "....such a Cause as this, where the Object is neither Glory nor Extent of Territory, but a Defence of all that is dear & valuable in Life."[31]

In the spring of 1776 two events occurred that brought many of the colonist back to the cry for independence. First, King George of England issued a proclamation that declared the Americans to be rebels and outside his protection. This appeared to kill any hope of a peaceful reconciliation between the Americans and the Crown. Secondly, The British hired the hated German Hessians to fight for them in the colonies. The Americans saw this as the King hiring foreign mercenaries to do his dirty work and fight against British subjects on another continent.

Thomas Jefferson didn't hold back his feelings about this when he included the following statement it in the Declaration of Independence. "He is at this time transporting large Armies of foreign Mercenaries to complete the works of death, desolation and tyranny, already begun with circumstances of Cruelty & perfidy scarcely paralleled in the most barbarous ages, and totally unworthy the Head of a civilized nation."

In early 1776, Washington became a convert to independence that was fueled by the burning and cruelty at Falmouth, Massachusetts and Norfolk Virginia, by the British. In July 1776 Washington wrote about his fellow Virginians, "....my countrymen will come reluctantly into the idea of independence."[32] Washington realized that the British were determined to push its claims on the colonies and that reconciliation no longer was possible. When the pamphlet *Common Sense* by Thomas Paine was published advocating independence from England, Washington said it was a sound doctrine and unanswerable reasoning.

General Washington promoted, a little late:

The highest military rank in the United States Army is General of the Armies, and it has been conferred three times. First, to John J. Pershing in 1919 for commanding the American

Expeditionary Forces in W.W. I. Secondly, to George Washington in 1976 during the United states Centennial. Thirdly, Ulysses S Grant for commanding the Union Army in the Civil War.

The rank was first created by an act of Congress in 1799 with the intent of granting it to George Washington. However, President John Adams failed to make the appointment, because he felt it might infringe on his constitutional functions. The act lapsed in 1802 until it was revived by President Wilson.

Purple Heart Medal:

The Continental Congress forbid General Washington from granting commissions and promotions in rank to recognize merit. Washington wanted to honor merit, especially among enlisted soldiers, so he established the Badge of Military Merit on August 7, 1782. This badge was given to three men along with a brace of silver-mounted pistols.

On May 3, 1783 a badge was presented to William Brown of the 5th Connecticut Regiment. No record of his citation exists, but it is believed that he was given the badge because of his bravery on the assault of redoubt No. 10 at Yorktown. Years later the badge of Military Merit was replaced with the Purple Heart Medal.

Washington the cattle rustler:

While at Valley Forge, the army was suffering from a shortage of food. The farmers in the area were reluctant to accept highly inflated continental dollars for goods. As a result, Washington was forced to resort to ordering his men to rustle cattle. Most of the farmers were able to hide their herds deep in the Pine Barrens, but in all some 800 head were seized from loyalist farmers in Salem County in southwestern New Jersey.

Washington Achieves a Victory Without a Battle

British finally leave Boston:

For nearly a year after the Battles of Lexington and Concord, the Americans and British faced each other at Boston. Neither side felt they had the manpower to attack the other so they engaged in a stalemate. That changed in March 1776. On March 4th Washington seized Dorchester Heights and trained his cannons, recently arrived from Fort Ticonderoga, on the British in Boston and their ships in the harbor.

The British, taken by surprise, had been running short of supplies and disease had taken a toll on the troops, so British commander Howe decided to evacuate the city. The British said they would not burn Boston if they were allowed to leave the town without being attacked. Washington did not agree to this but he allowed them leave unmolested. On March 17, 1776 the winds were favorable and by noon 120 British ships with more than 11,000 people on board sailed out of Boston Harbor.

The retreating British made Washington an instant hero. Most in the colonies expected the British to mount a counterattack and, like Washington, believed it would be aimed at New York City. Washington departed for Manhattan on April 4 with his army to establish defenses. A small force under General Ward was left behind to guard Boston. Spirits among the men were high as they happily left Boston, even though they did not know where they were going, or of the hardships they would soon encounter.

Congress declared independence from England that July, and in the same month the largest expeditionary force ever launched by England sailed into New York harbor. Washington's problems were just starting. The warm glow the people felt when the British departed was now gone and would not return for many years.

Washington's Body Guards

The Life Guard:

Washington knew that he had enemies both domestic and abroad. In 1776 a unit was formed known as Washington's Life Guard with the job of protecting the General. The guard was with him in all of his battles and was disbanded in 1783. The number of guards varied from 180 to 250 and care was given to select men from every colony.

The men selected for this prestigious duty had to meet strict standards. They had to be good men that were recommended for their sobriety, honesty, and good behavior. They had to stand between five feet eight inches to five feet ten inches tall. They should be handsome and well made, clean, and neat. Cleanliness was very important to Washington, and he encouraged all the troops under him to try to remain clean. He also wanted men born in America, but he did not want the men aware that this was a requirement because he did not want to "create any invidious distinction between them and the foreigners." Their uniform consisted of a blue coat, with white facings, white waistcoat and breeches, black stock and black half-gaiters, and a round hat with blue and white feather. They carried muskets and side arms, and their motto was conquer or die. [33]

What happen to Mount Vernon during the War?

Washington is unhappy his plantation was not burned:

Mount Vernon, unlike many plantations, was spared from destruction during the war. However, it was nearly burned to the ground in 1781. That April a British sloop of war, *HMS Savage,* anchored in the Potomac River very near Mount Vernon. The ship had been raiding up and down the river and was now in need of supplies. British Captain Graves demanded provisions from the plantation or be burned to the ground. When the slaves on the plantation learned that the British were close, they thought this would be a good chance to escape to freedom. Seventeen of them fled Mount Vernon and took refuge onboard the *Savage.*

Lund Washington was currently in charge of the plantation and he decided to turn down the British demand for supplies. This angered the captain who brought his ship closer to the plantation as if to fire upon the plantation.

Lund grew nervous so he met the captain on his ship and after the two talked, Lund reconsidered the demand. He thought that if he did comply it might save the plantation from being burned, and as an added incentive he hoped that the British might return the escaped slaves. So, Lund sent the captain sheep, hogs, and an abundant of other supplies. The captain was happy to receive the supplies, so he spared the plantation, but he kept the slaves.

When Washington learned what had happen from General Lafayette who was in the area. He became angry that Lund had given the British aid, which he thought cast a stain on his reputation. In a letter to Lund on April 30, 1781, Washington expressed his displeasure,

> I am very sorry to hear of your loss; I am a little sorry to hear of my own; but which gives me most concern, is, that you should go on board the enemys Vessels, and furnish them with refreshments. It would have been a less painful circumstance to me, to have heard, that in consequence of your non-compliance with their request, they had burnt my House, and laid the Plantation in ruins. You ought to have considered yourself as my representative, and should have reflected on the bad example of communicating with the enemy, and making a voluntary offer of refreshments to them with a view to prevent a conflagration…But to go on board their Vessels; carry them refreshments; commune with a parcel of plundering Scoundrels, and request a favor by asking the surrender of my Negroes, was exceedingly ill-judged, and 'tis to be feared, will be unhappy in its consequences, as it will be a precedent for others…Unless a stop to [the British raids occurs], I have little doubt of its ending in the loss of all my Negroes, and in the destruction of my Houses; but I am prepared for the event….[34]

15

George Washington: A Great General or Just Lucky

"...tactics ...is only a small part of generalship. For a general must also be capable of furnishing military equipment and providing supplies for the men; he must be resourceful, active, careful, hardy and quick-witted; he must be both gentle and brutal, at once straightforward and designing, capable of both caution and surprise, lavish and rapacious, generous and mean, skillful in defense and attack; and there are many other qualifications, some natural, some acquired, that are necessary to one who would succeed as a general."-----attributed to Socrates

Washington Was Not a Good Tactician

Washington commanded in seven battles and one siege (Boston) from June 1775, until June, 1778. After that he was not in another battle for three years and four months. From June 1778, until the end of 1779, the British were inactive. After that the British took the war to the south, mainly in North and South Carolina and Virginia. The final great battle of the war took place at Yorktown in October 1781. During this time General Washington had no part, personally, in any campaign in the south except at Yorktown. General Washington fought in seventeen battles during the war, and his record was a mediocre: six wins, seven loses, and four draws. But he realized early in the war that he did not have to win every battle in order to win the war.

Washington was not a brilliant strategist or tactician, and he did not improve that much as the war continued. At several critical moments he showed indecisiveness, and he made serious mistakes in judgement. He wasn't great at directing troops and taking charge of battle planning as the fight unfolded. At times, Washington favored plans that were too complicated and depended on perfect timing. Because of that he lost some battles that could have gone in his favor.

His bravery, however, was never in question. He often put himself at great personal risk on the front lines. For example, Washington watched the assault on Yorktown from the grand battery with his staff, and with General Lincoln, General Knox, and their staffs. While the assault was going on, the English kept up a very heavy fire of cannon and musketry along the whole line. One of Washington's aids, Colonel Cobb, said to him, "Sir, you are too much exposed here. Had you not better step a little back?" "Colonel Cobb," answered Washington, "if you are afraid, you have the liberty to step back."[1]

Let's analyze some of the battle flaws of Washington. Luckily for the country, he was not the type of person to give up when things went wrong. Fortunately, he had the skill to learn from his mistakes and to avoid them in the future.

The loss of New York:

There were numerous eulogies delivered after the death of Washington that talked of his extensive and masterly military plans. They stressed that he observed what was happening and took advantage of every situation. So, it was only natural that most of us were taught in school that George Washington was a brilliant military tactician.

If you examine this, particularly in the early years of the war, you will see that he failed in most cases as a tactician. Before his engagement with the British in New York in 1776, he mentioned his limitations to Congress. He confessed that he had a lack of experience to move on a large scale and had limited knowledge in military matters.

Yet, after his army was chased out of New York he wrote to his cousin Lund that he placed the blame for the loss on the militia he commanded. "I am told that if I quit the command inevitable ruin will follow from the distraction that will ensue. In confidence I tell you that I never was in such an unhappy, divided state since I was born."[2]

It is true that the militia was not a reliable fighting force, but Washington failed to recognize that his leadership did not provide the conditions for an American victory. He tried too soon and without the proper supplies or men, to win a large decisive battle on Long Island in 1776.

The Continental Army lost the Long Island battle because Washington failed to carry out the needed reconnaissance and he tried to defend an area too large for the limited size of his army. Since Washington lacked intelligence on the British, he was uncertain where the enemy intended to strike. British General Howe's troops landed unopposed on Staten Island in early July, and it was repeated in August when he landed on Long Island. In September, the British landed at Kips Bay which was a great tactical surprise to the Americans.

By the end of August, the British had trapped Washington's smaller army at Brooklyn Heights with their backs to the East River. Rather than attack the Americans, Howe knowing his losses would be great, decided to wait for the Americans to surrender. What happens next added to the belief that Washington was a great general.

Luck is with Washington for the first time:

Washington was able to save his army by moving all his men across the East River during the middle of the night without the British being aware. After that miracle, Washington was declared a hero and praised as a great general. There is no doubt that it was an immense feat to move 9,000 men across a river in the middle of the night without the enemy detecting it. But it involved more luck that great leadership. Let's not forget that the lack of good leadership put the army in this position to begin with.

It was luck that made the retreat a complete success. On August 29, a storm blew in from the northeast and prevented the British from sailing up the East River to block any retreat across the water. By eleven that night the wind had died away and the surface of the water was smooth, so both sail and rowboats were able to cross the river without any problems. As daybreak approached, the retreat was not complete, but providence intervened again and a thick fog rolled in. It was so dense that some men reported they could not even see six feet in front of themselves. By seven in the morning as the fog started to lift, all 9,000 men were safely across the East River into Manhattan.

U.S. Army – Artillery Retreat from Long Island 1776 (1899) public domain.

Washington received well deserved praise for his successful night retreat off Long Island. The success, however, was due more to luck than leadership. It was fortunate that Howe decided not to attack while Washington was trapped. Had it not been for strong winds that kept the British navy away and the morning fog that covered his retreat, events might have played out differently. Washington was indecisive and inept during this campaign and he managed to get his army trapped. He made several bad decisions during this time, but as bad as they were, it did not impact his ability to continue the fight.

Luck strikes for the second time:

During the retreat a woman, whose husband had been taken away because he was suspected of being disloyal to the American cause, sought her revenge. When she saw that the Americans were sneaking across the river she sent her slave woman to alert the British. Fortunately for the Americans, the slave woman fell into the hands of the German Hessians, who could not understand a word she said. They thought the woman might be a spy, so they waited until morning to turn her over to a British officer. That morning an officer sent a British patrol out and it was discovered that the Americans were gone.

New York Catches Fire on September 20, 1776

Did Washington burn New York City?

Five days after the British forced Washington out of New York City a great fire broke out. Nearly 25% of its buildings were consumed and about one-fifth of the inhabitants were left homeless. Only a shift in the winds kept the whole city from being destroyed.

Before the Americans left the city, General Greene strongly advocated for it to be burned and Washington agreed with him. By torching the city it would deprive the British comfortable winter quarters. In addition, many in the city supported the British and it would create a hardship for those traitors. Washington asked Congress to allow him to burn New York. This request was made in a letter to them on September 2, 1776,

> If we should be obliged to abandon this Town, ought It to stand as Winter Quarters for the Enemy? They would derive great conveniences from It on the one hand—and much property would be destroyed on the other—It is an important question, but will admit of but little time for deliberation—At present I dare say the Enemy mean to preserve It if they can—If Congress therefore should resolve upon the destruction of It, the Resolution should be a profound secret as the knowledge of It will make a Capital change in their plans.[3]

John Hancock, President of Congress, wrote back to Washington on September 3,

> I do myself the Honour to enclose you sundry Resolves, by which you will perceive that Congress having taken your Letter of the 2d Inst. into Consideration, came to a Resolution, in a Committee of the whole House, that no Damage should be done to the City of New York.[4]

Congress wanted New York to be spared, but around eleven at night on September 20, fire broke out in New York City and continued to burn all night. The fire began near Whitehall Slip at the southern end of Manhattan Island. All of the houses in the area directly north of the slip were destroyed as were most of the structures west of Broadway as far north as King's College, including Trinity Church and the Lutheran church. St. Paul's Chapel on Broadway near Vesey Street was saved by citizens who climbed to its flat roof and extinguished the burning debris blown there by the wind.

The British and Loyalist immediately asserted that Washington started it. They claimed that Washington had earlier sent all the church bells out of the city so that they could not sound an alarm about the fire. It's true that Washington removed the church bells, but it was to melt them down and cast them as cannons.

Reports from people within the city claimed that the fire appeared to start at several places at once. This may have just been embers spreading the fire due to the strong wind. Other witnesses say they saw rebels carrying torches and doing things to keep the fires burning. The British executed some of the suspected arsonist on the spot. Others were arrested, and all claimed their innocence. No one was ever brought to trail, and no evidence of an American conspiracy has been found.

Washington wrote to Congress on September 22, to alert them of the fire,

> On Friday night, about Eleven or Twelve OClock, a Fire broke out in the City of New York, near the New or St Pauls Church, as It is said, which continued to burn pretty rapidly till after Sun rise the next morning. I

have not been Informed how the Accident happened, nor received any certain account of the damage. Report says many of the Houses between the Broadway and the River were consumed.[5]

He later wrote about it to his cousin Lund Washington on October 6, 1776. It was apparent that the general was not upset over the fire, "In speaking of New York, I had forgot to mention that Providence—or some good honest Fellow, has done more for us than we were disposed to do for ourselves, as near One fourth of the City is supposed to be consumed, however enough of it remains to answer their purposes."[6]

Artist's depiction of the Great Fire of New York on September 19, 1776. Public domain.

So the question remains...did George Washington order New York City to be burned? From a military standpoint it made sense. Also, his generals were in support of the act. The majority of historians do not believe that he ordered the burning. Washington was a man who believed in obeying orders from his superiors. He asked Congress, they said no, so case closed as far as he was concerned.

Some historians believe that some overzealous rebels may have torched the city for either military reasons or their hatred for the many Loyalist that lived there and supported the British. Other historians thought the fire might have been an accident. There was much dry wood debris in the city that could have caught fire from someone's torch or cooking fire. It is also possible it could have been started by the British in order to blame it on the Americans and create more hatred for the American cause. All we know for sure is that it happen and it can't be proven who or what caused it. This writer believes it was started by a small group of fanatical patriots.

Blunders Are Costly

Indecision cost the Americans two forts:

After the loss of New York, Washington's poor decisions in November 1776 resulted in the capture of two forts and a fourth of his men, as well as much needed supplies and provisions. Washington had planned to abandon Fort Washington on Manhattan Island and Fort Lee in New Jersey. He believed that the forts could not be defended and had issued a discretionary order to vacate them. General Nathanael Greene pushed to hold the forts, and Washington went along with the suggestion even though he did not believe it was a good idea.

The decision was Washington's to make, however earlier in the war, Washington rarely gave a direct order to his officers. Instead he would refer to the majority on his Council of War. An early example of this occurred at the siege of Boston in the summer of 1775. Washington wanted to attack the British using an amphibious assault. His council was against it and it was fortunate they were. The Americans did not have enough powder for the attack and they were going to send boats across the harbor, each carrying fifty men. British cannons from land and sea would have destroyed most of them and the survivors who made it ashore would have been killed by the British troops.

He may have relied on this council during the early part of the war because he was unsure of himself, overly cautious, or afraid if it was a bad decision he would receive the full blame. When he took command in June 1775, his lack of confidence in his ability, may have been the reason for referring to the council. By the time of the Battle of Trenton at the end of 1776 he would become more assertive of his own opinions.

Greene never received a direct order to abandon or hold Fort Washington, instead Washington left it up to his discretion. Greene, who would later be considered a great general, was young and very inexperienced and made the decision to defend the fort. As a result, Fort Washington easily fell into British hands on November 16, 1776 causing the Americans to lose many men and supplies. Half of the Americans captured were among the best soldiers in the army. This was a devastating blow to Washington because his army was already shrinking due to ending enlistments and desertions. Three days later Fort Lee was abandoned and Washington was on the run from the British.

General Greene felt badly because he had talked Washington into defending the fort. After this disaster, Cornwallis chased Washington's remaining army across New Jersey and into Pennsylvania. Cornwallis was convinced that the war was over and all that was left to do was to mop-up the remains of the American Army. He was so confident that he made arrangements to go back to England. He had to cancel his plans because the pesky Americans made a surprise attack on Trenton and Princeton at the end of 1776 and scored two stunning victories.

Washington's blunder at the Battle of Brandywine:

On September 11, 1777, Washington and Howe clashed in battle again at Brandywine Creek in Pennsylvania. Howe decided to repeat the flanking move that was successful against Washington at Long Island. Howe split his army by sending General Cornwallis on a seventeen mile march around Washington's army. Washington was not aware of the maneuver, but was alerted of the movement by "Squire" Thomas Cheyney.

Cheyney had been less than a hundred yards from the British, when he saw what they were doing. He hurried back to Washington to warn him, telling the general that he was about to be surrounded, but Washington did not believe him. Chaney then said, "You are mistaken general, my life for it, you are mistaken."[7]

Washington finally believed him but by that time the American right flank had been left exposed. Once again the American general was outwitted and his army almost destroyed. The British victory allowed them to capture Philadelphia. This was the American capital and it sent members of Congress scurrying for their lives.

Still another blunder the next month:

On October 4, 1777 the two armies met again at Germantown nearly forty miles from Brandywine Creek. At the start of the battle a heavy fog rolled in and 100 British soldiers, with ample powder, ran inside the large mansion owned by Benjamin Chew. Washington's plan of attack was similar to what had been successful at Trenton against the Hessians. The main attack would be against the British center directly towards Howe's headquarters.

Rather than sticking to the plan and ignoring the Chew mansion where the British troops had taken refuge, Washington attacked it in an attempt to dislodge them. Washington used his reserve forces to make repeated failed assaults on the mansion resulting in heavy American losses. Washington would have been better off to by-pass the house and carry his advance forward. Once again the American army was defeated and limped away toward Valley Forge.

Things That Washington Should Have Done

Lack of mounted troops:

During the first two years of the war the use of cavalry was minimal. Washington had no experience with it during his early militia career and at the start of the revolution he did not comprehend its value. There was an abundance of horses, forage and horsemen in the colonies, yet Washington did not try to organize them into a strong fighting force.

In July 1776, 500 men in Connecticut organized and equipped as horsemen, offered their services to Washington. He turned them down telling them there was nothing the cavalry could do. He sent them home because he did not know what to do with them. In the early part of the war these horsemen could have been valuable by harassing the enemy, cutting their supply lines, and using hit and run tactics against the British.

By 1777 regiments of light dragoons were being formed and Washington began to use them in battle. These horse soldiers became very important in the war in the south. Units of mounted guerillas led by Francis Marion in the south proved to be an effecting fighting force against the

British. In fact, it was in the south where the largest cavalry battle of the war took place. On October 3, 1781 British cavalry under the command of Colonel Tarleton fought with the French cavalry at Gloucester Point.

———✦———

Washington ignored the south:

In the later stages of the war Washington was slow to grasp the significance of the war in the south. He failed to see the potential of a campaign against his home state of Virginia in 1780 and 1781, and he sent troops there only after Congress ordered him to do so. Washington was more concerned in pushing British commander Clinton out of New York City. He wanted the French troops under Rochambeau and the French fleet to help him do that. This led to the French commander Rochambeau writing that Washington, "did not conceive the affair of the south to be such urgency."[8]

Rochambeau was not in favor of attacking New York and the admiral of the French fleet said he would sail to Yorktown and not to New York. So Washington was forced sent his army to Yorktown where Cornwallis became surrounded and was forced to surrender. Both the public and Congress were unaware that the strategy that led to the final victory had been formulated by the French and not by Washington.

———✦———

Washington should have made less complicated battle plans:

At times, Washington came up with overly complicated battle plans in which success depended on perfect timing. During their execution unexpected factors could disrupt these type of plans. An example of this occurred at the attack on Trenton in December 1776.

Washing split his army into three groups with each crossing the Delaware River miles apart of each other. The three groups would march a different distance and would meet at Trenton at the same time. This would be quite a feat, as time pieces were not always reliable during this period. Also, the attack was carried out during the middle of the night just as an unexpected storm blew up. Washington's group quickly fell behind the schedule and he was not aware that the other two groups had failed to even make the crossing. His group got to Trenton hours behind the set timetable, and found themselves alone.

Fortunately for Washington the Hessians were still caught by surprise and most of them were either killed or captured. This victory kept the American's hope for victory alive. Even when things went wrong, Washington pressed on during a terrible storm. Luck had intervened for a third time for Washington, and what could have been a disaster turned into a great victory.

During the first two years of the war, Washington made many serious blunders and the war might have been lost several times. A combination of luck and poor decisions by the British kept the Americans from losing the war. Washington never forgot what was at stake and he never gave up. He learned from his mistakes and eventually led the Americans to an improbable victory.

164

The Strengths of Washington Carry the Day

Washington took command of an army that had almost no discipline, little supplies, a lack of training, no firm commitment to the cause, and no money to pay the troops. In addition, he lacked the experience to lead this group of rabble. In addition, some key officers wanted his job, and many of the troops considered him an outsider.

Yet, with all this against him he managed to defeat the greatest army in the world, earn the respect and love of his men, and keep his army intact even though the men were rarely being paid. So, there must be something great or special about a man that could do this. How was he able to achieve this impossible goal?

Washington developed a new type of warfare:

The type of war that Europeans were accustomed to waging was large armies facing and fighting each other on an open field. The armies would withdraw and later repeat the maneuver until one side quit. The leaders did this because they were after a large battle victory to end the war. Sometimes just capturing the enemy's capital would help end the war.

After his loss on Long Island, Washington realized that a big victory was not possible. His army was out manned and out gunned, so he developed the tactic of smaller battles, breaking off and running to fight another day. The British were fixated on controlling Philadelphia, which was the capital of the rebels. If they captured it then they thought the war would soon be over. Instead, when Philadelphia was captured, the rebel leaders simply left and set up the government at another location. Through much of the war the British armies were constantly chasing after the American army trying to engage them in a big battle. The Americans tried to avoid large battles, rather they wanted to wear the British down in a protracted war. Washington wanted the British to tire of fighting and go home, which was much like what happen later to the American Army in Viet-Nam.

Washington also approved of other tactics that went against the European rules of conducting war. He encouraged the use of guerilla warfare, particularly in the south. This was similar to the type of combat the Indians used against him years before on the Virginia frontier. He also approved the patriot habit of targeting officers during battle. General Morgan had a group of sharpshooters who made it their mission to shoot officers. This practice was especially despised by the British. They believed that officers were needed to control the men under them and without leadership the troops would become an unruly mob.

Washington looks to the future:

On September 6, 1776 the first submersible, an underwater vessel, was used by the Americans. It was launched at eleven o'clock at night to sink the British flagship *HMS Eagle*. The lone crew member of the *Turtle* was Sergeant Ezra Lee, a volunteer. He made two attempts to attach a bomb to the hull of the British ship and both failed. Because of fatigue and the effects of breathing too much carbon dioxide, Lee abandoned his mission. It was the first recorded use of a submarine to attack a ship. In 1785 Washington wrote to Thomas Jefferson, "I then thought, and still think, that it was an effort of genius."[9]

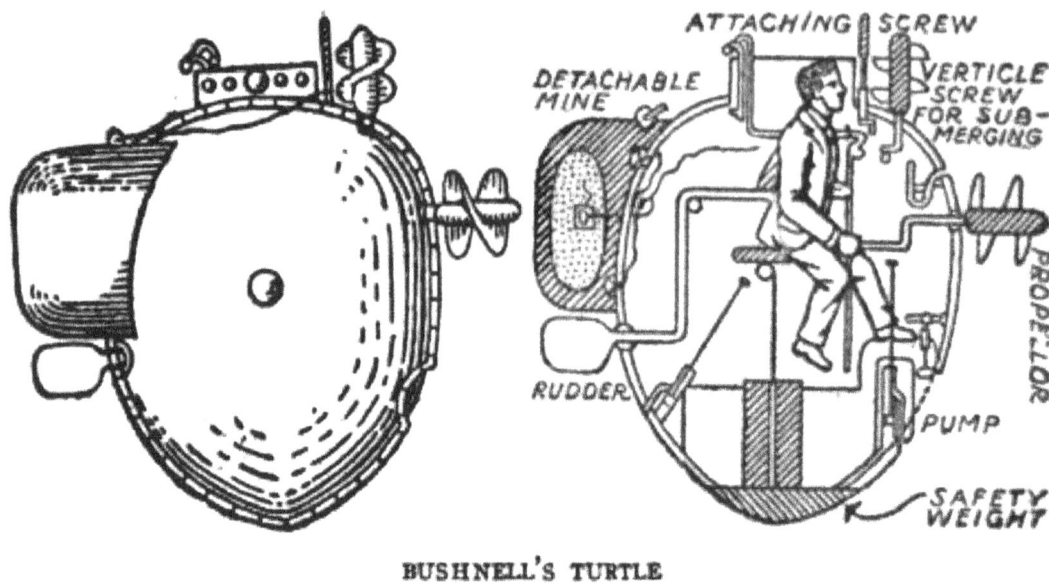

BUSHNELL'S TURTLE

A History of Sea Power by William Oliver Stevens & Allan Westcott, Published by G. H. Doran Company, 1920, pg. 294. {PD-1923}

Using spies

Although spies had been used in war for centuries, Washington took their use to the next level by placing a greater emphasis on them. Washington's decision to use espionage did not win the American Revolution for the Americans, but it certainly helped. At times, the use of spies evened the "playing field" for the American Army and likely saved many lives. He used women, slaves and children effectively as spies.

Washington excelled as a judge of character:

General Washington assembled a "military family" around him and actively sought their opinions. He did not encourage "yes men" in this family as many leaders wanted, rather he valued men who argued against him and offer their own suggestions. As he became more experienced, Washington started trusting his own decisions more. He would allow his officers to argue and pick apart his ideas, then he would examine their suggestions and make his decision. He also expected his decisions to be carried out by them.

The appointment of General Greene to command the armies in the south was an example of Washington being a good judge of character. Washington had confidence in Greene's ability and gave him total control of the southern army. Greene began to wage different tactics in the south, which help to defeat the British. Before Greene took command of the south, it appeared that the British would gain control of the southern states.

Washington recognized immediately the contributions Baron von Steuben could make to the army. He turned over the training of his army to the Prussian and allowed him to make sanitation improvements. In a few short months the baron had turned the American Army into a healthier, more effective fighting force.

When Lafayette first met Washington he was nineteen years old, and he told the general he came over from France to help the Americans fight for their freedom. Washington quickly saw something special in the young lad. Lafayette was made a major general and quickly began to prove his value to the army. He served without pay and in time he was placed in command of American troops. His greatest accomplishment was forcing General Cornwallis to remain at Yorktown, where he was later surrounded and forced to surrender.

Washington Was Not Afraid To Make bold Decisions

Attack on Trenton:

The British generals had several opportunities to end the war in their favor, but fear of failure kept them from making the needed decisions to give them victory. Washington had to make several decisions that, if not successful, could cost him his army and the war. It was these bold decisions that placed him in the camp of great leaders.

His first bold decision occurred at Trenton on Christmas Day 1776. The morale of his army was at a low point, and in a week the enlistment of many of his men would expire. He was about to lose most of his army and the revolution would be over. In mid-December Washington sent a depressing letter to his cousin Lund Washington, "The unhappy policy of short enlistments, and a dependence upon militia will, I fear, prove to be the downfall of our cause. Our only dependence now, is upon the speedy enlistment of a new army; if this fails us, I think the game will be pretty well up."[10]

Washington knew that he had to do something to raise the confidence of his men, to encourage new recruits, and save his army. He decided to launch an attack against the Hessians in Trenton. It would require him to transport his men across the Delaware River in the middle of the night, reach Trenton before sunrise, and launch a surprise attack against them. He divided his men into three forces that would converge together at the same time in Trenton. A very complicated plan that as previously discussed, required perfect timing.

As the Americans began to cross the river, a terrible winter storm blew in, and heavy rain was followed by sleet and snow. This made the crossing difficult and put the operation behind schedule. Instead of reaching Trenton before sunrise they would now arrive well after the sun was up. Washington knew the element of surprise was now gone. He was fearful that the two other groups of troops had made the crossing and would reach town without him to lead them in the attack. Washington was unaware they the other two groups turned back and did not make the crossing.

Washington sat on the Trenton side of the river with just minutes to decide what to do. His options were to go on and press the attack that might destroy his army, or to cross back over the river and return to camp and then wait a week to see how much of an army he would have left. Washington looked down at a piece of paper on which he had written the words: Victory or Death. He then made his decision…to press on and gamble the fate of his men and the Revolution by marching to Trenton. The next time an American general would have to make such an important decision would occur on June 6 1944, off the coast of Normandy.

[Note: Among the famous men at the crossing of the Delaware was John Marshall, future Chief Justice of the Supreme Court, Aaron Burr future vice president, Alexander Hamilton, future Secretary of Treasury and future president James Madison, who was shot in the shoulder during the battle and would carry the bullet for rest of his life.]

Washington at the Battle of Trenton, public domain. Washington did not lead the battle in the middle of town. Instead, he directed his forces from a small hill just outside of town.

Inoculating his men against smallpox:

At Valley Forge in January 1778, smallpox began to break out once again in Washington's army. If he decided to inoculate a third of his army at a time, it would put those men out of service for several weeks. The British were at winter camp just eighteen miles away and if they learned of this they could attack and easily destroy the American Army. If Washington decided not to inoculate the men, then many would be dead by spring, and new recruits would be afraid to enlist in an army that was sick with smallpox.

Washington made the decision to take a chance and inoculate his men. By late March his soldiers were going through the various stages of inoculation at Valley Forge. Washington, fearing an attack by the British if they learned that much of his army was incapacitated due to inoculation, ordered the doctors to perform inoculations using all possible secrecy.

This decision saved the army and enlistments went up, so that by the end of winter the American army was nearly equal in strength to the British army. That June, the Americans fought the British to a draw at Monmouth Court House. In addition smallpox never again became a problem for the American Army.

Washington changes his decision and admits blacks into the army:

Despite their proven bravery, black soldiers were not included in the overall plan for waging the war, and therefore, General Washington, military leaders, and the Continental Congress decided that the service of black soldiers would not be needed to defeat the British. The Committee of Safety in Windham, New Hampshire passed the following on April 12, 1776, "All able-bodied men aged twenty-one and above are required to sign a declaration pledging hostilities against the British, with the exception of lunatics, idiots, and Blacks." [11]

This banishment from the regular army was done to appease the southern colonies and gain their support for the cause. Slave owners, especially in the south, were concerned that training and arming black men could lead to an uprising. The south threaten to withdraw their support in the revolution if blacks did serve.

In 1777 things were not going well for the American Army and Washington was desperate for more men. They had suffered huge losses, desertions, and recruitment began to dwindle as morale sank. Congress lengthened the service time to one year for the Continental Army, which slowed the signing of new recruits even more than before. To meet the crisis, Congress called for eighty-eight new battalions from the colonies. Despite paying bonuses and bounties to new recruits, many men were did not want to enlist. In early January 1777, Washington retracted his early order which barred free blacks from serving, and Congress ordered the states to fill their units by drafting from the militia, or in any other way.

Unfortunately, the gains that African Americans had achieved in the military were erased after the war ended. In 1784 Connecticut and Massachusetts banned all blacks, free or slaves, from serving in the military. In 1792 the United States Congress excluded African Americans from military service, allowing only free able-bodied white male citizens to serve.

Washington Kept His Ego In Check

Washington did not let his ego get in the way of achieving his goals. In some cases he was willing to allow others who were more experienced take charge. The British commanders on the other hand, displayed jealously toward each other at times. On several occasions Generals Clinton and Cornwallis would undermine each other and place blame on the other when things went wrong.

Valley Forge:

Washington did not let his ego prevent him from turning over the training of the American Army to Baron von Steuben at Valley Forge in 1778. He knew that his men were poorly trained and that this foreigner could provide the training he could not. There was no man in America capable of doing what Baron von Steuben did during the winter of 1778 at Valley Forge. Washington was probably the only commander in the American army not afraid to admit that his army had problems and to have the courage and confidence to appoint this stranger to solve the problem. Washington decisions at Valley Forge probably saved the army and the Revolution.

Dealing with General Gates:

When General Gates defeated the British at Saratoga, he notified Congress of the victory before he notified Washington because of his dislike for his superior officer. This violated military code of conduct of following the chain of command. Most generals would have punished Gates for this violation which was not only out of line but, disrespectful to the commanding officer. Washington did admonish Gates in a private letter but he did not punish him. The victory was more important to Washington than his bruised ego.

Siege of Yorktown:

When Washington reached Yorktown and surrounded the British it was decided that they should lay siege to the British forces. Washington knew nothing of siege warfare, and he felt comfortable turning over the operation to the French, since they had the needed experience.

Taking credit:

When victories were achieved, especially the last one at Yorktown, Washington took no personal credit for the outcomes. Instead, he gave credit to the officers and men under him. This was much different than what happen after the British were defeated at Saratoga. General Gates was not shy about accepting personal responsibility for the victory, even though others knew that was not the case.

More Lucky Events For Washington

Sea power missing:

General Washington was very lucky that the British, for some reason, did not use their sea power effectively. The war was decided at Yorktown in 1781, by the use of sea power, but it was the French navy using it rather than the British navy. Many British officers felt that the war could not be won only on land and that the American ports should be blockaded. With the coast blockaded the British might have brought the Americans to the peace table in just a couple of years. Several years after the war, Alexander Hamilton remarked, "All the English need have done was to blockade our ports with twenty-five frigates and ten ships of the line. But, thank God, they did nothing of the sort."[12]

Another lucky event occurred at Yorktown:

When Cornwallis was bottled up by the American army he decided that he would transport his men across the York River to Gloucester under the cover of darkness. Once across he could attack and defeat the smaller American force there. From there he could quickly advance northward and with a little luck he might be able to join forces with Clinton in New York.

If their forces were joined then they could match the Allied army numbers and continue the war. Without the American victory at Yorktown, the French fleet would have sailed back to the West Indies and the French support for the war would begin to vanish. The Americans would be forced to the peace table and they would have to bargain from a position of weakness. The Americans might have been given a few political concessions but they would have still remained under British control. Washington and some of the leaders of the revolt most likely would have been put on trial for treason and made an example of.

On the night of October 16, 1781, Cornwallis began to move his army across the river to escape. As the first group of men rowed across the York River, the winds began to pick up and a thunderstorm blew in. The boats started to bounce around in the high waves, heavy rain fell, and the winds grew in intensity. Two of the boats were blown off course and landed back on the Yorktown side shore where the frightened men were taken prisoner by the Americans. Fourteen boats made it across the river, and the water soaked men went ashore safely. It was impossible to bring any more men across until the storm blew itself out.

The weather did not break until around two in the morning. Cornwallis knew this would not be enough time to gather the scattered boats, so the escape was called off. Around noon the next day, he had the men that crossed earlier to Gloucester brought back. It was now clear to the British that their choice was annihilation or surrender.

16

Disrespect Towards General George Washington

"My temper leads me to peace and harmony with all men." ....George Washington

~ↄ⊗ⓖⓢⓞ⊗ᴄ~

Slander Strikes At Washington

There is no man so high that some will always be found who wish to pull him down. Washington was no exception to this rule. He was very sensitive to criticism and to any comments that could damage his reputation. Privately he took these attacks personally, but publically he tried to rise above them and ignore what was said and who it came from.

Accused of being a womanizer:

As soon as Washington was appointed commander of the new American Army the attacks on him began. Newspapers, usually under British control, suggested that Washington was a womanizer. One such story appeared in the summer of 1775, just after he took command of his army. On August 17, a newspaper inside of Boston published a story that the British navy captured a letter that Washington had sent to Congressman Benjamin Harrison.

In the letter it claimed that Washington wrote of a "pretty little woman" Kate, who was the washer woman's daughter. The article suggested that something either had or was going to happen between the two of them. Washington did like the women when he was a young man, but once married to Martha he had eyes only for her. It was later uncovered that the letter was written in England, possible by a member of the British admiral's office by the name of Gefferini.

━·◦⧢◦·━

In June 1776, Thomas Hickey was hanged for his part in a plot to kill George Washington. Immediately the British attacked the general's reputation once again. A pamphlet was published in London titled, "Minutes of the Trial and Examination of Certain Persons in the Province of New York."

In it William Cooper reported that Washington was constantly visiting a woman late at night by the name of Mary Gibbons. Mary, a spy for the British, passed along everything Washington confided in her. According to Cooper, after Mary had relations with the general and when he was asleep, she went through his pockets and make copies of letters and documents he had.[1]

As the story spread, many variations emerged. For example, in one account Mary lived in New Jersey and Washington rowed across the Hudson River at night to meet her. This would have been quite a feat because there were numerous British warships in the river, and at this particular time the American Army was retreating from the British Army.

━·◦⧢◦·━

Personal attacks:

The first attack was from George Muse, a lieutenant-colonel under Washington in 1754. At Fort Necessity Muse was found guilty of cowardice and was discharged in disgrace. Washington seemed to have harbored no personal ill-will for Muse's conduct, and when the division of the "bounty lands" was being pushed, he used his influence so that the disgraced officer would receive some. Not knowing this, or else being ungrateful, Muse seems to have written a letter (copy has not been found) to Washington which angered George and he wrote back,

> Sir, Your impertinent letter was delivered to me yesterday. As I am not accustomed to receive such from any man, nor would have taken the same language from you personally, without letting you feel some marks of my resentment, I would advise you to be cautious in writing me a second of the same tenor.[2]

A pamphlet came out in 1777 titled, "Letters from George Washington to several of his friends in 1776." The letters supposedly contained insults by George Washington toward New Englanders. One letter suggested that he thought the war to be hopeless because he had terrible allies. Another claimed that Washington thought the Revolution was a misunderstanding and that his loyalty was still to the King. It was suspected that the letters were written by John Randolph who was loyal to the Crown and had fled to England before war broke out. Rarely did anyone on either side of the ocean believe them.

General Charles Lee, who faced the wrath of Washington at the battle at Monmouth Courthouse, later launched a campaign of vengeance against the general. He charged Washington with cruelty to his slaves and that he used them immorally. When asked to produce proof, Lee maintained that it was done in secret and therefore difficult to detect.

Allegations of illegitimate children:

Even after the death of Washington, attacks against his character emerged. For example, it was suggested that the fatal illness that struck Washington on December 13, 1788 was brought about by a secret meeting with an overseer's wife. When he was at Mount Vernon, Washington took daily rides around his plantation and sometimes times stopped at farm houses due to severe weather conditions. Many times those stops brought rumors of secret meeting with women, the cause due to weather was disregarded. Then there is the story of his illegitimate son, Thomas.

Thomas Posey was born in Virginia in 1750 on a farm adjacent to Mount Vernon. Throughout the boy's life there was speculation that he was an illegitimate child of George Washington. Historians are not sure who his parents really were and most agreed that Washington was not his father. The fact that Washington supposedly paid for the education of Thomas added fuel to the rumors the he was the father of the boy. Washington, however, contributed to the education of numerous other children so this was not unusual. Other "proofs" of Thomas being Washington's son have emerged over the years, but none of them can be backed by fact, and they are not really worth going into.

In 1940, stories began to appear that Washington fathered a son, West Ford, by a slave named Venus. The family claimed that they had proof from various documents of the period such as photos, books, and newspaper mentions. West was born between March 3, 1783 and June 22, 1784, however Washington was not at his plantation from November 1781 and Christmas Eve of 1783. During that time he was with the army. Also, West was born on his brother's plantation and records show that Washington did not visit the plantation during this time.

Portrait of West Ford in 1859, by Benson John Lossing. Public domain

Even Martha was not immune against slander from the press:

When she joined Washington at his camp at Cambridge in 1775, it was said that, "…she being a warm Loyalist, had separated from her husband since the commencement of the present war, and now lived very much respected in the city of New York."[3] This malicious rumor convinced her to make the dangerous 600 mile trip to join her husband at his first winter camp. She now realized that she was a public figure and would be under a public microscope.

Loss of support from friends in Congress:

When Washington took his men to winter quarters at Valley Forge in 1777, it appeared that the war was lost. The army had just suffered two defeats at the hands of the British, there was a lack of supplies, sickness plagued the troops, and men began deserting. In Congress, Washington's reputation was at an all-time low and it appeared that the country and Congress had abandoned the general.

John Adams, the man who had nominated Washington for the job of leading the army, led the opposition. Even Washington's old friend Richard Henry Lee wrote, "Gates [General Horatio Gates] was needed to procure the indispensable changes in our army." Clark of New Jersey said, "We may talk of the enemy's cruelty as we will, but we have no greater cruelty to complain of than the management of our army."[4] Even some of Washington's own generals such as Nathanael Greene and Timothy Pickering, leveled mild complaints against him.

Dr. Benjamin Rush, who always spoke well of Washington, wrote several anonymous letters of which one was sent to Patrick Henry. The letter stated, "The people of American have been guilty of idolatry by making a man their God."[5] He also wrote something about Baal and his worshippers, and implied that Washington was Baal. The letter was forwarded to Washington who recognized Rush's handwriting, but the general did not think it worthy of comment. Congressman Jonathan D. Sargent declared, "Thousands of lives and millions of property are yearly sacrificed to the insufficiency of our commander-in-chief, ... and yet we are so attached to this man that I fear we shall rather sink with him than throw him off our shoulders."[6]

If this was a sample of what Washington's friends was saying about him, imagine what his enemies were saying. He did, however, have some supporters. Officers in the lower ranks continued to support Washington. One Captain said they could remove any general except Washington. General Lafayette, to his credit, maintained a steadfast support of Washington, even though others tried to sway him to their side.

It appeared that the only thing keeping Washington from being dismissed of his command was the continued absences of the two delegates from New York. While they were gone there were not enough votes to discharge him.

The Conway Cabal against Washington

A "cabal" is a secret group against a person with the object to hurt or injury.

General Horatio Gates was disappointed that George Washington was given command of the American Army rather than him. The two men professed to be friends and Washington gave Gates his first appointment. Yet, early in the war, Gates suggested that a committee of Congress be sent to camp to keep an eye on Washington. Meanwhile, Gates began to curry favor with some members of Congress against his commander. Washington became aware of the behavior of Gates, and was alarmed that the enemies he faced were not just the British, but men under his own command and in Congress.

What became known as the Conway Cabal was a group of Washington's senior officers in the army in late 1777 and early 1778 who lobbied to have him replaced as the Commander-in-

Chief. It was named after General Thomas Conway, who was a member, along with Gates and General Thomas Mifflin. To what extent some members of Congress were part of it is not clear. But it was clear that some members did support the three Generals.

Horatio Gates   Thomas Conway   Thomas Mifflin

The aim of the cabal was to force Washington to resign and be replaced with Gates. The cabal began in October 1777 when General Conway lobbied to be promoted to major general. Washington, who distrusted the man did not support his promotion. Regardless, Congress appointed Conway which disappointed Washington. This was followed by numerous letters from the cabal and its supporters being sent to Congress about Washington criticizing him personally and professionally. What prompted the letters were the defeats at Brandywine, Germantown, the loss of Philadelphia, the loss of forts in Delaware, and the victory of General Horatio Gates at Saratoga.

The victory at Saratoga was claimed by Gates, but it was really due to the efforts of Generals Arnold, Schuyler, and Morgan. In addition, Washington had reduced the size of his own army to reinforce the Northern Army of Gates. Congress did not take this into account when they began to criticize Washington. Even so, Gates had been so intoxicated by his success against Burgoyne that he thought himself the man of the day. Conway believed Gates was a rising star, and he meant to rise with him.

The cabal maintained that General Gates's army was like "a well-regulated family, and General Washington's like an unformed mob."[7] To the alarmed Washington, it appeared that at least two of his generals were plotting to overthrow him, something that seemed not only disloyal but virtually treasonous. He wrote from Valley Forge, "My enemies take an ungenerous advantage of me. They know the delicacy of my situation, and that motives of policy deprive me of the defence I might otherwise make against their insidious attacks."[8]

General Thomas Mifflin, the last major member of the Cabal, was the first man appointed to Washington's staff at the start of the war, but he did not remain long in that position, being

promoted by Washington to be quartermaster-general. Mifflin was one of the most outspoken against the commander-in-chief as his opponents gathered force. Mifflin resigned from the army and took a position on the Board of War, but when the influence of the cabal began to collapse he applied for a reappointment to the army.

⸎

Appointment of officers:

Washington also had difficulty with Congress over their power to appoint his generals. Several members of Congress wanted to seize control of the army away from Washington and create a Board of War to which Congress would appoint their chosen generals. Congress persisted in promoting politically well-connected officers out of turn without consulting Washington. Benedict Arnold was among the generals who had been passed over for promotion and in a fit of anger he resigned. It was only through the efforts of Washington's insistence that Arnold reenlisted. The general could not afford to lose good officers because of the interference from Congress. Washington became engaged in a running battle with Congress to make appointments according to seniority, a battle in which he later won.

The constant wrangling over rank and regional interest had pushed Washington beyond disgust. He wrote to Richard Lee in October 1777, "To sum up the whole, I have been a Slave to the service: I have undergone more than most men are aware of, to harmonize so many discordant parts but it will be impossible for me to be of any further service if such insuperable difficulties are thrown in my way."[9] Washington was hinting at resigning and thus putting his career on the line to block the cabal of their scheming and the meddling of Congress.

⸎

Results in dealing with the cabal:

It is the nature of cabals and conspiracies that they flourish in the dark. They cannot bear the light. As soon as these hostile intentions began to reach the ears of the public, a great indignation stirred, and one after another of the conspirators made haste to disown any evil purpose.

When the cabal realized that Washington had the support of most of Congress and was not going to be replaced, they scrambled to disavowal themselves from any wrong doing. Also other generals began to send letters to Congress supporting Washington. This prompted the three generals in the cabal to struggle to save their careers and make amends.

Gates was forced to apologize for things he had said, written, and lied about in his correspondence with Conway. A friend of Washington, with urging, challenged Gates to a duel. Gates wept, and apologized for any offense he caused and the duel was called off.

Conway was placed in command of an insignificant post in Albany. From his obscure corner, Conway later wrote an impertinent letter of resignation to Congress, and his resignation was immediately accepted. General John Cadwalader, also with the urging of Washington, had a duel with Conway, shot him in the mouth and the bullet exited through his head. Cadwalader later remarked that it stopped the rascal's lying tongue. Conway, before he left for France wrote Washington an apology, which was never answered. Here is his letter,

178

I find my self just able to hold the penn During a few Minutes, and take this opportunity of expressing my sincere grief for having Done, Written, or said any thing Disagreeable to your excellency. my carreer will soon be over, therefore justice and truth prompt me to Declare my Last sentiments. you are in my eyes the great and the good Man. May you Long enjoy the Love, Veneration and Esteem of these states whose Libertys you have asserted by your Virtues. I am With the greatest respect sir your Excellency's Most obedt humble Servant[10]

Thomas Mifflin rejoined the army after he resigned from the Board of War in 1778. He did not take an active part in the military and was later accused of embezzlement while he served as quartermaster. He resigned from the military in 1779, returned to Pennsylvania, and became involved in politics.

General Lee had a small role in this sortied affair and once said of Washington, "He is not fit enough to command a Sergeant's Guard."[11] He was brought up on charges for not following orders at the battle of Monmouth Court House, and was later removed from the army.

After the Conway Cabal, the nation largely rallied behind Washington, who was now seen more as a figure of national unity. No noticeable attempt was made to replace him for the remainder of the war. It was a long time before anyone challenged his command again, but the episode left Washington shaken with the knowledge that there were generals and congressmen who he could not trust.

It was a striking illustration of Washington's generosity that he never allowed the memory of this devious plot against himself to interfere in his relations in later years to the men who had taken part in it. When he became President he appointed some of them to important offices.

Mutiny in Washington's Army

Pennsylvania line mutiny:

In November 1780, the Continental Army went into winter quarters. The Pennsylvania line suffered from shortages and their commander wrote to Congress, "We are reduced to dry bread and beef for our food, and to cold water for our drink. . . . Our soldiery are not devoid of reasoning faculties, they have now served their country with fidelity for near five years, poorly clothed, badly fed, and worse paid; of the last article, trifling as it is, they have not seen a paper dollar in the way of pay for near twelve months."[12]

On January 1, 1781 all eleven regiments under General Anthony Wayne, 1,500 soldiers, claimed that their three year enlistment had expired. They left the winter camp after they killed three officers in a drunken rage. It is not clear what sparked the men to such action, nor is it clear if they even planned to mutiny. Lt. John Reeves described what happen,

> The column of now mutinous soldiers moved down the line of huts, seized four cannons, fired muskets into the air, and called for more men to join them. Many soldiers hid in their huts until the tumult passed. Mutineers forced the men of the 2nd Pennsylvania to join at bayonet point and fired a few cannon shots over the ranks of the 5th and 9th Regiments to convince them to join the revolt. While the main group of mutineers gathered (or coerced) men, others seized horses, wagons, tents, and provisions. Some officers made fruitless attempts to gain control.[13]

British General Henry Clinton saw a chance to be disruptive by offering the mutineers pay owed to them and a full pardon if they would join the British Army. The mutineers, rejected the offer, and marched on to Congress. General Wayne and Congressional President Joseph Reed met with them and three days later, January 10, they reached an agreement. Half of the men accepted discharges, and the rest took furloughs in addition to a bonus if they reenlisted. Later, those men went on to participate in the southern campaign.

The Pompton Mutiny:

The success of the Pennsylvania mutiny encourage the Pompton Mutiny on January 20, 1781. About 300 troops from the New Jersey Line revolted at Pompton Camp in New Jersey. These men had the same complaints as the Pennsylvania men and they were given the same benefits that the Pennsylvania men received. However, this did not satisfy the men and they still mutinied.

General Washington immediately ordered troops under General Robert Howe to confront the men. Howe surrounded the mutineers and forced them to surrender, and the worst offenders were tried on the spot and immediately shot. In a letter to General Greene on February 2, 1781, Washington wrote, "The execution of two of their Instigators on the spot—This has totally quelled the spirit of Mutiny, and everything is now quiet."[14]

The British Disrespect George Washington

During the Revolution the British generals did not consider Washington their equal in rank. To them he was just a wealthy farmer who was playing at being a general. This attitude toward Washington and the rest of the American Army would eventually help cause their defeat.

Say my rank:

In July 1775, during the siege of Boston, General Howe sent Lieutenant Brown, under a flag of truce, to General Washington. Brown presented a letter to Washington which was addressed to George Washington, Esq. Brown met with Joseph Reed and told him that he had a letter for Mr. Washington. Reed quickly replied that there was no one present by that name.

Brown then inquired, by what title did Mr. Washington wish to go by? Reed replied that he should be addressed by the rank of General. The letter was decline to be received and Lieutenant Brown returned to report the conversation to General Howe.

Three days letter Brown returned to the American headquarters with another letter. This time it was addressed to George Washington, Esq., etc., etc. Once again the letter was declined. The next day a new messenger appeared from the British, this time a captain named Nisbet Balfour, asked if General Washington would receive the adjutant general to General Howe, Colonel James Paterson. This time the American reply was yes.

When Paterson and Washington met, he placed on the table the same letter addressed to George Washington, Esq., etc., etc. Washington refused to touch it. Each man then explained their position in the matter over the unopened letter.

When General Clinton took over command of the British Army in the United States, he tried to use the same insult that General Howe had earlier used. A dispatch was sent to Washington and addressed to Mr. Washington. The general took the letter, and saw that it was not addressed using his proper title, and said, "This letter is directed to a planter in the state of Virginia. I shall have it delivered to him after the end of the war. Until that time it shall not be opened."[15] The next letter was addressed to his Excellency.

Surrender of the sword:

When General Cornwallis surrendered to the Americans at Yorktown he was so devastated and humiliated by the defeat to the rebel army that he refused to attend the surrender ceremony. This was a break in protocol that required the leader of the defeated army to offer his sword to the leader of the victorious army. Instead, he sent his second in command, General O'Hara to hand over the sword.

At the surrender ceremony, the British officers rode toward the allied generals, O'Hara quickened the pace of his horse, so that he could surrender his sword to the French general. O'Hara did not want to surrender to an American. However, as O'Hara approached Rochambeau, the French general pointed out General Washington, and he led the British general to him. General O'Hara apologized to Washington for General Cornwallis not coming out and said his commander was sick. As General O'Hara raised his sword to give it up, Washington stopped him.

Washington knew that if a second in command was sent to surrender, then it was proper for his own second in command to receive the sword. Washington then directed O'Hara to present the sword to General Lincoln, who accepted the sword and pointed O'Hara in the direction where his men should go to surrender their weapons.

Payback by Washington:

After the surrender at Yorktown the allied generals threw parties for the British officers. Now that the fighting was over they could be friends and eat, drink, and toast one another. After all they were gentlemen and civilized. At one such meal, the French commander, Rochambeau, raised his glass to toast and said, "To the United States." Washington did likewise and said, "To the King of France." Next it came the turn for Cornwallis, who raised his glass and said, "To the King." Washington quickly added, "Of England. Confine him there and I'll drink him a full bumper,"[16] and then he filled his glass until it ran over. (A bumper means filled to the brim.)

17

Close Calls for George Washington

"I expected any moment to see Washington fall; his duty and situation exposed him to every danger. Nothing but the superintending care of Providence could have saved him from the fate of all around him." … Dr. James Craik

During George Washington's military career he had many brushes with death. His first close call took place in 1753, when the governor of Virginia sent him out to warn the French trespassers to stop construction of military posts on the Ohio. During the encounter, Washington escaped death when an Indian he thought was friendly appeared to fire at him from just twelve yards away and missed.

This led to the Indians believing that Washington, or the "Great White Chief" as they referred to him, led a charmed life. The belief was later reinforced at the Battle of the Monongahela where British General Braddock suffered a terrible defeat. Washington was on horseback during the battle and made a tempting target. As a result, he had two horses shot from under him and received four bullet holes through his clothing. He was one of the few officers that escaped the battle uninjured.

Dr. James Craik, Washington's personal friend and physician, who ministered to the dying General Braddock during the battle said, "I expected any moment to see Washington fall; his duty and situation exposed him to every danger. Nothing but the superintending care of Providence could have saved him from the fate of all around him."[1]

One close call that may or may not have happened occurred at the Battle at Trenton. According to the story, when Washington raised his sword and ordered his men to charge, a bullet struck the hilt of his uplifted sword. While the story is possible, but it may just be a legend.

Several days later at the Battle of Princeton, Washington rode his horse at full speed between the American and British lines, ordering his men to charge while the firing between both armies was going on. It was reported that Colonel Fitzgerald, his aide, covered his eyes with his hat so that he would not see his general shot. Washington emerged unharmed and rallied his men to victory.[2]

After the battle, Colonel Fitzgerald rode over to Washington and exclaimed, "Thank God your excellency is safe." Washington grasp his hand and replied, "Away, my dear colonel, and bring up the troops, the day is won."[3]

On August 27, 1777, General Washington, accompanied by Generals Lafayette, Greene, and Weedon, reconnoitered the previous day to within three miles of the Head of Elk, the place where the British had just landed. They were in imminent danger of being captured, having to remain all night at a farm-house, due to a terrible storm. The men were able to evade the British and at dawn they returned to Wilmington.[4]

During his stay at West Point in the early part of the war, General Washington frequently dined at the home of a nearby family. Suspicions had arisen about the honesty of his host, and some had accused the person of treachery to the American cause. One time the man was very insistent that Washington dine with him on a certain day and at a certain hour. The host, aware of the suspicions that circled around him, suggested that Washington come alone without his usual guard. He said that this would prove that the General trusted him and the suspicions were unfounded. This insistence of a certain day and time aroused the suspicions of Washington, so he arrived at one o'clock which was an hour early for the dinner.

The host insisted that the two of them take a walk and enjoy a conversation. During the walk Washington noticed that the man seemed nervous and excitable. The General led the conversation to topics that might make the host betray his agitation. At one point Washington pointed out toward the British camp in the distance. He remarked to the man about the lack of principle that could induce men of American birth to trade the interests of their country and their patriotism by helping the British on the promise of a little gold.

The man became very tense and nervous at the remarks and had no reply. At 1:45 the sound of horsemen interrupted the men's conversation. Washington turned toward the noise and said, "Bless me, sir. What cavalry are these approaching the house?"

The host replied with a shaking voice, "A party of British light horse who mean no harm, but are sent for my protection!" Washington replied in a stern voice, "British horse sent here while I am your guest! What does this mean sir?"

As the horsemen arrived and dismounted, the host spoke with a little more courage in his voice, "General, you are my prisoner." "I believe not," replied Washington in a calm voice. "But sir, I know you are mine! Officer, arrest this traitor."[5]

The host was shocked to learn that Washington had ordered a company of Americans to disguise themselves as British cavalry and to arrive at the home at a designated time. Washington had suspected that his host was a false friend, and this ruse was designed to expose the man. The man later confessed that the British had offered him a large sum of money to betray General Washington. The British Calvary was to arrive at the house that day at 2 o'clock to capture the General. At first Washington was going to make an example of the man, but the traitor's family begged for mercy. Washington pardoned the man.

Captain Patrick Ferguson was considered to be the finest shot in the British army. He and a few of his marksmen came upon a small group of American officers during the Battle of

Brandywine on September 11, 1777. Ferguson and his men were hidden about 100 yards from the American officers.

One of the officers wore a dark green and blue uniform with a high cocked hat, the badge of the Commander-in-Chief. The Americans were in the sights of the British marksmen, when Ferguson gave the order not to fire but to advance on the unsuspecting men. Ferguson had decided to take the Americans prisoners.

The British approached the officers and ordered the Americans to dismount. Ferguson yelled, "You are marked by rifles. Come in as my prisoners." The Americans turned their horses and began to ride away. Ferguson aimed his rifle at the back of the fleeing man with the high cocked hat. Ferguson lowered his rifle and allowed the men to escape. He later said he did not want to shoot the officer in the back.

Was the man with the high cocked hat General Washington? It was later confirmed that Washington was out doing recon in the area. Some historians doubt that the general would have been out riding near the enemy. However, on several different occasions Washington did just that, placing himself in danger.

Ferguson later remarked, "The next day, the surgeon told me that a wounded rebel officer informed him that General Washington was all the morning with the light troops, and only attended by a French officer in the hussar dress, he himself dressed and mounted as I have before described."[6]

Taking chances at Yorktown:

Washington and other general officers rode near the British lines at Yorktown to Pigeon Quarter at an early hour to survey the British defenses. During this time they knew they were in view of the enemy. The group, quickly attracted the British's attention, and were fired at by cannons which struck the trees above them. Washington remained under fire until he had finished his observations.

During the siege of Yorktown, Washington was in continuous activity, and at times he was in the saddle the entire night. He was constantly observing the British lines, and at times he placed himself in danger. The following account occurred when Washington was at the Poplar Redoubt that had been earlier captured from the British,

> At the battle of Yorktown, Mr. Evans was standing beside Washington when a cannon ball in full sweep struck the earth at his very feet and sent s shower of dirt over his hat. Washington glanced at the chaplain to see how he took it, but the latter was as imperturable as himself. Without stirring from the spot, he took off his hat, and seeing it covered with sand, said quietly as he held it up, "See here, general." Washington smiled and replied, "Mr. Evens, you had better take that home and show it to your wife and children."[7]

Washington watched the assault on the British lines from the grand battery with his staff, General Lincoln, General Knox, and their staffs. While the assault was going on, the English kept up a very heavy fire of cannon and musketry along the whole line. One of Washington's aids, Colonel Cobb, said to him, "Sir, you are too much exposed here. Had you not better step a little back?" "Colonel Cobb," answered Washington, "if you are afraid, you have the liberty to step back."[8]

Dr. Munson was at the main battery with Washington watching the assault. Munson reported, "While the attack was progressing a musket ball rolled along a cannon, and fell at the feet of Washington. General Knox seized him by the arm, and said; 'My dear General, we can't spare you yet!' Washington replied, 'It is a spent ball, and no harm is done."[9]

Assassination Attempt on General Washington:

William Tyron, the Royal Governor of New York was the ringleader of an attempted assassination on General Washington's life in 1776. The plan was not just to take out Washington, but all the rest of his generals and then carry out guerrilla warfare in New York City. It might had been successful if not for Sgt. Thomas Hickey, a member of Washington's life guard.

In 1776 Washington formed a unit in the Continental Army called the Life Guard. Their function was to protect him during the war. During the siege of Boston four men were selected by Colonels from each army regiment and they had to meet the following requirements, "...recommend for their sobriety, honesty, and good behavior; he [Washington]wishes them to be from five feet, eight inches high, to five feet, ten Inches; handsomely and well made, and as there is nothing in his eyes more desirable, than Cleanliness in a Soldier, he desires that particular attention may be made, in the choice of such men, as are neat, and spruce."[10]

Thomas Hickey had been a British deserter that had joined the militia and was handpicked by Washington. Hickey was later jailed for passing counterfeit money and while in his cell he confessed to Isaac Ketchum, another prisoner, his role in the conspiracy to kill the general.

Hickey was court-martialed and found guilty of mutiny, treachery, and sedition and one of his fellow conspirators testified against him to save his own neck. Once found guilty he was quickly hanged on June 28, 1776, in what is now the Bowery section of the city. With his last words, Hickey said he hoped his accusers would meet the same fate.

This execution, attended by 20,000 people, was up to this time the largest public hanging in the history of the colonies. It was quite a social event for the people of New York City. Some people attended and had a picnic, some used it as an excuse to start drinking early, women of the evening looked for new customers, and pickpockets scored big time. For some reason, no other conspirators stood trial and paid the price for their involvement. After the hanging, George Washington issued General Orders that included a part about Hickey,

The unhappy Fate of Thomas Hickey, executed this day for Mutiny, Sedition and Treachery; the General hopes will be a warning to every Soldier, in the Army, to avoid those crimes, and all others, so disgraceful to the character of a Soldier, and pernicious to his country, whose pay he receives and Bread he eats—And in

186

order to avoid those Crimes the most certain method is to keep out of the temptation of them, and particularly to avoid lewd Women, who, by the dying Confession of this poor Criminal, first led him into practices which ended in an untimely and ignominious Death.[11]

In Washington's itinerary dated June 28, 1776 it also included information about the assassination plot,

Thomas Hickey, one of Washington's Guard, was tried by a court-martial and sentenced to death, being found implicated in a plot to murder the American general officers on the arrival of the British, or at best to capture Washington and deliver him to Sir William Howe. The plot had been traced to Governor Tryon, the mayor (David Matthews) having been a principal agent between him and the persons concerned in it.[12]

18

President George Washington

"His Highness, the President of the United States of America and the Protector of Their Liberties."....suggested title for the new President.

ᴐ᷿᷿᷿᷿ᴐ

George Washington Becomes the Leader

Even though they called themselves the United States of America, they were very loosely united. Congress held them together, but actually had no power over the states. After the war, the individual states considered themselves independent and it was difficult to get them to work together as one nation. Each state was afraid of another state taking advantage over them. In addition, the American Army was in a state of disarray because they wanted payment that was promised for services rendered the past eight years.

The majority of the country knew that only George Washington could unite and lead them unto the world stage. On May 22, 1782, Colonel Lewis Nicola wrote a letter to George Washington urging him to take a royal title and lead the country as king. Washington replied back in a stern manner, "Let me conjure you, if you have any regard for your country, concern for yourself, or posterity, or respect for me: to banish these thoughts from your mind, and never communicate a sentiment of the like nature."[1] Nicola quickly sent Washington two letters of apology.

George Washington was in debt:

One of the biggest problems facing the new nation was the debt due to the war, which amounted to, with interest, a whopping fifty-four million dollars. The country was not alone in being in debt, George Washington suffered from the same problem. He had been away from Mount Vernon since 1775 and after those eight years Mount Vernon was in terrible shape. He wrote to his nephew Fielding Lewis, who had written to Washington requesting financial aid, "You very much mistake my circumstances when you suppose me in a condition to advance money. I made no money from my Estate during the nine years I was absent from it, and brought none home with me. Those who owed me took advantage of the depreciation and paid me off with six pence on the pound."[2]

Truth be told, Washington was usually hard up for money. Even though he was one of the wealthiest men in the country, his money was in the land and other property. Daily living expenses drained him of any cash he could accumulate. When he was elected president he had to borrow money to make the trip to New York to be inaugurated.

The Constitutional Convention was called:

This convention met from May 25 to September 17, 1787 in Philadelphia with the intention to revise the league of states and the first system of government under the Articles of Confederation. For four moths delegates met and their finished product became our Constitution.

Washington was asked to be a delegate to the convention, but he did not want to be a part of the meeting. He felt he had too much work to catch up on at Mount Vernon. Also, if he attended, he was afraid that people would think he was trying to seize power. But the delegates and the people trusted him more than anyone else and insisted he play a part in it. He reluctantly agreed and was selected as the president of the convention and when the job was completed he was the first to sign the document.

Washington could be a good politician:

A good politician must know how to play the game and how to work around people. Washington wrote early in his career, "I have found it of importance and highly expedient to yield to many points in fact without seeming to have done it." On one occasion he offered Patrick Henry a position, knowing in advance he would refuse it. When the well-known revolutionist of France, Volney, asked him for a general letter of introduction to the American people, he dodged the dangerous issued raised by the request and sent back this reply, "Volney needs no recommendation from George Washington."[3]

An unusual letter sent by Washington:

During the war Washington gave women little recognition for their efforts in helping win the war. Shortly after the Constitution was ratified, Washington did a strange thing. He wrote an interesting letter to Annis Boudinot in August 1788.

Annis was known for her prolific and patriotic poetry. She had earlier written about Washington's bravery and leadership and the two had developed a mutual friendship. In a letter written to her, Washington acknowledged the role that women played in the Revolution, "Nor would I rob the fairer Sex of their share in the glory of a revolution so honorable to human nature, for, indeed, I think you Ladies are in the number of the best Patriots America can boast."[4]

Portrait of Annis Boudinot Stockton (Mrs. Richard Stockton) at the Princeton University Art Museum. Public domain.

He went on in the same letter to make a most unusual request of her.

> And now that I am speaking of your Sex, I will ask whether they are not capable of doing something towards introducing federal fashions and national manners? A good general government, without good morals and good habits, will not make us a happy People; and we shall deceive our selves if we think it will. A good government will, unquestionably, tend to foster and confirm those qualities, on which public happiness must be engrafted. Is it not shameful that we should be the sport of European whims and caprices? Should we not blush to discourage our own industry & ingenuity by purchasing foreign superfluities & adopting fantastic fashions, which are, at best, ill suited to our stage of Society?[5]

A new job for Washington:

In 1788 the College of William & Mary decided to re-establish the position of Chancellor at the college. Washington was asked to accept the position and he agreed, and continued to serve in the post until his death. Not bad for a man with a limited formal education.

A leader was chosen for the new government:

Once it appeared that the constitutional would be adopted, the people began to look toward George Washington to lead them. Even though he didn't want the job the people knew, if called, he would not turn it down. It was Robert Morris who proposed George Washington for president of the new nation. Benjamin Franklin was supposed to do it, but he fell ill.

So, the first presidential election this country ever had was completely undemocratic. There were no primaries, no convention to nominate, no debates, no speeches, and no opposition candidate. In fact the people didn't even get to vote for the president. The Electoral College would pick the pick the man for the job and the only person considered was George Washington. He didn't want the job or even think he was up to the task.

Just as he felt he might not be able to command the army back in 1775, Washington again was afraid that he was not up to being president. Several months into his first term he wrote to Edward Rutledge, "I greatly apprehend that my Countrymen will expect too much from me."[6]

When it appeared that he would be chosen as the first leader of the country, Washington was not exactly elated. He wrote to Henry Knox on April 1, 1789 that he felt, "...not unlike a culprit who is going to the place of his execution, so unwilling am I, in the evening of a life nearly consumed in public cares, to quit a peaceful abode for an Ocean of difficulties."[7]

Likewise, Martha Washington was not happy that George was chosen as president. She wrote to her nephew, John Dandridge on April 20, 1789,

> I am truly sorry to tell you that the General is gone to New York, Mr. Charles Thompson came express to him, on the 14th, when or whether he will ever come home again god only knows. I think it was much too late for him to go in to publick life again, but it was not to be avoided, our family will be deranged as I must soon follow him.[8]

Thomas Jefferson, like some others, thought that Washington should be president for life.

> ....the perpetual re-eligibility of the president. But three states out of 11. Having declared against this, we must suppose we are wrong according to the fundamental law of every society. And should the majority change their opinion, and become sensible that this trait in their constitution is wrong, I would wish it to remain uncorrected as long as we can avail ourselves of the services of our great leader, whose talents and whose weight of character I consider as peculiarly necessary to get the government so under way.[9]

When Washington was notified on April 14th that he had been elected the new president, he immediately prepared to leave Mount Vernon for New York. Two days later he wrote in his diary,

> About ten o'clock I bade adieu to Mount Vernon, to private life, and to domestic felicity; and with a mind oppressed with more anxious and painful sensations than I have words to express, set out for New York in company with Mr. Thompson, and colonel Humphries, with the best dispositions to render service to my country in obedience to its call, but with less hope of answering its expectations.[10]

What title should the new leader have?

In April, as Washington was traveling to New York, Congress had to grapple with the question, what do we call our leader once he takes office? When something new is created it becomes a task to decide on the right name. One of the first titles for the famous movie, "Gone With the Wind" was "Bugles Sang the Blue", and Scarlett O'Hara was going to be called Pansy. So it is important to come up with just the right title.

The debate had already been going on for weeks and many suggestions were discussed. Elective majesty, sacred majesty, elective highness, illustrious highness, and serene highness were all discarded. John Adams offered the following title, "His Highness, the President of the United States of America and the Protector of Their Liberties." One Congressman suggesting calling him President George which encouraged another to suggest George IV.

Washington also came up with a suggestion, "His Mightiness the President of the United States. This caused the Speaker of the House to chuckle, which hurt the feelings of Washington and the Speaker was never forgiven.

The House was in favor of the simple title of "President," which the Senate thought it was too plain. The House believed that by adding more words to the title it made the leader sound like a monarch. Congress was then reminded that the newly formed constitution forbid titles. Eventually the vote was taken and Mr. President was selected, following in second place was the title His Superfluous Excellency. John Adams was later sworn in with the title as Vice President. Washington was very pleased with the choice.

Martha was called Lady Washington since she was expected to act as a queen. The term "First Lady" may have been used as early as 1838, when Martha was referred to as the First Lady of the nation, in a newspaper article in the "St. Johnsbury Caledonian". The title gained nationwide acceptance in 1877 when the wife of Rutherford B. Hayes, Lucy, was called in an article, "the first Lady of the Land."

How much do you pay a president?

Washington did not want to be paid as president because it might cause the appearance of corruption and he wanted the people to be reassured that his administration was not going to be corrupt. The American people had experienced government corruption under the rule of England and he did not want it to happen again. Also, Washington didn't want to be obligated to anyone for his income, including Congress. Since the Constitution required him to accept a salary, Congress voted to pay him $25,000 a year, which he could really use.

Washington needed this paid job as he indicated in a letter to George Augustine, the oldest son of his brother Charles. Washington wrote on March 31, 1789,

> I have heard of and I have seen with pleasure, a remarkable change in the mode of living from what it was a year or two ago—and nothing but the event, which I dreaded would take place soon [being President], has prevented my following the example. Indeed necessity (if this had not happened) would have forced me into the measure as my means are not adequate to the expence at which I have lived since my retirement to what is called private life.[11]

Opposition to Washington:

When Washington became President, many thought that since he was elected unanimously, everyone was pleased with the choice of Congress. Actually there were large groups of Americans who feared and disliked the Constitution and the new government it had created. They focused much of their hostility on the presidency. They were afraid that the newly created office would be a threat to their rights and liberties. They watched the president closely, waiting for him to turn into the American version of King George III.

Inauguration:

The day Washington was to be inaugurated as the first president of the United States, he arose and began to prepare himself. He powdered his hair, put on a brown suit, white silk stockings, and shoes with silver buckles.

On April 30, 1789, the Chancellor of New York, Robert Livingston administered the oath of office to George Washington on the second floor balcony of Federal Hall. Washington added the phrase "So help me God" to the end of the Presidential Oath of Office during his inauguration and it has been delivered in that manner ever since.

At two o'clock, after Washington had taken the oath of office as President of the United States, the crowd waited to hear his comments. Senator William Maclay from Pennsylvania noted in his diary, "This great man was agitated and embarrassed more than ever he was by the leveled cannon pointed musket."[12]

Washington delivered his first inaugural address to Congress assembled at Federal Hall in the Senate chamber. This address was not required by law, and every president since has delivered one. Washington urged Congress to add a bill of rights to the Constitution in his speech. His first draft of his speech was a lengthy 73 pages, which he fortunately discarded. Historians believe that James Madison may have drafted Washington's speech.

His second inaugural address was the shortest ever given, it consisted of around 135 words. If you had trouble finding your seat at the event you would have missed it. The longest ever given belonged to William Henry Harrison at 8,445 words. He gave the two hour speech on a cold, wet day without the benefit of wearing a hat or overcoat. He later caught pneumonia and a month after the speech he died.

After the speech was given the inaugural party left for St. Paul's Chapel in New York. When the service was over, President Washington was taken by carriage to the Franklin House where he dined alone. Martha had missed the event because she had to wrap up affairs at Mount Vernon.

That evening the new President watched celebration fireworks from the homes of Chancellor Livingston and his friend General Henry Knox. By 10:00 o'clock the tired president left in his carriage to his resident at Franklin House. There were so many people out celebrating that the carriage had trouble getting Washington home. As a result, the president and his escort walked the rest of the way home.

Oil painting of George Washington's inauguration as the first President of the United States which took place on April 30, 1789. Public domain

First presidential reception:

There were no inaugural balls given on the day Washington took the oath. The first Presidential reception was given days later and arranged by Colonel Humphreys, one of Washington's aids. People were standing around in a large room waiting for the president when Humphreys flung open the doors and shouted, "The President of the United States." Washington entered the room, people bowed and it remained silent as Washington greeted each person.

Apparently Washington was not pleased with the introduction because when it was over he remarked to Humphreys, "By God, you've taken me in once, but you shall never do it again."[13] After that his receptions had less ceremony.

Washington as president:

Washington was well aware that anything he said or did was important because it could start a precedent. Congress wisely had left much of his functions unresolved, leaving Washington to fill in the details. This certainly indicated the trust they had in Washington. He did one thing as president that did not create a precedent. Once he became president he refused to shake hands with anyone. He thought it was beneath the presidency to do so, and so instead he would bow.

As president, Washington never lost touch with Mount Vernon. He expected weekly reports of his plantation from his manager and would send back instructions. When Congress was not in session he would try to visit, however the visits were short and rare.

A precedent is establish:

Today, rather than visiting the Senate and discussing with them what he wanted, the president sends them a message or calls them to his office. That precedent started on August 22, 1789, when President Washington went to the Senate Chamber to receive "advice and consent" on various provisions in a treaty with the Creek Indians.

He gave Vice-President John Adams some papers to read to the Senate. Adams read the papers but the Senators had difficulty hearing him due to the noise of carriages driving by outside the chambers. Adams read them a second time and then asked "Do you advise and consent?"

After a short silence, Senator William Maclay said that the Senate need more information and he asked for more documents. A vote was taken to postpone their decision and then Senator Morris moved that the treaties be referred to committee. It was obvious that the President was very agitated with their lack of action. Maclay heard the President say, "This defeats every purpose of my coming here."[14]

Washington left and returned the following Monday thinking the Senate would finally reach a decision. The Senators then engaged in a long debate on two of the treaty's provision. This further frustrated the President, who then left the Senate and vowed never to return. After that he sent the Senate written messages, which set a precedent for subsequent Presidents to follow. The treaty was accepted two days later.

Dining with the president:

Washington never accepted invitations to private dinners, but he did invite foreign ministers, government officials, and sometimes strangers to dine with him. Washington wanted his meal time to be punctual. He established Thursday as his weekly dining day for company, and his hour to dine was always four in the afternoon. Sometimes he entertained as many as twenty guests. As a rule he would allow five minutes due to the variations of clocks and watches, and then go to the table.

He kept his own clock in the hall, just within the outward door, and always exactly regulated. When lagging members of Congress came in, as they often did, after the guests had sat down to dinner, the president's only apology was, "Gentlemen (or sir) we are too punctual for you. I have a cook who never asks whether the company has come, but whether the hour has come." The company usually assembled in the drawing-room, about fifteen or twenty minutes before dinner, and the president spoke to every guest personally on entering the room.[15]

What foods did the president eat?

Washington was especially fond of fish. It was the habit for New England ladies frequently to prepare the codfish in a very nice manner, and send it enveloped in cloths, so as to arrive quite warm for the president's Saturday dinner.

His personal tastes in food were somewhat boring and simple. Homegrown vegetables and fruits, meats, game, a wide variety of nuts were among Washington's favorite foods. For breakfast he was fond of hoecakes smothered in butter and honey with hot tea.

Samuel Fraunces came out of retirement to serve as steward of the presidential household. He quickly learned of Washington desire to not be extravagant. On one occasion, making his purchases at the market, he observed a fine shad, the first of the season. He did not take long in making a bargain, and the fish was sent home with his other provisions.

The next morning it was duly served, in the best style, for breakfast. As Washington sat down he observed the fragrant delicacy, and asked what it was, the steward replied, that it was "a fine shad." "It is very early in the season for shad, how much did you pay for it?" "Two dollars." "Two dollars! I can never encourage this extravagance at my table, take it away. I will not touch it." The shad was removed, and Fraunces, who had no such economical scruples, made a hearty meal of it in his own room.[16]

Too much pomp complaint:

In 1790, Washington, referring to the criticism that there was more pomp at his receptions than at the court of St. James, said, "Between the hours of three and four every Tuesday, gentlemen, often in great numbers, come and go. A porter shows them into the room, and they retire from it when they please, without ceremony. At their first entrance, they salute me, and I them, and as many as I can talk to, I do. What pomp there is in all this, I am unable to discover. Perhaps it consists in not sitting."[17]

Selection of a new capital:

Congress passed the Residence Act in July 1790, which called for a new permanent capital. George Washington carefully chose the site for the new capital of the nation which was on the Potomac River near two well-established port cities. Washington was involved in nearly all aspects of the project until his death.

Because of a shortage of white craftsmen to hire for the project, enslaved laborers from the surrounding states were also used. Congress moved the government from Philadelphia to Washington D.C. as the project neared completion in 1800.

First to lead an army as president

In January 1791, Secretary of the Treasury Alexander Hamilton proposed a tax on alcohol made in the United States. Some producers of whiskey living on the frontier of Pennsylvania rose up to protest it and the event became known as the Whiskey Rebellion. They were not against taxes, but against what they thought were unfair taxes.

The rebellion grew and in July 1794, 400 protesters burned the house of John Neville, the regional tax collector. A militia force of 12,950 troops were organized and led by Washington. By the time the militia reached the area the rebels had disbanded and disappeared. Two men were later found guilty of treason and were afterwards pardoned by Washington.

Did Washington want a second term?

Toward the end of his first term, George and Martha discussed the possibility of a second term. They both agreed to an emphatic NO! Washington asked James Madison to write a farewell speech to the American people. However, many of the politicians, including Jefferson and Hamilton, told him they feared the country would come apart if he did not serve a second term. He gave in to their wishes even though Martha was disappointed with his decision.

Did he have a pleasant second term?

George Washington spent eight years away from his home and family while leading the nation's army to defeat the British and win freedom for his country. He wanted to live out the rest of his days at home, and be a farmer, but in 1787 his country called him back to service. Against his wishes, he presided as the president over the Constitutional Convention. The next year he was asked to become Chancellor for the College of William & Mary, which he agreed to do. In 1789, he was unanimously elected to serve as the first United States President, a position he did not seek. After four years he wanted to go back home and once again he was elected by unanimous vote to a second term. Four years later the people wanted him for a third term, this time he rejected it and went back home for a well deserve rest.

After all of this you might think that his support and love of country would never be questioned. You would think that people would never speak ill of him after all the years he gave the country. Yet, once he became president it appeared that memories for some had grown short and once again he was subjected to slander and nasty criticism.

Attacks against Washington intensified as the government began to divide into two parties. In his first term, the attacks were usually about domestic and foreign policy, which you would expect. However, during the second term the attacks became more personal. Thomas Jefferson wrote to James Madison that the President was "extremely affected by the attacks made and kept up on him in the public papers."[18]

As his second term began, news reached America that French King Louis XVI and his wife, Marie Antoinette had been guillotined and a revolution had taken place. England and other nations joined to crush the French Revolution. Even though France was an ally of the United States, Washington knew that the country could not afford a war at this time because of a fragile economy. So the President declared that the country would not take sides.

Many of the common people, politicians, and newspapers were pro-French and protested the decision. At one gathering, Virginia journalist James Thomas Callender proposed a toast, "to a speedy death to General Washington."[19] Vice-President John Adams wrote that, "Ten thousand people in the streets of Philadelphia, day after day, threatened to drag Washington out of his house, and effect a revolution in the government, or compel it to declare war in favour of the French revolution and against England."[20]

In 1796 Washington was attacked by Thomas Paine. There had been good feelings between the two for many years. When Paine had financial problems, Washington used his influence to secure him a position that would help him recover. In addition, Washington even tried to get the Virginia Legislature to grant him a pension or a land grant for his service, which they later did. However, Paine became angry at the President because he felt that he did not do enough to free him when Paine was imprisoned during the French Revolution.

In a letter dated July 30, 1796, Paine questioned, of all things, Washington's ability during the war and he implied that the general did nothing to help win it.

Mr. Washington had the nominal rank of Commander in Chief; but he was not so in fact. He had in reality only a separate command. He had no controul over, or direction of, the army to the northward, under Gates, that captured Burgoyne; nor of that to the south, under Green, that recovered the southern States. The nominal rank, however, of Commander in chief, served to throw upon him the lustre of those actions, and to make him appear as the soul and centre of all the military operations in America

Nothing was done in the campaigns of 1778, 1779, 1780, in the part where Gen. Washington commanded, except the taking Stony Point by Gen. Wayne. The Southern States in the mean time were over-run by the enemy. They were afterwards recovered by Gen. Greene, who had in a very great measure created the army that accomplished that recovery. In all this Gen. Washington had no share.[21]

After reading this letter, and knowing what Washington did and achieved in the war, a person might ask himself if Paine was even in the country during the war, or kept up with what was going on during this time.

Then in late 1796, Thomas Paine again went after the president and wrote an open letter in which he attacked him, "The world will be puzzled to decide whether you are an apostate or an imposter; whether you have abandoned good principles or whether you ever had any."[22].

Benjamin Franklin Bache, the grandson of Benjamin Franklin, frequently attacked President Washington in his newspaper. He once wrote that Washington was "treacherous, mischievous, inefficient, and dwelt upon his farce of disinterestedness."[23] He also said that had Washington been promoted when he fought for the British during the French and Indians War, then he would be fighting for them during the Revolution.

Bache, the editor of the Aurora newspaper, continued his attacks and wrote, "If ever a nation was debauched by a man, the American nation has been debauched by Washington."[24] Yet, through attacks such as these, Washington never took public notice of them. Privately he did let of steam to the people close to him.

Hearing loss:

Toward the end of his second term as president, Washington's hearing began to decline. One of his assistance noted that at one of the President's dinners, "he seemed in more good humor than I ever saw him, though he was so deaf that I believe he heard little of the conversation." Three years later the President was reported as saying to Jefferson that he was "sensible, too, of a decay of his hearing, perhaps his other faculties might fall off and he not be sensible of it."[25]

The end of the second term:

By the end of the second term, Washington's administration was on the rocks. It suffer from a loss of prestige around the country and it appeared that the country was waiting for the end to come. Many of the opponents of Washington thought that he had not been up to the task of leading the country and was being influenced by unscrupulous people in his administration. Fortunately, the esteem and love of Washington that had been held by the majority of the people before he became president, resurfaced once the great man left office. On his way back to Mount Vernon he was met with cheers by groups and leading citizens in towns he passed through.

Who wrote the farewell address? :

Before leaving office, Washington issued a farewell address that he did not write. Instead, it was written by his close friend Alexander Hamilton at the suggestion of Washington. It was thought that Washington submitted a rough draft to Hamilton to improve and make changes. Hamilton rewrote the address from start to finish.

Return to Mount Vernon and a secret is revealed:

Washington had finished his second term as president and the elderly couple had arrived back home at Mount Vernon for a deserved rest. While George and Martha were unpacking, he received a letter from Elizabeth Willing Powell in March 1797. The house they had in Philadelphia had a desk they could not use at Mount Vernon, so they sold it to their good friend Elizabeth for $245.00.

Elizabeth wrote to Washington that she had found a secret drawer in the desk that contain some love letters addressed to Washington. She teases him about how shocked she was to find such letters. She told him that she had not read them and that Mrs. W, (Martha) would not be informed of them. This is the letter she wrote to Washington,

Like a true Woman (as you will think) in the Moment of Exultation, and on the first Impulse (for you know we are never supposed to act Systematically or from attentive Consideration, I take up my Pen to address you, as you have given me a complete Triumph on the Subject of all others on which you have I suppose thought me most deficient, and most opposite to yourself; and what is still more charming—your Candor shall preside as Judge, nay you shall pass Sentence on yourself, and I will not appeal from your Decision. Suppose I should prove incontestably that you have without Design put into my Possession the love Letters of a Lady addressed to you under the most solemn Sanction; & a large Packet too. What will the Goddess of Prudence and Circumspection say to her favorite Son and Votary for his dereliction of Principles to which he has hitherto made such serious Sacrifices. Was the Taste of your Sex predominant in your Breast; and did the Love of Variety so preponderate, that because you had never blundered as President, was you determined to try its Delights as a private Gentleman; but to keep you no longer in Suspense, tho' I know that your Nerves are not as irritable as a fine Ladies, yet I will with the Generosity of my Sex relieve you, by telling you—that upon opening one of the Drawers of your writing Desk I found a large Bundle of Letters from Mrs Washington bound up and labled with your usual Accuracy.

Mr Lear was present, I immediately desired him to take Charge of the Package which he declined—alleging that he thought it was safer in my Hands, at least for some Time—at first I urged it; but finding him Inflexible as I suppose from Motives of Delicacy I sealed them up And I trust it is unnecessary for me to add that they will be keept Inviolably until I deliver them to him or to your Order. As Mr Lear has been connected both with you and Mrs Washington, and as it is probable that some family Circumstances may have been mingled into her Communications to you, to save his Feelings I have sealed the Package with Three Seals bearing the Impression of my blessed Friends Arms, such as that I myself use. Should Mrs Washington appear to have any unpleasant Sensations on this Subject you will I am certain remove them by reminding her—that tho' Curiosity is supposed to be a prominent feature of the female Mind, yet it will ever be powerfully counteracted when opposed by native Delicacy, or sense of Honor, and I trust a pious Education.

I shall my good Sir give to Mr Lear 245 Dollars which I find was the first Cost of the writing Desk. In my Estimation its Value is not in the least diminished by your use of it; nor from its having been the Repository of those valuable Documents that originated with you during your wise and peaceful Administration for Eight Years. I am sensible many true & handsome Compliments might be paid to you on this Occasion; but as they have been resounded with Elegance & Sincerity through the Whole Continent, and will be re-echoed by Posterity, as you must be conscious they are just and as you are not a Man of Vanity, I will not in my blundering Way attempt a Theme that I feel myself totally inadequate to, as Blundering would not have to me even the Charm of *variety to* recommend it.

N.B. March 13th Mr Lear dined with me Yesterday. I desired him not to mention the Circumstance alluded to in the first (Para)-graph of this Letter, therefore Mrs W. need not be informed of it unless you choose to tell her yourself. E.P.[26]

Washington quickly replied back to Elizabeth Powell. He thanked her and explained that they were letters expressing friendship rather than love, and that he had no love letters to lose.

My dear Madam,

A Mail of last week brought me the honor of your favor, begun the 11th, and ended the 13th of this instant.

Had it not been for one circumstance, which by the bye is a pretty material one—viz.—that I had no love letters to lose—the introductory without the explanatory part of your letter, would have caused a serious alarm; and might have tried how far my nerves were able to sustain the shock of having betrayed the confidence of a lady. But although I had nothing to apprehend on that score, I am not less surprized at my having left those of Mrs Washington in my writing desk; when as I supposed I had emptied all the drawers; mistaken in this however, I have to thank you for the delicacy with which they have been treated. But admitting that they had fallen into more inquisitive hands, the corrispondence would, I am persuaded, have been found to be more fraught with expressions of friendship, than of *enamoured* love, and, consequently, if the ideas of the possessor of them, with respect to the latter passion, should have been of the *Romantic order* to have given them the warmth, which was not *inherent,* they might have been committed to the flames.[27]

Called to service one final time:

In May 1798, a French privateer captured an American merchant ship off of New York Harbor which resulted in American ships harassing French ships. Worries about a possible invasion from France brought calls to build up the army. Once again Washington was called to command the army, and it would mark the third time that he had been made Commander-in-Chief. He conducted most of his business by letter, though he spent a month in Philadelphia. Once again he took up the burden he had laid down, quietly, readily, since it was necessary, and without complaint, but he had not very long to bear it. On December 14, 1799, Washington passed away at home.

George Washington slept here signs begins to appear:

There have been signs up and down the east coast saying that the president had slept here. Because they are so numerous, over the years they have become a joke. Actually, President Washington did sleep at many of those places. During the war he was constantly moving his army and much of the time he stayed with them in camp. In the eight years of war he established headquarters at more than 200 places in seven states. Many times he did take up residence in private homes. There were also several long trips the president took while he was in office. Most travelers in the 1700s stayed at private homes because there were not that many inns available.

Conclusion

"If men have a common factor, it seems to me it's their ability to err. If a man's mistakes determine who he was, then what he does about those mistakes should determine what he is"…Paladin, *Have Gun, Will Travel, episode 161*

George Washington, a man much like us, was concerned about money, possessions, reputation, family, and success. He also doubted his abilities at times and was sensitive to criticisms. In many ways he was just an average man going about life. He did not seek greatness, but had it forced upon him. Because of this, he became a figure on the world's stage, to be talked about and written about.

For more than a hundred years after his death, he rose to mythical proportions and greatness not seen by any other American. Yet today there is a call to cancel his life and achievements, because this hero has been found to have ordinary faults. There are those who wish to cast Washington on the trash pile of history, because he does not meet the current standards of acceptable behavior. This former hero was a slave owner and trader, in addition to having other human faults.

What this man did was wrong by our societal beliefs today, but they were accepted by the society at the time. Will our actions and beliefs that guide us today be able to stand up to scrutiny two hundred years from now? Would it not be better to judge this man by the standards of his day? Should we not look at the entirety of his life's contributions? Perhaps we should ask ourselves if his life had a positive effect on those that came after him.

As George Washington matured in life, he began to see that slavery of another human was not the proper thing to engage in, and toward the end of his life he did want to rid himself of slave ownership. It is certainly true that he could have done more to help rid the country of slavery, such as speaking out against it. However, public speaking and pushing for cultural change was not part of his make-up.

His contributions toward ensuring our independence and establishing a strong government must be taken into consideration as he is judged. Without his efforts and sacrifice, our independence would have certainly been delayed. Instead of removing his portraits from schools and removing his accomplishments from our textbooks, we should honor his lasting achievements.

We should recognize that George Washington had flaws, is more than a mythical person, and not a man of marble, but of flesh and blood. He did many great things during his life, but at the end of the day he was just like us, a human who tried to do the right thing. If we cancel George Washington, then we cancel ourselves. To paraphrase Pogo, "We have met the man and he is us."

End notes

Introduction

1. Thomas Jefferson to Walter Jones, 2 January 1814, *Founders Online,* National Archives.
2. Sophie Lee Foster, *Revolutionary Reader, Reminiscences and Indian Legends.* (Atlanta, Georgia: Byrd Printing Company, 1913), 139.

Chapter 1 The Myth of George Washington

1. M.L. Weems, *The Life of George Washington with Curious Anecdotes 6th edition,* (Philadelphia: Printed by R. Cochran, 1808), 13.
2. Wayne Whipple, *The Story of the American Flag.* Philadelphia, PA: (Henry Altemus Company, 1910), 40-50.
3. _____, *The Friend a Religious and Literary Journal, Vol. LXXX.* (Philadelphia, PA: Wm. H. Pile's Sons, 1907), 367.
4. Parker C. Thompson, *From Its European Antecedents to 1791—The United States Army Chaplaincy.* (Washington D.C., Department of the Army, 1978), 250-272.
5. William Makepeace Thackray, *The Virginians, A Tale of the Last Century. Vol. I.* (New York, NY: Oxford University Press, 1858), 4.
6. Ibid, 8.
7. Nathaniel Hawthorne, *The Complete Writings of Nathaniel Hawthorne in Twenty-Two Volumes, Volume XXII.* (Boston, MA: Houghton Mifflin, 1900), 43.

Chapter 2 Young George Washington

1. Elizabeth Johnson, *George Washington Day by Day.* (New York, NY: The Baker & Taylor Co., 1895), 22.
2. Rupert Hughes, *George Washington The Human Being & the Hero.* (New York, NY: William Morrow & Company, 1926), 21.
3. J.M. Toner, *Washington's Rules of Civility and Decent Behavior in Company and Conversation.* (Washington D.C.: W.H. Morrison), 1888.
4. From George Washington to Samuel Griffin, 20 February 1788, *Founders Online,* National Archives.
5. Wayne Whipple, *The Story of Young George Washington.* (Philadelphia, PA: Henry Altemus Company, 1915), 9.
6. _____, *Memoirs of the Long Island Historical Society Vol. IV, George Washington and Mount Vernon,* (Brooklyn, New York: Published by the society, 1889), xii.
7. Ibid, xiii.
8. To George Washington from Mary Ball Washington, 13 March 1782, *Founders Online,* National Archives.
9. From George Washington to Mary Ball Washington, 15 February 1787, *Founders Online,* National Archives.
10. _____, *Memoirs of the Long Island Historical Society Vol. IV, George Washington and Mount Vernon,* (Brooklyn, New York: Published by the society, 1889), xiiv.
11. Daniel Moncure, *Baron's of the Potomack and the Rapphannock.* (New York, NY: Grolier Club, 1892), 238.
12. Marion Harlan, *The Story of Mary Washington.* (Boston, MA: The Riverside Press, 1893), 79-80.
13. Ibid, 239-240.
14. Paul Leicester Ford, *The True George Washington.* (Philadelphia, PA: J.B. Lippincott Company, 1896, 135.
15. Ibid, 113.
16. Ibid, 114.

Chapter 3 George Washington Body and Soul

1. Paul Leicester Ford, *George Washington.* (Philadelphia, PA: J.B. Lippincott Company, 1896), 38-39.
2. George Washington Custis, *Recollections and Private Memories of Washington by his Adopted Son.* (New York, NY: Derby & Jackson, 1860), 485.
3. Ibid, 486.
4. Ibid, 519.
5. Letter from Abigail Adams to John Adams, 16 July 1775, *Founders Online,* National Archives.
6. George Washington Custis, *Recollections and Private Memories of Washington by his Adopted Son.* (New York, NY: Derby & Jackson, 1860), 484.
7. Paul Leicester Ford, *George Washington.* (Philadelphia, PA: J.B. Lippincott Company, 1896), 44.
8. George Washington Custis, *Recollections and Private Memories of Washington by his Adopted Son.* (New York, NY: Derby & Jackson, 1860), 485.
9. Kevin J. Hayes, *George Washington A life in Books.* (New York, NY: Oxford Press, 2017), 28.
10. Horace E. Scudder, *George Washington an Historical Biography.* (New York, NY: Houghton Mifflin Company, 1882), 28.
11. Paul Leicester Ford, *The True George Washington.* (Philadelphia, PA: J.B. Lippincott Company, 1896), 187.
12. Rupert Hughes, *George Washington The Human Being & the Hero.* (New York, NY: William Morrow & Company, 1926), 190.
13. Ibid, 458.
14. Washington Irving, *Life of George Washington in Five Vols., Vol. 1.* (Philadelphia, PA: J.B. Lippincott & Co., 1871), 69-70.
15. Letter from Thomas Jefferson to Walter Jones, 2 January 1814, *Founders Online,* National Archives.
16. Paul Leicester Ford, *The True George Washington.* (Philadelphia, PA: J.B. Lippincott Company, 1896), 82.
17. Harper's Monthly magazine December, 1864.
18. Elizabeth Johnson, *George Washington Day by Day.* (New York, NY: The Baker & Taylor Co., 1895), 174.
19. Charles E. Claghorn, *Women Patriots of the American Revolution: a Biographical Dictionary.* (Lanham, MD: Scarecrow Press, 1991), 128.
20. Rupert Hughes, *George Washington The Human Being & the Hero.* (New York, NY: William Morrow & Company, 1926), 164-165.
21. Elizabeth Johnson, *George Washington Day by Day.* (New York, NY: The Baker & Taylor Co., 1895), 15.
22. _____, *Orderly Book of the Siege of Yorktown from September 26th, 1781, to November 2nd, 1781.* (Philadelphia, PA: Horace Smith, 1865), 31.
23. Washington's Address to Congress Resigning his Commission, 23 December 1783, *Founders Online,* National Archives.
24. G. R., Allison Goethals, S. T., *Heroic Leadership: An Influence Taxonomy of 100 Exceptional Individuals.* (United States: Taylor & Francis, 2013).
25. From George Washington to Elias Dayton, 4 June 1782, *Founders Online,* National Archives.
26. From George Washington to John Hanson, 19 August 1782, *Founders Online,* National Archives.
27. To George Washington from Charles Asgill, 18 October 1782, *Founders Online,* National Archives.
28. From George Washington to Charles Asgill, 13 November 1782, *Founders Online,* National Archives.
29. To George Washington from James Tilghman, 26 May 1786, *Founders Online,* National Archives.
30. From George Washington to James Tilghman, 5 June 1786, *Founders Online,* National Archives.
31. Act Giving Canal Company Shares to General Washington, [4–5 January] 1785, *Founders Online,* National Archives.
32. From George Washington to Benjamin Harrison, 22 January 1785, *Founders Online,* National Archives.
33. From George Washington to Patrick Henry, 29 October 1785, *Founders Online,* National Archives.
34. Winslow Watson, Editor, *Men and Times of the Revolution or, Memoirs of Elkanah Watson.* (New York, NY: Dana and Company, 1856), 279-280.
35. From Abigail Adams to Mary Smith Cranch, 12 July 1789, *Founders Online,* National Archives.
36. Thomas G. Cary, *Memoir of Thomas Handasyd Perkins.* (Boston, MA: Little, Brown and Co., 1856), 199.
37. Oliver Bell Bunce, *The Romance of the Revolution.* (Philadelphia, PA: Porter & Coats, 1870), 36-38

38. _____, *They Fight Our Fires for Free*, Kiplinger's Personal Finance, May 1952. (Washington D.C.), 43.

Chapter 4 The Emotions of George Washington

1. _____, *Documents of the Assembly of the State of New York, Vol. XXXII, No. 59.* (Albany, NY: The Argus Company, 1912), 639.
2. Norman Hapgood, *George Washington.* (New York, NY: The Macmillan Company, 1915), 309-310.
3. James Parton, *Life of Thomas Jefferson.* (Boston, MA: James R. Osgood and Company, 1874), 369.
4. Letter from Thomas Jefferson to Walter Jones, 2 January 1814, *Founders Online,* National Archives.
5. George C. Mason, *The Life and Works of Gilbert Stuart.* (New York, NY: Charles Scribner's Sons, *1879),* 54.
6. Orders to Major General Israel Putnam, 25 August 1776, *Founders Online,* National Archives.
7. Bill O'Riley, *Killing England.* (New York, NY: Henry Holt and Company, 2017), 106.
8. George F.Scheer, and Hugh Rankin, editors, *Rebels and Redcoats.* (New York, NY: De Capo Press, 1957), 171.
9. From George Washington to John Hancock, 16 September 1776, *Founders Online,* National Archives.
10. William Heath, *Heaths Memories of the American War.* (New York, NY: A. Wessels Company, 1904), 70.
11. W.E. Woodward, *George Washington the Image and the Man.* (New York, NY: Boni and Liveright, 1926), 316.
12. _____, *Graham's American Monthly Magazine of Literature & Art, Vol. XLV.* (Philadelphia, PA: Richard H. See & Co., 1854), 14.
13. George Washington Custis, *Recollections and Private Memories of Washington by his Adopted Son.* (New York, NY: Derby & Jackson, 1860), 218-219.
14. Elizabeth Johnson, *George Washington Day by Day.* (New York, NY: The Baker & Taylor Co., 1895), 95.
15. Henry Cabot Lodge, *Early Memories.* (New York, NY: Charles Scribner & Sons, 1913), 169-170.
16. General Orders, 3 August 1776, *Founders Online,* National Archives.
17. Willard Wallace, *Traitorous Hero: The Career and Fortunes of Benedict Arnold.* (New York, NY: Harper & Row, 1954), 251.
18. Sir George Otto Trevelyan, *George the Third and Charles Fox, The Concluding Part of the American Revolution.* (New York, NY: Longmans, Green, and Co., 1912), 315.
19. To George Washington from Lieutenant Colonel John Jameson, 27 September 1780, *Founders Online,* National Archives.
20. From John Adams to Benjamin Rush, 11 November 1807, *Founders Online,* National Archives.
21. To George Washington from Thomas Paine, 30 July 1796, *Founders Online,* National Archives.
22. Thomas Fleming, *The Intimate Lives of the Founding Fathers.* (New York, NY: Harper Collins, 2009), 49.
23. _____, *Memoirs of the Long Island Historical Society Vol. IV, George Washington and Mount Vernon,* (Brooklyn, NY: Published by the Society, 1889), xi.
24. From George Washington to Major General Horatio Gates, 30 October 1777, *Founders Online,* National Archives.
25. George Washington Custis, *Recollections and Private Memories of Washington by his Adopted Son, with a Memoir of the Author, by His Daughter.* (Philadelphia, PA: J.W. Bradley, 1861), 416-417.
26. Pension Application S30171 for Israel Trask from the Nation Archives.
27. Pension Application S39943 for Isaac Artis from the National Archives.
28. From George Washington to Lieutenant Colonel Joseph Reed, 28 November 1775, *Founders Online,* National Archives.
29. From George Washington to Lieutenant Colonel Joseph Reed, 14 January 1776, *Founders Online,* National Archives.
30. From George Washington to Henry Laurens, December 22, 1777, *Founders Online,* National Archive.
31. From George Washington to Henry Laurens, December 23, 1777, *Founders Online,* National Archive.
32. From George Washington to Henry Laurens, January 1, 1778, *Founders Online,* National Archive.
33. From George Washington to John Laurens, 15 January 1781, *Founders Online,* National Archives.

34. From George Washington to John Laurens, April 9, 1781. Founders Online, National Archives.
35. _____, *Family Relationships of George Washington.* (United States George Washington Bicentennial Commission, Washington D.C., 1932), page 18.
36. Samuel Hazard, editor, *Hazard's United States Commercial and Statistical Register.* (Philadelphia, PA: 1841), 220.
37. From George Washington to Lund Washington, 30 September 1776, *Founders Online,* National Archives.

Chapter 5 The Humor of George Washington

1. From George Washington to Theodorick Bland, 15 August 1786, *Founders Online,* National Archives.
2. John Stegeman and Janet Stegeman, *Cath A Biography of Catharine Littlefield Greene.* (Athens, GA: University of Georgia Press, 1977), 76.
3. Paul Leicester Ford, *The True George Washington.* (Philadelphia, PA: J.B. Lippincott Company, 1896), 179.
4. Edward Everett Hale, *Memories of a Hundred Years, Two Volumes in One.* (New York, NY: The MacMillan Company, 1904), 174.
5. John Bernard, *Retrospections of America 1797-1811.* (New York, NY: Harper & Brothers, 1887), 93.
6. Paul Leicester Ford, *The True George Washington.* (Philadelphia, PA: J.B. Lippincott Company, 1896), 180.
7. Washington Irving, *George Washington: A Biography,* (New York, NY: Da Capo Press, 1994), 633-634.
8. Ibid, 634-635.
9. Washington Irving, *Life of Washington, Vol IV.* (Leipzig: Bernard Tauchnitz, 1857), 418.
10. Elizabeth Johnson, *George Washington Day by Day.* (New York, NY: The Baker & Taylor Co., 1895), 165.
11. Paul Leicester Ford, *The True George Washington.* (Philadelphia, PA: J.B. Lippincott Company, 1896), 179.
12. From George Washington to Lieutenant Colonel Joseph Reed, 31 January 1776, *Founders Online,* National Archives.
13. Paul Leicester Ford, *The True George Washington.* (Philadelphia, PA: J.B. Lippincott Company, 1896), 181.
14. Edmund C. Burnet, ed., *Letters of Members of the Continental Congress, Vol. 7.* 1934, 292.
15. James Whitehead, editor., *Notes and Documents: The Autobiography of Peter Stephen Du Ponceau.* (The Pennsylvania Magazine of History and Biography, 63, No. 2, April 1939), 210-211.
16. Gilbert Chinard, editor, *George Washington as the French Knew Him.* (Princeton: Princeton University Press, 1940), 36 and 65.
17. Ibid, 42.
18. Ibid, 42-43.
19. Ibid, 50.
20. From George Washington to John Cochran, 16 August 1779, *Founders Online,* National Archives.
21. Paul Zall, editor, *George Washington Laughing.* (North Haven, CT: Archon Books, 1989), 6-7.
22. _____, *Graham's Illustrated Magazine of Literature, Romance, Art, and Fashion.* (Philadelphia, PA: Vol. 1, #1, January, 182)8, 137.
23. Memorandum Prepared for the President's Blue Ribbon Commission on Defense Management, Llmc, 121.
24. From George Washington to Francis Hopkinson, 16 May 1785, *Founders Online,* National Archives.
25. Winslow Watson, Editor, *Men and Times of the Revolution or, Memoirs of Elkanah Watson.* (New York, NY: Dana and Company, 1856), 119.
26. Max Farrand, *The Framing of the Constitution of the United States.* (New Haven, CT: Yale University Press, 1913), 74.
27. Henry Cabot Lodge, *Early Memories.* (New York, NY: Charles Scribner & Sons, 1913), 170-171.
28. John F. Watson, *Notes on the Private Character of General Washington, Collections of the Historical Society of Pennsylvania.1, 1853,* 139.
29. From George Washington to Tobias Lear, 9 March 1797, *Founders Online,* National Archives.
30. From George Washington to William Stoy, 14 October 1797, *Founders Online,* National Archives.
31. Paul Zall, editor, *George Washington Laughing.* (North Haven, CT: Archon Books, 1989), 18.
32. Ibid, 21.
33. Elizabeth Johnson, *George Washington Day by Day.* (New York, NY: The Baker & Taylor Co., 1895), 168.
34. From George Washington to Burwell Bassett, 28 February 1776, *Founders Online,* National Archives.

35. From George Washington to Major General Lafayette, 30 September 1779, *Founders Online,* National Archives.

36. From George Washington to Major General Lafayette, 30 September 1779, *Founders Online,* National Archives.

37. From George Washington to Annis Boudinot Stockton, 2 September 1783, *Founders Online,* National Archives.

Chapter 6 George Washington the Ladies Man

1. Paul Leicester Ford, *George Washington.* (Philadelphia, PA: J.B. Lippincott Company, 1896), 84.

2. W.E. Woodward, *George Washington the Image and the Man.* (New York, NY: Boni and Liveright, 1926), 39.

3. _____, *Memoirs of the Long Island Historical Society Vol. IV, George Washington and Mount Vernon,* (Brooklyn, New York: Published by the society, 1889), xi.

4. Founders Online December 3, 1751.

5. W.E. Woodward, *George Washington the Image and the Man.* (New York, NY: Boni and Liveright, 1926), 39.

6. Ibid, 40.

7. Ibid, 41.

8. Charles Frederic Nirdlinger, *Washington's First Defeat, A Comedy in One Act.* (New York, NY: Samuel French), 1906.

9. Mary Newton Standard, *Colonial Virginia, It's People and Customs.* (Philadelphia, PA: J.B. Lippincott Co., 1917), 178.

10. Sally Nelson Robins, *Love Stories of Famous Virginians.* (Richmond, VA: The Dietz Printing Co., 1923), 17.

11. Paul Leicester Ford, *George Washington.* (Philadelphia, PA: J.B. Lippincott Company, 1896), 88.

12. _____, *Memoirs of the Long Island Historical Society Vol. IV, George Washington and Mount Vernon,* (Brooklyn, New York: Published by the society, 1889), xxxix.

13. Bishop Meade, *Old Churches, Ministers and Families of Virginia Vol. 1.* (Philadelphia, PA: J.B. Lippincott, 1906), 108-109.

14. Paul Leicester Ford, *George Washington.* (Philadelphia, PA: J.B. Lippincott Company, 1896), 90.

15. To George Washington from Joseph Chew, 13 July 1757, *Founders Online,* National Archives.

16. Sally Nelson Robins, *Love Stories of Famous Virginians.* Richmond, VA: The Dietz Printing Co., 1923, 19.

17. George Washington to Sarah Cary Fairfax, April 30, 1755, *Founders Online,* National Archives.

18. George Washington to Sarah Cary Fairfax, Founders Online, September 12, 1758, *Founders Online,* National Archives.

19. Wilson Miles Cary, *Sally Cary A Long Hidden Romance of Washington's Life.* (New York, NY: The Devinne Press, 1916), 29-30.

20. Ibid, 54.

Chapter 7 Martha Dandridge Custis Washington

1. Anne Hollingsworth Wharton, *Martha Washington.* (New York, NY: Charles Scribner's Sons, 1897), 56.

2. Sally Nelson Robins, *Love Stories of Famous Virginians.* (Richmond, VA: The Dietz Printing Co., 1923), 40.

3. Anne Hollingsworth Wharton, *Martha Washington.* (New York, NY: Charles Scribner's Sons, 1897), 35.

4. Joseph E. Fields editor, *Worthy Partner:The Papers of Martha Washington.* (Westport, CT: Greenwood Press, 1994), 26-26.

5. Rupert Hughes, *George Washington The Human Being & the Hero.* (New York, NY: William Morrow & Company, 1926), 358.

6. W.E., Woodward *George Washington the Image and the Man.* (New York, NY: Boni and Liveright, 1926), 99.

7. Elizabeth Johnson, *George Washington Day by Day.* (New York, NY: The Baker & Taylor Co., 1895), 4.

8. Rupert Hughes, *George Washington The Human Being & the Hero.* (New York, NY: William Morrow & Company, 1926), 454.
9. Ibid, 103.
10. Paul Leiceste Ford, *The True George Washington.* (Philadelphia, PA: J.B. Lippincott Company, 1896), 95.
11. From a letter to Dr. Walter Jones to Thomas Jefferson, 2 January, 1814. Quoted in Bryan, William Alfred, *George Washington in American Literature, 1775-1865.* New York, NY: Columbia University Press, 1952, 49.
12. From George Washington to Lund Washington, 20 August 1775, *Founders Online,* National Archives.
13. Sally Nelson Robins, *Love Stories of Famous Virginians.* (Richmond, VA: The Dietz Printing Co., 1923), 74.
14. George C. Mason *The Life and Works of Gilbert Stuart.* (New York, NY: Charles Scribner's Sons, 1879), 54.
15. Anne Hollingsworth Wharton, *Martha Washington.* (New York, NY: Charles Scribner's Sons, 1897), 55.
16. Rupert Hughes, *George Washington The Human Being & the Hero.* (New York, NY: William Morrow & Company, 1926), 458-459.
17. Anne Hollingsworth Wharton, *Martha Washington.* (New York, NY: Charles Scribner's Sons, 1897), 75.
18. Elizabeth Johnson, *George Washington Day by Day.* (New York, NY: The Baker & Taylor Co., 1895), 139.
19. Anne Hollingsworth Wharton, *Martha Washington.* (New York, NY: Charles Scribner's Sons, 1897), 164.
20. From George Washington to Eleanor Parke Custis, 21 March 1796, *Founders Online,* National Archives.
21. Anne Hollingsworth Wharton, *Martha Washington.* (New York, NY: Charles Scribner's Sons, 1897), 276.
22. From George Washington to George Washington Parke Custis, 15 November 1796, *Founders Online,* National Archives.
23. Henry Laurens, *The Army Correspondence of Colonel John Laurens in the Years 1777-8.* (New York, NY: Bradford Club, 1867), 138.
24. Martha Washington, "Letter, Martha Washington to Elizabeth Ramsay, December 30, 1775," in Martha Washington, Item #85, https://marthawashington.us/items/show/85.
25. George Washington Custis, *Recollections and Private Memories of Washington by his Adopted Son.* (New York, NY: Derby & Jackson, 1860), 403.
26. Richard K. Showman, *The Papers of General Nathanael Greene. Nathanael Greene to Mrs. Catharine Greene, April 8, 1777.* (Chapel Hill, NC: 1980), 2:54

Chapter 8 George Washington and Religion

1. Paul Leicester Ford, *The True George Washington.* (Philadelphia, PA: J.B. Lippincott Company, 1896) 78.
2. _____, *Biographical Memoirs of the Illustrious General George Washington Late President of the United States of America, 4th Edition.* (Battleborough, NC: William Fessenden, 1811), 198.
3. William J. Johnson, *George Washington the Christian.* (New York, NY: The Abingdon Press, 1919), 68.
4. Paul Leicester Ford, *The True George Washington.* (Philadelphia, PA: J.B. Lippincott Company, 1896), 79-80.
5. William J. Johnson, *George Washington the Christian.* (New York, NY: The Abingdon Press, 1919), 153.
6. George Washington Cusis, *Recollections and Private Memories of Washington by his Adopted Son.* (New York, NY: Derby & Jackson), 1860, 173.
7. Sidney Hayden, *Washington and his Masonic Compeers.* (New York, NY: Masonic Publishing and Manufacturing Co., 1866), 23.
8. William J. Johnson *George Washington the Christian.* (New York, NY: The Abingdon Press, 1919), 55.
9. Ford, Paul Leicester, *The True George Washington.* (Philadelphia, PA: J.B. Lippincott Company, 1896), 82.
10. William J. Johnson *George Washington the Christian.* (New York, NY: The Abingdon Press, 1919), 191.
11. General Orders, 9 July 1776, *Founders Online,* National Archives.
12. William J. Johnson, *George Washington the Christian.* (New York, NY: The Abingdon Press, 1919), 68.
13. General Orders, 2 May 1778, *Founders Online,* National Archives.
14. William J. Johnson, *George Washington the Christian.* (New York, NY: The Abingdon Press, 1919), 44.
15. General Orders, 3 August 1776, *Founders Online,* National Archives.
16. From George Washington to Bushrod Washington, 15 January 1783, *Founders Online,* National Archives.

Chapter 9 George Washington: Teeth, Illness, and Death

1. James Thomas Flexner, *Gilbert Stuart A Great Life in Brief.* (New York, NY: Alfred A. Knopf, 1955), 124.
2. Paul Leicester Ford, *The True George Washington.* (Philadelphia, PA: J.B. Lippincott Company, 1896), 123.
3. Ibid, 57-58.
4. From George Washington to Lund Washington, 25 December 1782, *Founders Online,* National Archives.
5. From George Washington to John Greenwood, 16 February 1791," *Founders Online,* National Archives.
6. From George Washington to John Greenwood, 20 January 1797, *Founders Online,* National Archives.
7. From George Washington to John Greenwood, 25 January 1797, *Founders Online,* National Archives.
8. To George Washington from John Greenwood, 28 December 1798, *Founders Online,* National Archives.
9. Ledger B, 1772-1793, page 179, Library of Congress.
10. From George Washington to John Baker, 29 May 1781, *Founders Online,* National Archives.
11. _____, *Dining with the Washingtons: Historic Recipes, Entertainment, and Hospitality from Mount Vernon.* (Chapel Hill, NC: UNC Press Books, 2011), 38.
12. Paul Leicester Ford, *The True George Washington.* (Philadelphia, PA: J.B. Lippincott Company, 1896), 49.
13. James Thomas Flexner. *Washington, The Indispensable Man.* (Boston, MA: Little, Brown, 1974), 24.
14. Ibid, 25.
15. Paul Leicester Ford, *The True George Washington.* (Philadelphia, PA: J.B. Lippincott Company, 1896), 50.
16. From George Washington to Charles Green, 26-30 August 1761, *Founders Online,* National Archives.
17. Paul Leicester Ford, *The True George Washington.* (Philadelphia, PA: J.B. Lippincott Company, 1896), 51.
18. Ibid, 52.
19. Ibid, 53.
20. David S. Heidler & Jeanne T. Heidler, *Washington's Circle, The Creation of the President.* (New York, NY: Random House, 2016), 73.
21. Paul Leicester Ford, *The True George Washington.* (Philadelphia, PA: J.B. Lippincott Company, 1896), 53.
22. Ibid, 57.
23. Sally Nelson Robins, *Love Stories of Famous Virginians.* (Richmond, VA: The Dietz Printing Co., 1923), 40.
24. Jared Sparks, *The Life of George Washington.* (Boston, MA: Ferdinand Andrews., 1839), 534.
25. Tobias Lear, *Letters and Recollections of George Washington.* (London: Archibald Constable and Co., 1906), 131.
26. To George Washington from Martha Washington, 30 March 1767, *Founders Online,* National Archives.

Chapter 10 George Washington the Planter

1. _____, *A Poetical Epistle to His Excellency George Washington, A Short Sketch of General Washington's Life and Character.* (Privately reprinted, 1863), 20.
2. Paul Leicester Ford, *The True George Washington.* (Philadelphia, PA: J.B. Lippincott Company, 1896), 113.
3. Ibid, 116.
4. From George Washington to Lund Washington, 26 November 1775, *Founders Online,* National Archives.
5. From George Washington to Lund Washington, 19 November 1776, *Founders Online,* National Archives.
6. Horace E. Scudder *George Washington an Historical Biography.* (New York, NY: Houghton Mifflin Company, 1882), 110.
7. Ibid, 111.
8. Ibid, 113.
9. Paul Leicester Ford, *The True George Washington.* (Philadelphia, PA: J.B. Lippincott Company, 1896), 123.
10. Ibid, 116.
11. John C. Fitzpatrick, Editor, *The Writings of George Washington from the Original Manuscript Sources 1745-1799, Vol. 37.* (Washington: United States Government Printing Office, 1940), 415.
12. From George Washington to Lafayette, 10 May 1786, *Founders Online,* National Archives.
13. Paul Leicester Ford, *The True George Washington.* (Philadelphia, PA: J.B. Lippincott Company, 1896), 125.
14. Horace E. Scudder, *George Washington an Historical Biography.* (New York, NY: Houghton Mifflin Company, 1882), 116.

Chapter 11 George Washington and Slavery

1. W.E. Woodward *George Washington the Image and the Man.* (New York, NY: Boni and Liveright, 1926), 165.
2. Willard Sterne Randall, *George Washington, A Life.* (New York, NY: Henry Holt and Company, 1997), 207.
3. Ibid, 208.
4. W.E. Woodward, *George Washington the Image and the Man.* (New York, NY: Boni and Liveright, 1926), 167.
5. George Washington "Newspaper Advertisement for Runaway Slaves, George Washington (August 20, 1761)" *Encyclopedia Virginia.* Virginia Humanities, (05 Feb. 2021). Web. 18 Feb. 2023.
6. Richard Parkinson *A Tour in America, in 1798, 1799, and 1800.* (London: Printed for J. Harding and J. Murray, 1805), 420.
7. J.E. Budka Metchie, editor, and Julian Ursyn Niemcewiez *Under Their Vine and Fig Tree: Travels through America in 1797-1799, with some further account of life in New Jersey.* (Elizabeth, NJ: Grassman Publishing Company, 1965), 101.
8. From George Washington to Arthur Young, 18–21 June 1792, *Founders Online,* National Archives.
9. To George Washington from Anthony Whitting, 16 January 1793, *Founders Online,* National Archives.
10. From George Washington to Anthony Whitting, 20 January 1793, *Founders Online,* National Archives.
11. W.E. Woodward, *George Washington the Image and the Man.* (New York, NY: Boni and Liveright, 1926), 166.
12. George Washington "Reflections on Slavery" c. 1788-89 in *George Washington: Writings.* (Editor John Rhodehamel, NY: Library of America, 1997), 701-2.
13. To George Washington from William McGachen, 13 March 1774, *Founders Online,* National Archives.
14. Elizabeth Johnson, *George Washington Day by Day.* (New York, NY: The Baker & Taylor Co., 1895), 61.
15. Jack Darrell Crowder, *African Americans and American Indians in the Revolutionary War.* (Jefferson, NC: McFarland, 2019), 4.
16. General Orders, 12 November 1775, *Founders Online,* National Archives.
17. General Orders, 31 October 1775, *Founders Online,* National Archives.
18. General Orders, 12 November 1775, *Founders Online,* National Archives.
19. Jack Darrell Crowder, *African Americans and American Indians in the Revolutionary War.* (Jefferson, NC: McFarland, 2019), 4.
20. General Orders, 30 December 1775, *Founders Online,* National Archives.
21. From George Washington to John Hancock, 31 December 1775, *Founders Online,* National Archives.
22. Jack Darrell Crowder, *Strange, Amazing, and Funny Events that Happen during the Revolutionary War.* (Baltimore, MD: Clearfield, 2019), 100.
23. To George Washington from Marquis de Lafayette, 5 February 1783, *Founders Online,* National Archives.
24. From George Washington to Lafayette, 5 April 1783, *Founders Online,* National Archives.
25. Elizabeth Johnson, *George Washington Day by Day.* (New York, NY: The Baker & Taylor Co., 1895), 133.
26. Ibid, 121.
27. From George Washington to George Lewis, 13 November 1797, *Founders Online,* National Archives.
28. From George Washington to Oliver Wolcott, Jr., 1 September 1796, *Founders Online,* National Archives.
29. Paul Leicester Ford, *The True George Washington.* (Philadelphia, PA: J.B. Lippincott Company, 1896), 152.
30. Ibid, 153.
31. _____, *Biographical Memoirs of the Illustrious General George Washington Late President of the United States of America, 4th Edition.* (Battleborough, NC: William Fessenden, 1811), 200.
32. Elizabeth Johnson, *George Washington Day by Day.* (New York, NY: The Baker & Taylor Co., 1895), 108.

Chapter 12 George Washington Begins His Military Career 1752-1757

1. Paul Leicester Ford *George Washington.* (Philadelphia, PA: J.B. Lippincott Company, 1896), 88.
2. Rupert Hughes *George Washington The Human Being & the Hero.* (New York, NY: William Morrow & Company, 1926), 99.
3. Horace E. Scudder, *George Washington an Historical Biography.* (New York, NY: Houghton Mifflin Company, 1882), 76.
4. Jared Sparks, *The Writings of George Washington, Vol. II.* (Boston, MA: Russell, Odiorne, and Metcalf and Hilliard, Gray, and Co., 1834), 40.

5. Rupert Hughes, *George Washington The Human Being & the Hero.* (New York, NY: William Morrow & Company, 1926), 204.
6. Ibid, 205.
7. Ibid, 229.
8. Jared Sparks, *The Life of George Washington.* (Boston, MA: Ferdinand Andrews., 1839), 67.
9. Wayne Whipple, *The Story of Young George Washington.* (Philadelphia, PA: Henry Altemus Company, 1915), 218.
10. Rupert Highes, *George Washington The Human Being & the Hero.* (New York, NY: William Morrow & Company, 1926), 302.
11. Ibid, 303.

Chapter 13 George Washington the Politician

1. Rupert Hughes, *George Washington The Human Being & the Hero.* (New York, NY: William Morrow & Company, 1926), 334.
2. Elizabeth Johnson, *George Washington Day by Day.* (New York, NY: The Baker & Taylor Co., 1895), 109.
3. Washington Irving, *Life of Washington.* (New York, NY: Mast, Crowell & Kirkpatrick, 1896), 83.
4. Horace E. Scudder, *George Washington an Historical Biography.* (New York, NY: Houghton Mifflin Company, 1882), 122.
5. From George Washington to Robert McKenzie, 9 October 1774, *Founders Online,* National Archives.
6. Elbridge Brooks, *The True Story of George Washington.* (Boston, MA: Lothrop, Lee & Shepard, 1895), 73.

Chapter 14 George Washington Takes Command

1. John Adams to Abigail Adams, 29 May 1775, *Founders Online,* National Archives.
2. W.E. Woodward, *George Washington the Image and the Man.* (New York, NY: Boni and Liveright, 1926), 265.
3. L.H. Butterfield, et al, editors, *Diary and Autobiography of John Adams Vol. 3.* (Cambridge, MA: Belknap Press, 1961), 322-23.
4. W.E. Woodward, *George Washington the Image and the Man.* (New York, NY: Boni and Liveright, 1926), 266.
5. Wayne Whipple, *The Story of George Washington.* (Philadelphia, PA: Altemus Co., 1915), 207.
6. Elbridge Brooks, *The True Story of George Washington.* (Boston, MA: Lothrop, Lee & Shepard, 189), 76.
7. Letter from George Washington to Martha Washington, June 18, 1775, *Founders Online,* National Archives.
8. George Washington letter to John Parke Custis June 19, 1775, Founders Online, National Archives.
9. George W. Corner, editor, *The Autobiography of Benjamin Rush, His Travels Through Life Together with his Commonplace Book for 1789-1813.* (American Philosophical Society, 1948), 113.
10. Paul Smith et al., editors, *Letters of Delegates to Congress, 1774-1789.* (Washington D.C.: Library of Congress, Vol. 1), 516.
11. Ibid, 529.
12. W.E. Woodward, *George Washington the Image and the Man.* (New York, NY: Boni and Liveright, 1926), 274.
13. George Washington letter to Martha Washington, July 20, 1775, Founders Online, National Archives.
14. Elizabeth Johnson, *George Washington Day by Day.* (New York, NY: The Baker & Taylor Co., 1895), 112.
15. William B. Willcox, editor, *The American Rebellion: Sir Henry Clinton's Narrative of His Campaigns, 1775-1782.* (New Haven, CT: 1954), 19.
16. Richard Frothingham, *History of the Siege of Boston and of the Battles of Lexington, Concord and Bunker Hill.* (Boston, MA: Charles C. Little and James Brown, 1849), 210.
17. From George Washington to Lund Washington, 26 November 1775, *Founders Online,* National Archives.
18. National Archives RG 56, General Records, Treasury Department.
19. From George Washington to Martha Washington, 23 June 1775," *Founders Online,* National Archives.
20. From George Washington to Lund Washington, 20 August 1775, *Founders Online,* National Archives.
21. Horace E. Scudder, *George Washington an Historical Biography.* (New York, NY: Houghton Mifflin Company, 1882), 150-151.
22. General Orders, 1 August 1776, *Founders Online,* National Archives.

23. Jared Sparks, *The Writings of George Washington, Vol. II.* (Boston, MA: Russell, Odiorne, and Metcalf and Hilliard, Gray, and Co., 1834), 486.
24. Paul Leicester Ford, *The True George Washington.* (Philadelphia, PA: J.B. Lippincott Company, 1896), 282.
25. William J. Johnson *George Washington the Christian.* (New York, NY: The Abingdon Press, 1919), 69.
26. Ibid, 72.
27. Elizabeth Johnson, *George Washington Day by Day.* (New York, NY: The Baker & Taylor Co., 1895), 30.
28. Letter from George Washington to Lund Washington, September 30, 1776, *Founders Online,* National Archives.
29. Paul Leicester Ford, *The True George Washington.* (Philadelphia, PA: J.B. Lippincott Company, 1896), 282.
30. Daniel E. Harmon, *John Burgoyne British General.* (Philadelphia, PA: Chelsea House, 2002), 18.
31. From George Washington to Brigadier General John Thomas, 23 July 1775, *Founders Online,* National Archives.
32. Sydney George Fisher, *The true History of the American Revolution.* (Philadelphia, PA: J.B. Lippincott, 1902), 199.
33. Elizabeth Johnson, *George Washington Day by Day.* (New York, NY: The Baker & Taylor Co., 1895), 71.
34. Letter from George Washington to Lund Washington, April 30, 1781, *Founders Online,* National Archives.

Chapter 15 George Washington: A Great General or Just Lucky

1. Elizabeth Eggleston Seelye, *The Story of Washington.* (New York, NY: D. Appleton, 1893), 303.
2. From George Washington to Lund Washington, 30 September 1776, *Founders Online,* National Archives.
3. From George Washington to John Hancock, 2 September 1776, *Founders Online,* National Archives.
4. To George Washington from John Hancock, 3 September 1776, *Founders Online,* National Archives.
5. From George Washington to John Hancock, 22 September 1776, *Founders Online,* National Archives.
6. From George Washington to Lund Washington, 6 October 1776, *Founders Online,* National Archives.
7. _____,*Some Account of the British Army, Under the Command of General Howe and of the Battle of Brandywine,* (Philadelphia, PA: Townsend Ward, 1846), 31.
8. M.W.E. Wright, translated, *Memoirs of the Marshal Count De Rochambeau, Relative to the War of Independence of the United States.* (Paris: 1838), 41.
9. From George Washington to Thomas Jefferson, 26 September 1785, *Founders Online,* National Archives.
10. Letter from George Washington to Lund Washington, December 10-17, 1776, Founders Online, National Archives.
11. Jack Darrell Crowder, *African Americans and American Indians in the Revolutionary War.* (Jefferson, NC: McFarland, 2019), 4.
12. W.E. Woodward, *George Washington the Image and the Man.* (New York, NY: Boni and Liveright, 1926), 291.

Chapter 16 Disrespect Towards General George Washington

1. _____,*The History of George Washington, Bicentennial Celebration Vol. III.* (Washington D.C., 1932), 314-16.
2. Paul Leicester Ford, *The True George Washington.* (Philadelphia, PA: J.B. Lippincott Company, 1896), 240-241.
3. Alice Curtis Desmond, *Martha Washington Our First Lady.* (New York, NY: Dodd Meade & Company, 1942), 142.
4. Louis Clinton Hatch, *The Administration of the American Revolutionary Army.* (New York, NY: Longmans, Green, and Co., 1904), 25-26.
5. W.E. Woodward, *George Washington the Image and the Man.* (New York, N.Y.: Boni and Liveright, 1926), 337-336.
6. Louis Clinton Hatch, *The Administration of the American Revolutionary Army.* (New York, NY: Longmans, Green, and Co., 1904), 25.
7. Ibid, 25.
8. David Ramsay, *The Life of George Washington.* (London: Luke Hanford & Sons, 1807), 103.
9. From George Washington to Richard Henry Lee, 16 October 1777, *Founders Online,* National Archives.

10. To George Washington from Thomas Conway, 23 July 1778, *Founders Online*, National Archives.
11. Jack Darrell Crowder, *Strange, Amazing, and Funny Events that Happen during the Revolutionary War.* (Baltimore, MD: Clearfield, 2019), 42.
12. From Anthony Wayne to Joseph reed, December 16, 1780, *Founders Online*, National Archives.
13. John B. Reeves, *Extracts from the Letter-Books of Lieutenant Enos Reeves, of the Pennsylvania Line.* (The Pennsylvania Magazine of History and Biography, Vol. 21, No. 1 1897), 73.
14. From George Washington to Nathanael Greene, 2 February 1781, *Founders Online*, National Archives.
15. Paul Leicester Ford, *The True George Washington.* (Philadelphia, PA: J.B. Lippincott Company, 1896), 243.
16. Ibid, 244.

Chapter 17 George Close Calls for George Washington

1. _____,*The History of George Washington, Bicentennial Celebration Vol. III.* (Washington D.C., 1932), 239.
2. Ibid, 70.
3. Oliver Bell Bunce, *The Romance of the Revolution.* Philadelphia, (PA: Porter & Coats, 1870), pages 43.
4. Elizabeth Johnson, *George Washington Day by Day.* (New York, NY: The Baker & Taylor Co., 1895), 126.
5. Jack Darrell Crowder, *Strange, Amazing, and Funny Events that Happen during the Revolutionary War.* (Baltimore, MD: Clearfield), 2019, 49.
6. Oliver Bell Bunce, *The Romance of the Revolution.* (Philadelphia, PA: Porter & Coats, 1870), 45-46.
7. John Calvin Thorne, *Rev. Israel Evans, Chaplain of the American Army.* (Concord, NH: William Abbatt, 1902), 18.
8. _____,*The History of George Washington, Bicentennial Celebration Vol. III.* (Washington D.C., 1932), 71.
9. Elizabeth Eggleston Seely, *The Story of Washington.* (New York, NY: D. Appleton, 1893), 302-303.
10. General Orders, 11 March 1776, *Founders Online*, National Archives.
11. General Orders, 28 June 1776, *Founders Online*, National Archives.
12. Thomas S. Barker, *Itinerary of General Washington from June 15, 1775 to December 23, 1783,* (J.R. Lippincott Company: Philadelphia, PA: 1892), 41.

Chapter 18   George President George Washington

1. Elizabeth Johnson, *George Washington Day by Day.* (New York, NY: The Baker & Taylor Co., 1895), 76.
2. Ibid, 30.
3. Albert Shaw, editor, *The American Monthly Review of Reviews, Vol. XXIII, January-June, 1901.* (New York, NY: The Review of Reviews Company, 190), 193.
4. From George Washington to Annis Boudinot Stockton, 31 August 1788, *Founders Online*, National Archives.
5. From George Washington to Annis Boudinot Stockton, 31 August 1788, *Founders Online*, National Archives.
6. From George Washington to Edward Rutledge, 5 May 1789, *Founders Online*, National Archives.
7. From George Washington to Henry Knox, 1 April 1789, *Founders Online*, National Archives.
8. Joseph E. Fields, editor, *Worthy Partner: The Papers of Martha Washington.* (Westport, CT: Greenwood Press, 1999), 213.
9. From Thomas Jefferson to David Humphreys, 18 March 1789, *Founders Online*, National Archives.
10. George Washington, Diary entry: 16 April 1789, *Founders Online*, National Archives.
11. From George Washington to George Augustine Washington, 31 March 1789, *Founders Online*, National Archives.
12. Albert Shaw, editor, *The American Monthly Review of Reviews, Vol. XXIII, January-June, 1901.* (New York, NY: The Review of Reviews Company, 1901), 194.
13. W.E. Woodward, *George Washington the Image and the Man.* (New York, NY: Boni and Liveright, 1926), 437.

14. Edgar S. Maclay, ed., *Journal of William Maclay, United States Senator from Pennsylvania 1789-1791.* (New York, NY: D. Appleton and Company, 1890), 131.

15. George Washington Custis, *Recollections and Private Memories of Washington by his Adopted Son, with a Memoir of the Author, by His Daughter.* (Philadelphia, PA, J.W. Bradley, 1861), 435.

16. Rufus Wilmot Griswol, *Republican Court on American Society in the Day of Washington.* (New York, NY: D. Appleton Company, 1854), 149.

17. Elizabeth Johnson, *George Washington Day by Day.* (New York, NY: The Baker & Taylor Co., 1895), 88.

18. Paul Leicester Ford, *The True George Washington.* (Philadelphia, Pa: J.B. Lippincott Company, 1896), 206.

19. Thomas Fleming, *The Intimate Lives of the Founding Fathers.* (New York, NY: Harper Collins, 2009), 49.

20. W.E. Woodward, *George Washington the Image and the Man.* New York, (NY: Boni and Liveright, 1926), 449.

21. To George Washington from Thomas Paine, 30 July 1796, *Founders Online,* National Archives.

22. Michael P. Richards, *A Republic If You Can Keep It. The Foundation of the American Presidency 1700-1800.* (Westport, Conn: Greenwood Press. 1987), 186.

23. Paul Leicester Ford, *The True George Washington.* (Philadelphia, PA: J.B. Lippincott Company, 189), 264.

24. W.E. Woodward, *George Washington the Image and the Man.* (New York, NY: Boni and Liveright, 1926), 451.

25. Paul Leicester Ford, *The True George Washington.* (Philadelphia, Pa: J.B. Lippincott Company, 1896), page 57.

26. To George Washington from Elizabeth Willing Powel, 11–13 March 1797, *Founders Online,* National Archives.

27. From George Washington to Elizabeth Willing Powel, 26 March 1797, *Founders Online,* National Archives.

Bibliography

Abbot, W.W., ed. *The Papers of George Washington, Colonial Series 1, 1748-1755.* Charlottesville Va.: University of Virginia, 1893.

Alden, John R., *George Washington A Biography.* Baton Rouge, LA: Louisiana State University Press, 1984.

Barker, Thomas S., *Itinerary of General Washington from June 15, 1775 to December 23, 1783,* J.R. Lippincott Company: Philadelphia, PA: 1892.

Baker, W.S., *Bibliotheca Washingtoniana, a Descriptive List of the Biographies and Biographical Sketches of George Washington.* Philadelphia, PA: Robert Lindsay, 1889.

Bancroft, Aaron, *An Essay on the Life of George Washington.* Worchester, England: Thomas & Sturtevant, 1807.

Barker, Thomas S., *Itinerary of General Washington from June 15, 1775 to December 23, 1783,* J.R. Lippincott Company,: Philadelphia, PA: 1892.

Bellamy, Partridge, *Sir Billy Howe.* London: Green & Company, 1932.

Bernard, John, *Retrospections of America 1797-1811.* New York, NY: Harper & Brothers, 1887.

_____, *Biographical Memoirs of the Illustrious General George Washington Late President of the United States of America, 4th Edition.* Battleborough, North Carolina: William Fessenden, 1811.

Brooks, Elbridge, *The True Story of George Washington.* Boston, MA: Lothrop, Lee & Shepard, 1895.

Bryan, William Alfred, *George Washington in American Literature, 1775-1865.* New York, NY: Columbia University Press, 1952.

Bugbee, James M., *The Journal of Ebenezer Wild 1776-1781, Who Served as an Corporal, Sergeant, Ensign, and Lieutenant in the War of the Revolution.* Cambridge, MA: John Wilson & Son, 1891.

Bullock, A.M., *Head Lights: Washington.* Wentworth Press, 1903.

Bunce, Oliver Bell, *The Romance of the Revolution.* Philadelphia, PA: Porter & Coats, 1870.

Burnet, Edmund C., ed., *Letters of Members of the Continental Congress, Vol. 7.* 1934.

Cary, Thomas G., *Memoir of Thomas Handasyd Perkins.* Boston, MA: Little, Brown and Co., 1856.

Cary, Wilson Miles, *Sally Cary A Long Hidden Romance of Washington's Life.* New York, NY: The Devinne Press, 1916.

Chinard, Gilbert, editor, *George Washington as the French Knew Him.* Princeton, NJ: Princeton University Press, 1940.

Claghorn, Charles E., *Women Patriots of the American Revolution: a Biographical Dictionary.* Lanham, MD: Scarecrow Press, 1991.

Crowder, Jack Darrell, *African Americans and American Indians in the Revolutionary War.* Jefferson, NC: McFarland, 2019.

Crowder, Jack Darrell, *Strange, Amazing, and Funny Events that Happen during the Revolutionary War.* Baltimore, MD: Clearfield, 2019.

Custis, George Washington, *Recollections and Private Memories of Washington by his Adopted Son.* New York, NY: Derby & Jackson, 1860.

Custis, George Washington, *Recollections and Private Memories of Washington by his Adopted Son, with a Memoir of the Author, by His Daughter.* Philadelphia, PA: J.W. Bradley, 1861.

Desmond, Alice Curtis, *Martha Washington Our First Lady.* New York, NY: Dodd Meade & Company, 1942.

_____, *Dining with the Washingtons: Historic Recipes, Entertainment, and Hospitality from Mount Vernon.* Chapel Hill, NC: UNC Press Books, 2011.

_____, *Documents of the Assembly of the State of New York, Vol. XXXII, No. 59.* Albany, NY: The Argus Company, 1912.

_____, *The Edinburgh Magazine or Literary Miscellany, Vol. XVI.* Edinburgh: J. Murray, 1792.

_____, Excerpt from Notes of Debate in the Federal Convention of 1878, Bill of Rights Institute, online.

Farrand, Max, *The Framing of the Constitution of the United States.* New Haven, CT: Yale University Press, 1913.
_____, *Family Relationships of George Washington.* United States George Washington Bicentennial Commission, Washington D.C., 1932.

Ferris, Robert, Series Editor, *The Presidents.* Washington D.C.: United States Department of the Interior National Park Service, 1977.

Fields, Joseph E., *Worthy Partner: The Papers of Martha Washington.* Westport, CT: Greenwood Press. 1994.

Fisher, Sydney George, *The True History of the American Revolution.* Philadelphia, PA: J.B. Lippincott, 1902.

Fithian, Philip Vickers, *Philip Vickers Fithian, Journal and Letters, 1767-1774.* Carlisle, MA: Applewood Books, 1900.

Fitzpatrick, John C., Editor, *The Writings of George Washington from the Original Manuscript Sources 1745-1799, Vol. 37.* Washington: United States Government Printing Office, 1940.

Fleming, Thomas, *The Intimate Lives of the Founding Fathers.* New York, NY: Harper Collins, 2009.

Flexner, James Thomas. *Washington, The Indispensable Man.* Boston, MA: Little, Brown, 1974.

Flexner, James Thomas, George Washington in the American Revolution. Boston, MA: Brown & Company, 1968.

Flexner, James Thomas, *Gilbert Stuart A Great Life in Brief.* New York, NY: Alfred A. Knopf, 1955.

Ford, Paul Leicester, *The True George Washington.* Philadelphia, PA: J.B. Lippincott Company, 1896.

Foster, Sophie Lee, *Revolutionary Reader, Reminiscences and Indian Legends.* Atlanta, Georgia: Byrd Printing Company, 1913.

_____, *The Friend a Religious and Literary Journal, Vol. LXXX.* Philadelphia, PA: Wm. H. Pile's Sons, 1907.

Frothingham, Richard, *History of the Siege of Boston and of the Battles of Lexington, Concord and Bunker Hill.* Boston, MA: Charles C. Little and James Brown, 1849.
_____, *Graham's Illustrated Magazine of Literature, Romance, Art, and Fashion.* Philadelphia, Vol. 1, #1, January, 1828.
_____, *Graham's American Monthly Magazine of Literature & Art, Vol. XLV.* Philadelphia, PA: Richard H. See & Co., 1854.

Godfrey, Carlos Emmer, *The Commander in Chief's Guard, Revolutionary War.* Washington D.C.: Stevenson-Smith Company, 1904.

Goethals, G. R., Allison, S. T., *Heroic Leadership: An Influence Taxonomy of 100 Exceptional Individuals.* United States: Taylor & Francis, 2013.

Griswold, Rufus Wilmot, *Republican Court on American Society in the Day of Washington.* New York, NY: D. Appleton Company, 1854.

Hale, Edward Everett, *Memories of a Hundred Years, Two Volumes in One.* New York, NY: The MacMillan Company, 1904.

Hapgood, Norman, *George Washington.* New York, NY: The Macmillan Company, 1915.

Harland Marion, *The Story of Mary Washington.* Boston, MA: The Riverside Press, 1893.

Harmon, Daniel E. , *John Burgoyne British General.* Philadelphia, PA: Chelsea House, 2002.

_____, Harper's Monthly magazine December, 1864.

Hatch, Louis Clinton, *The Administration of the American Revolutionary Army.* New York, NY: Longmans, Green, and Co., 1904.

Hawthorne, Nathaniel, *The Complete Writings of Nathaniel Hawthorne in Twenty-Two Volumes, Volume XXII.* Boston, MA: Houghton Mifflin, 1900.

Hayden, Sidney, *Washington and his Masonic Compeers.* New York, NY: Masonic Publishing and Manufacturing Co., 1866.

Hayes, Kevin J., *George Washington A life in Books.* New York, NY: Oxford Press, 2017.

Hazard, Samuel, editor, *Hazard's United States Commercial and Statistical Register.* Philadelphia, PA, 1841.

Heath, William, *Heaths Memories of the American War.* New York, NY: A. Wessels Company, 1904.

Heidler, David S. & Jeanne T. Heidler, *Washington's Circle, The Creation of the President.* New York, NY: Random House, 2016.

Hildreth, Richard, *The History of the United States of America, Vol. III.* New York, NY: Harper & Brothers, 1854.

_____,*The History of George Washington, Bicentennial Celebration Vol. III.* Washington D.C., 1932.

Hughes, Rupert, *George Washington The Human Being & the Hero.* New York, NY: William Morrow & Company, 1926.

Irving, Washington, *George Washington: A Biography,* New York, NY: Da Capo Press, 1896.

Irving, Washington, *Life of Washington.* New York, NY: Mast, Crowell & Kirkpatrick, 1896.

Irving, Washington, *Life of George Washington in Five Vols.,Vol. 1.*Philadelphia, PA: J.B. Lippincott & Co., 1871.

Irving, Washington, *Life of George Washington in Five Vols., Vol. II .*Philadelphia, PA: J.B. Lippincott & Co., 1856.

Irving, Washington, *Life of Washington, Vol IV.* Leipzig: Bernard Tauchnitz, 1857.

Johnson, Elizabeth, *George Washington Day by Day.* New York, NY: The Baker & Taylor Co., 1895.

Johnson, William J., *George Washington the Christian.* New York, NY: The Abingdon Press, 1919.

Kendall-Lowther, *Mount Vernon Arlington and Woodlawn.* Washington D.C., Chas H. Potter & Co., 1922.

_____, *Ladies Home Journal, Philadelphia December 1895 Vol. XIII, No. 1.*

Laurens, Henry, *The Army Correspondence of Colonel John Laurens in the Years 1777-8.* New York, NY: Bradford Club, 1867.

Lear, Tobias, *Letters and Recollections of George Washington.* London: Archibald Constable and Co., 1906.

Lodge, Henry Cabot, *Early Memories.* New York, NY: Charles Scribner & Sons, 1913.

Lodge, Henry Cabot, *George Washington.* Boston, MA: The Cambridge Press, 1894.

Lossing, Benson J., *Mary and Martha, The Mother and the Wife of George Washington*. New York, NY: Harper & Brothers, 1886.

Lossing, Benson J., *Pictorial Field Book of the Revolution Vol. 1*. New York, NY: Harper Brothers, 1851.

Maclay, Edgar S., ed., *Journal of William Maclay, United States Senator from Pennsylvania 1789-1791*. New York, NY: D. Appleton and Company, 1890.

Marshall, John, *The Life of George Washington, Commander in Chief of the American Forces, During the War Which Established the Independence of His Country, 2nd edition*. Philadelphia, PA: James Crissy, 1836.

Martin, Joseph Plumb, *Narrative of Some of the Adventures, Dangers and Sufferings of a Revolutionary Soldier*. Hallowell, Maine: Glazier, Masters & Co., 1830.

Mason, George C., *The Life and Works of Gilbert Stuart*. New York, NY: Charles Scribner's Sons, *1879*.

Meade, Bishop, *Old Churches, Ministers and Families of Virginia Vol. 1*. Philadelphia, PA: J.B. Lippincott, 1906.

_____, *Memoirs of the Long Island Historical Society Vol. IV, George Washington and Mount Vernon*, Brooklyn, New York: Published by the society, 1889.

_____, *Memoirs of the Long Island Historical Society Vol. III, The Campaign of 1776*. Brooklyn, New York: Published by the society, 1878.

Metchie J.E. Budka, editor, Niemcewicz, Julian Ursyn, *Under Their Vine and Fig Tree: Travels through America in 1797-1799, with some further account of life in New Jersey*. Elizabeth, NJ: Grassman Publishing Company, 1965.

Moncure, Daniel, *Baron's of the Potomack and the Rapphannock*. New York, NY: Grolier Club, 1892.

Moore, Frank, *American Eloquence: A Collection of Speeches and Addresses*. New York, NY: D. Appleton and Company, 1857.

Nirdlinger, Charles Frederic, *Washington's First Defeat, A Comedy in One Act*. New York, NY: Samuel French, 1906.

_____, *Orderly Book of the Siege of Yorktown from September 26th, 1781, to November 2nd, 1781*. Philadelphia, PA: Horace Smith, 1865.

O'Riley, Bill, *Killing England*. New York, NY: Henry Holt and Company, 2017.

Parkinson, Richard, *A Tour in America, in 1798, 1799, and 1800*. London: Printed for J. Harding and J. Murray, 1805.

Parton James, *Life of Thomas Jefferson*. Boston, MA: James R. Osgood and Company, 1874.

Paulding, James K., *A Life of Washington, Vol. II*. New York, NY: Harper & Brothers, 1835.

___. The Pennsylvania Magazine of History and Biography. Vol. 16, No. 1, Apr., 1892.

Pettigrew, Thomas Joseph, *Memoirs of the Life and Writings of the Late John Coakley Lettsom*. United Kingdom: Nichols, Son, and Bentley, 1817.

_____, *A Poetical Epistle to His Excellency George Washington, A Short Sketch of General Washington's Life and Character*. Privately Reprinted, 1863.

Ramsay, David, *The Life of George Washington*. London: Luke Hanford & Sons, 1807.

Randall, Willard Sterne, *George Washington, A Life*. New York, NY: Henry Holt and Company, 1997.

Reeves, John B., *Extracts from the Letter-Books of Lieutenant Enos Reeves, of the Pennsylvania Line*. (The Pennsylvania Magazine of History and Biography, Vol. 21, No. 1 1897.

Riccards, Michael P., *A Republic If You Can Keep It. The Foundation of the American Presidency 1700-1800*. Westport, Conn: Greenwood Press. 1987.

Robins, Sally Nelson, *Love Stories of Famous Virginians*. Richmond, VA: The Dietz Printing Co., 1923.

Saunders, Frederick, *The Washington Centennial Souvenir*. New York, NY: Thomas Whittaker, 1889.

Scheer, George F., and Hugh Rankin, eds, *Rebels and Redcoats*. New York, NY: De Capo Press, 1957.

Scudder, Horace E., *George Washington an Historical Biography*. New York, NY: Houghton Mifflin Company, 1882.

Seelye, Elizabeth Eggleston, *The Story of Washington*. New York, NY: D. Appleton, 1893.

Shaw, Albert, editor, *The American Monthly Review of Reviews, Vol. XXIII, January-June, 1901*. New York, NY: The Review of Reviews Company, 1901.

Showman, Richard K., *The Papers of General Nathanael Greene. Nathanael Greene to Mrs. Catharine Greene, April 8, 1777*. Chapel Hill: North Carolina, 1980, 2:54.

_____,*Some Account of the British Army, Under the Command of General Howe and of the Battle of Brandywine*, Philadelphia, PA: Townsend Ward, 1846.

Sparks, Jared, *The Life of George Washington*. Boston, MA: Ferdinand Andrews., 1839.

Sparks, Jared, *The Writings of George Washington, Vol. II*. Boston, MA: Russell, Odiorne, and Metcalf and Hilliard, Gray, and Co., 1834.

Standard, Mary Newton, *Colonial Virginia, It's People and Customs*. Philadelphia, PA: J.B. Lippincott Co., 1917.

Stegeman, John and Janet Stegeman, *Cath A Biography of Catharine Littlefield Greene*. Athens, GA: University of Georgia Press, 1977.

Stone, Edwin Martin, *Our French Allies Rochambeau and His Army, Lafayette and His Devotion, D'Estaing, DeTernay, Barras, DeGrasse and Their Fleets in the Great War of the American Revolution from 1778-1782*. Providence, RI: Providence Press Co., 1884.

Thackray, William Makepeace, *The Virginians, A Tale of the Last Century. Vol. I*. New York. NY: Oxford University Press, 1858.

_____, *They Fight Our Fires for Free, Kiplinger's Personal Finance, May 1952*. Washington D.C.

Thompson, Parker C., *From Its European Antecedents to 1791—The United States Army Chaplaincy*. Washington D.C., Department of the Army, 1978.

Thorne, John Calvin, *Rev. Israel Evans, Chaplain of the American Army*. Concord, NH, 1902.

Tiger, Caroline, *General Howe's Dog: George Washington, the Battle of Germantown, and the Dog who Crossed Enemy Lines*. Canada: Chamberlain Brothers, 2009.

Toner, J.M., *Washington's Rules of Civility and Decent Behavior in Company and Conversation*. Washington D.C.: W.H. Morrison, 1888.

Toner, J.M., *Journal of my Journey Over the Mountains by George Washington, While Surveying for Lord Thomas Fairfax in 1747-8*. Albany, NY: Joel Munsell's Sons, 1892.

Trevelyan, Sir George Otto, *George the Third and Charles Fox, The Concluding Part of the American Revolution*. New York, NY: Longmans, Green, and Co., 1912.

_____, *True Stories of the Days of Washington*. New York, NY: Phinney, Blakeman, & Mason, 1861.

Wallace, Willard, *Traitorous Hero: The Career and Fortunes of Benedict Arnold.* New York, NY: Harper & Row, 1954.

Washington, George. "Newspaper Advertisement for Runaway Slaves, George Washington (August 20, 1761)" *Encyclopedia Virginia.* Virginia Humanities, (05 Feb. 2021). Web. 18 Feb. 2023.
Washington, George, "Reflections on Slavery" c. 1788-89 in *George Washington: Writings.* Editor John Rhodehamel, NY: Library of America, 1997.

_____, *The Washingtoniana: Containing A Biographical Sketch of the Late Gen. George Washington with Various Outlines of His Character.* Baltimore, MD: Samuel Sower, 1800.

Watson, John F. *Notes on the Private Character of General Washington, Collections of the Historical Society of Pennsylvania.*1, 1853.

Watson, Winslow, Editor, *Men and Times of the Revolution or, Memoirs of Elkanah Watson.* New York, NY: Dana and Company, 1856.

Weems, M.L., *The Life of George Washington with Curious Anecdotes 6th edition,* Philadelphia: Printed by R. Cochran, 1808.

Wharton, Anne Hollingsworth, *Martha Washington.* New York, NY: Charles Scribner's Sons, 1897.

Whipple, Wayne, *The Story of the American Flag.* Philadelphia, PA: Henry Altemus Company, 1910.

Whipple, Wayne, *The Story of Young George Washington.* Philadelphia, PA: Henry Altemus Company, 1915.

Whitehead, James, editor, *Notes and Documents: The Autobiography of Peter Stephen Du Ponceau.* The Pennsylvania Magazine of History and Biography, 63, No. 2, April 1939.

Willcox, William B., editor, *The American Rebellion: Sir Henry Clinton's Narrative of His Campaigns, 1775-1782.* New Haven, CT: 1954.

Wilson, Woodrow, *George Washington.* New York, NY: Harper Brothers, 1905.

Woodward, W.E., *George Washington the Image and the Man.* New York, NY: Boni and Liveright, 1926.

Wright, M.W.E., translated, *Memoirs of the Marshal Count De Rochambeau, Relative to the War of Independence of the United States.* Paris: 1838.

Zall, Paul, editor, *George Washington Laughing.* North Haven, CT: Archon Books, 1989.

Index

A

Adams, Abigail, 33,35

Adams, John, 45,50,78,139,140,153,176,192,198

Adams, Samuel, 136,137,140,143,153

Alexander, Francis, 67

Aliquippa, Queen, 125

Alton, John, 114

Andre, Major John, 44

Anti-slave societies, 118

Arnold, Benedict, 44,177,178

Asgill, Charles, 32,33

B

Bache, Benjamin, Franklin, 199

Balfour, Nisbet, 180

Ball, Joseph, 19,78

Ball, Mary, 78

Bassett. Burwell, 63

Bassett, Nancy, 75

Battle of, Brandywine, 162,177,184; Bunker Hill, 136,143; Germantown, 163,177; Jumonville, 126,127; Kip's Bay, 40,53; Lexington & Concord, 48,85,137,139,152; Long Island, 39,40,52,158,165; Monmouth Court House, 42,174; Oriskany, 9; Princeton, 29,162,183; Saratoga, 170; Trenton, 29,162,164,167,168,183

Bernard, John, 56

Bland, Mary, 66,84

black soldiers, 169

Bland, Theodorick, 55

Board of War, 178,179

Boston, 48,56,69,83,139,141,146,151; siege of, 47,63,162,173,180

Boston Tea Party, 136

Boudinot, Annis, 190

Boucher, Rev. Jonathan, 80

Braam, Jacob von, 28,125,127

Braddock, General, 58,96,128,129,183

Brown, Dr. Gustavus, 100

Brown, Lt., 180

Burgess, House of, 81,102,132-135,139

Burgoyne, General John, 151,178

Burr, Aaron, 1568

C

Cadwalader, General John, 178

Calvert, Eleanor, 81

Cambridge, 47,89,145,150,175

Campbell, Alexander, 57

Carleton, Sir Guy, 33

Callender, Thomas, 198

Carter, Charles, 76

Cary, Mary, 68,69,76

Cary, Sally, see Sarah "Sally" Fairfax

Chew, Benjamin, 163

Chew, Joseph, 69,70

Cheyney, Squire Thomas, 163

chaplains, 89

Chich, John, 150

Cline, John, 149

Clinton, General Henry, 42,95,143,164,169,171,180,181

Cobb, Colonel, 157,185,186

Cochran, John, 60

Congress, Continental, 49,52,60,89,138,140,153,169

Congress, First Continental, 136,140

Congress, Second, Continental, 137,140

Convention, Constitutional, 38,46,61,190

Convention of 1787, 61

Conway, General Thomas, 177,178

Cooper, William, 173

Cornwallis, General Charles, 16,31,60,95,162,164,169,171

Craik, Doctor, 31,98,100,183

Cranch, Mary Smith, 35

Custis, Daniel, 75

X

Y

Z

www.ingramcontent.com/pod-product-compliance
Lightning Source LLC
Chambersburg PA
CBHW081434270326
41932CB00019B/3192